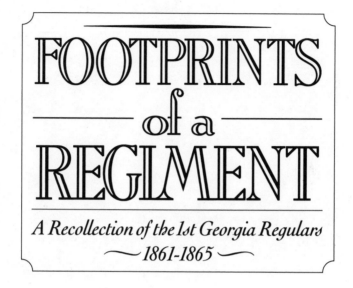

FOOTPRINTS
of a
REGIMENT

A Recollection of the 1st Georgia Regulars
1861-1865

The flag of the 1st Georgia Regulars bears the regimental colors on one side (*above*) and the Confederate stars and bars on the other (*below*). The Georgia state seal on the regiment side unfortunately has been lost. Photographs courtesy of the National Parks Service, Fort Pulaski Monument.

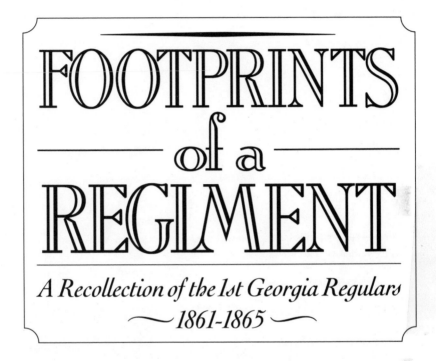

FOOTPRINTS
of a
REGIMENT

A Recollection of the 1st Georgia Regulars
~1861-1865~

W. H. Andrews, 1st Sergeant, Company M

ANNOTATED AND WITH AN INTRODUCTION BY RICHARD M. MCMURRY

LONGSTREET PRESS
Atlanta, Georgia

Published by
LONGSTREET PRESS, INC.
2140 Newmarket Parkway
Suite 118
Marietta, GA 30067

Printed in the United States of America
1st printing 1992
Library of Congress Catalog Card Number: 91-77195
ISBN 1-56352-030-3

This book was printed by Book Press, Inc., Brattleboro, Vermont.
The text was set in Goudy Old Style by In Other Words...
Book and jacket design by Jill Dible.

Jacket background illustration: "Rebel Soldiers advance to capture abandoned
guns at Gaines Mill, " by Alfred R. Waud. Photography by Katherine Wetzel.
Courtesy Eleanor S. Brockenbrough Library, The Museum of the Confederacy,
Richmond, Virginia.

CONTENTS

Mr. W. H. Andrews, Prominent Georgian, Dies Sunday Morning

Mr. William H. Andrews, a widely known and distinguished Confederate veteran, died Sunday morning at his home, 194 Grant street, following an extended period of illness.

Mr. Andrews had been a resident of Atlanta for more than thirty-five years, and up until about fifteen years ago, when his age and failing health necessitated his retirement, was actively engaged in the contracting business.

During his long life of eighty-two years he had lived in almost every section of Georgia, and his death is felt by his hundreds of friends as a distinct loss to the state. His early youth was spent in Fort Gaines, Ga., where he was born in 1838. After the War Between the States he moved to Dawson, Ga., where he was married to Miss Amanda Avent, and where he remained for several years. From Dawson he moved to Macon, and from there to Atlanta, where he had since made his home.

When the War Between the States broke out Mr. Andrews was one of the first of Georgia's sons to heed the call of the south. Enlisting when about twenty-two years of age with the First Georgia regulars he served with distinction throughout the duration of the war.

For many years he wrote many interesting stories and articles on the war. His articles, many of which were published in the magazine section of The Journal, contained an account of his own experiences in the war, and many interesting facts concerning the Confederacy.

Mr. Andrews was recognized as a man of a most lovable nature and the most unselfish type. These, coupled with a winning personality, won for him numerous friends.

Surviving Mr. Andrews are one daughter, Mrs. R. S. Cox, and a son, J. W. Andrews, both of Atlanta. The funeral services were held Monday afternoon at 2:30 o'clock from the chapel of Barclay & Brandon. Rev. Mr. Mann officiating. Interment was in Hollywood cemetery.

MR. WILLIAM H. ANDREWS, distinguished Georgian and Confederate veteran, whose death occurred Sunday at his home on Grant street.

Obituary of William H. Andrews, Atlanta *Journal*, November 15, 1920

INTRODUCTION

The Chattahoochee River rises in the hills of northeastern Georgia. It then flows to the southwest, passing just north of the bustling metropolis of Atlanta. About 150 miles from its source, the river turns from its southwestern course and flows almost due south to the Gulf of Mexico. For about 150 miles it marks the boundary between Georgia and Alabama. At the far southwestern corner of Georgia, it and the Flint River join to form the Apalachicola, and in that new incarnation, the Chattahoochee's waters flow on to the Gulf of Mexico.

Prior to the War of 1812 only a handful of white people lived in the lower Chattahoochee Valley. The area—as it had been for centuries—was the home of the Muscogee/Creek people. Their paths crisscrossed the region, and huge earthen mounds erected by even earlier inhabitants dotted the land. Under the terms of an 1802 agreement Georgia relinquished all of its claims to what are now Alabama and Mississippi. In return the national government agreed to pay to Georgia $1,250,000 and committed itself to extinguishing the Indian title to all land in the state.

Once the War of 1812 ended the Federal government accelerated its efforts to carry out the 1802 agreement. In a series of treaties (some of which were signed only by breakaway factions of the Muscogee/Creek nation) the government eliminated the Indians' legal claims to land in the state. By 1825, when the treaty of Indian Springs was signed, virtually all Muscogee/Creek land in Georgia had passed into white hands.

As it acquired legal possession of the land, the state acted to establish the machinery of local government and to encourage white settlement. Initially a few large counties were created. As the white population grew, these first counties were divided into smaller ones. As a part of this process, Lee County was organized in 1826. In 1828 several smaller counties were created, one of which was Randolph, named for the Virginia politician John Randolph of Roanoke.

In the 1820s and 1830s the frontier region of southwestern Georgia offered fine prospects to ambitious white settlers. The same opportunities were to be found across the Chattahoochee River in southeastern Alabama. Many families flocked to the area to seek their fortune from the rich cotton lands in the river valley. In 1830 the census enumerators found 2,191 people (1,508 whites, 682 slaves, and one free Negro) living in Randolph County.

The town of Fort Gaines, established on a high bluff along the eastern bank of the Chattahoochee near the site of an old military post, was chartered in 1830. First a ferry and later a bridge offered residents and travelers passage across the river (the bridge, however, was washed away by an 1855 flood and not replaced until 1869). Steamboats puffed 130 miles upriver from Apalachicola, Florida, on the Gulf to pick up cargoes of cotton. Entrepreneurs of all stripes came to pursue wealth in many different ways. John Dill, for example, was a South Carolinian who first visited the area with the army. He later returned, married well, and by the time of his death in 1856 was involved in such diverse activities as a tannery, a brick kiln, a cotton warehouse, and a mercantile establishment.

In 1854 Clay County (named for Henry Clay of Kentucky) was created with Fort Gaines as the county seat. At the beginning of the Civil War the town was a thriving cotton port, boasting several renowned hotels, a newspaper, the Fort Gaines Female College, a railroad, and the status that came from its being the most important point on the Chattahoochee between Apalachicola and Columbus, Georgia.

Among those who moved into the area in the decades after it was opened to white settlement were several men named Andrews. One of these—James Highsmith Andrews—was the father of the author of this memoir. His father, William Hill Andrews, was for at least a part of his life a resident of Buncombe County, North Carolina. We do not know when James H. Andrews moved to southwest Georgia, nor do we know exactly where he settled in what was then Randolph County. (Most of the early records of the area have been lost or destroyed.)

It seems that James Andrews acquired land several miles northeast of Fort Gaines near the now-abandoned settlement of Garnersville, not very far from Cotton Hill and Coleman. When James Andrews died in 1846 he was buried on the little hill behind Mount Gilead Baptist Church, some seven miles northeast of Fort Gaines on the old military road running from Cuthbert, via Cotton Hill, to Fort Gaines. His grave cannot now be identified. If it ever had a stone, it has disappeared or the inscription has become illegible.

After James Andrews' death, his widow, Jane Tucker Andrews, and her brood of children—six boys[1] and two girls[2]—remained on the land.[3] The second of the sons, William Hill Andrews (named for his paternal grandfather), had been born on April 15, 1838. We know virtually nothing about his early life other than the little that he tells us in his memoir. He did, however, acquire enough education to be literate. By 1861 he was living in Fort Gaines. His occupation then is unknown (the 1860 census listed him as an overseer). He did become a member of the Fort Gaines Guards, a famous local volunteer military company.

Upon its secession in January 1861, Georgia, like other Southern states, acted to organize a state military force for its defense. As part of this process, the Georgia secession convention created an army that was to include two infantry regiments. William J. Hardee and William H. T. Walker, both native Georgians and experienced army officers, were named as commanders of the regiments. The process of raising, organizing, and training the two units got underway. Recruiting officers were sent throughout the state to enlist volunteers. As Andrews relates at the beginning of his memoir, one of them soon arrived in Fort Gaines. It was then that Andrews decided to leave the Guards and to join the new state army.

Not long after William Andrews joined the Georgia army, the recently formed Confederate government assumed control of military activities and called upon the states to furnish troops for Confederate service. The companies that were then being organized for the two state regiments were consolidated into a single regiment designated the 1st Georgia Regulars, and that regiment was turned over to Confederate authorities.

It is that regiment's service that Andrews details in this memoir of his Civil War years.

A NOTE ON THE MEMOIR

In the summer of 1891 Andrews compiled and published a sixteen-page account entitled "1st Georgia Regulars Through the War Between the States." It may have been that attendance at a veterans' reunion or some other contact with wartime comrades inspired him to this undertaking. Published in Atlanta, the account is little more than an itinerary of the regiment's marches and battles. It contains virtually no personal information and, Andrews noted, was "drawn off from books carried with me during the war, and was written down as the incidents transpired."

Sometime in the years soon after Andrews published the 1891 account, he decided to compose a more complete narrative of his wartime service. Perhaps he simply wanted something to do to pass the time, or, like many old soldiers, he may have desired to leave a fairly detailed record of his wartime service for his family. Certainly the manuscript document, with its almost total absence of paragraphs, its lack of punctuation, and its numerous sentence fragments, does not read as though Andrews wrote it for readers outside his immediate family or with publication in mind. The memoir was an expansion of the diary that Andrews kept during the war.

Early in the new century the Atlanta *Journal* began to run a Saturday feature series (sometimes published under the heading SHOT AND SHELL) which was billed as "Thrilling Campfire Stories of Close Calls Recounted by Veterans." Each week's offering consisted of three or four articles—some a quarter of a page or so in length—in which veterans narrated some facet of their wartime experiences. Most of the authors contributed only one article to the series; others sent in several.

Reading the wartime reminiscences of some of his fellow veterans sparked Andrews' interest, and from his home in Sugar Valley he began to send selections of his memoirs to the *Journal*. "Being an old soldier," he wrote in what was probably the first of his contributions to the series (published February 23, 1901), "I love to read in the Journal the close calls by the boys from 1861 to 1865. Hoping that I may equally interest some one else I will, with your permission, give one of my many close calls during the years that tried men's souls."

Over the next two years Andrews published at least twenty-one articles in the series (see Appendix, following the memoir text). Each article was a section taken from the memoir that he had written in the 1890s, spruced up for publication and often changed slightly. He also published three articles in the *Confederate Veteran* about the regiment in which he had served. Two of these were also taken more or less intact from the memoir, and one of them had previously appeared in the *Journal*. The third, published in August 1909, was a roster of most of the officers who had served with the 1st Georgia Regulars.

Many Civil War veterans who wrote of their military service decades after the war tended to romanticize their experiences. Sometimes they remembered things that did not happen, and often they neglected to mention such unsavory aspects of army life as profanity in camp, gambling, cowardice in battle, straggling, and so on. Andrews remembered such subjects. On one occasion he even recorded how he and some friends had taken unauthorized leave from a battle. Andrews also demonstrated that he could be critical of the Confederate government for its failure to provide adequately for its soldiers and their families. In the 1890s very few old Confederates would have admitted the feelings about the Rebel government that Andrews expressed in the closing pages of his narrative.

William Hill Andrews' memoir presents no startling revelations about the war or about life in the Confederate army. The work does, however, give us an insight into how one enlisted man experienced the conflict, and it provides very valuable information on some oft-neglected areas of the Confederacy and about a little-known Rebel regiment.

EDITOR'S NOTE

In preparing Andrews' memoir for publication, we have made certain changes to enhance its readability. We have divided the work into ten major chapters, although the subdivisions within each chapter were made by Andrews. We have often had to separate the paragraphs within the subsections and the sentences within the paragraphs. Punctuation and spelling have generally been modernized, again for the sake of ease in reading. Where necessary, the names of prominent people have been corrected. For example, Andrews spelled the name of Maj. Gen. James E. B. Stuart as "Stewart." He also consistently spelled Chattahoochee as "Chattahoochie" and Culpeper as "Culpepper." In the cases of rank-and-file members of the regiment, names have been changed to match available records; where the records give variant spellings, we have left the name as Andrews wrote it. (All such cases, however, are noted.)

Several people were kind enough to drop their work and help with gathering material for this project. Special thanks are due to Judy Anthis of Richmond, Virginia; Franklin Garrett of Atlanta, Georgia; Lee Kennett of Athens, Georgia; P. C. King of Fort Gaines, Georgia; Bob Krick of Fredericksburg, Virginia; Dick Sommers of Carlisle, Pennsylvania; and Robert Watson of Cotton Hill, Georgia.

Not least, we thank W. H. Andrews' great-great-great-grandson Mark Reynolds and his family, of Atlanta, who found their ancestor's manuscript among their possessions and brought it to Longstreet Press for publication.

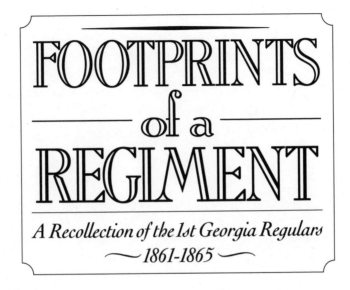

FOOTPRINTS
of a
REGIMENT

A Recollection of the 1st Georgia Regulars
~ 1861-1865 ~

Featherbed
Soldiers

Fort Gaines, Georgia

Fort Gaines is in Clay County on the banks of the Chattahoochee River, and took its name from the fort built by Gen. Gaines during the Indian War.[1] It has several hundred inhabitants, and before the Southwestern Railroad was built, was quite a business place in consequence of a number of steamboats plying the waters of the Chattahoochee.[2] My earliest recollections are of Fort Gaines and the surrounding country. My father owned a small farm near Mount Gilead Baptist Church, on which he was buried in 1846.[3] That ever memorable and never to be forgotten year 1861, found me in my 23rd year and temporarily a citizen of the fort.

In January the state had seceded from the Union with a number of other Southern states, and the war clouds were hanging dark and threatening over our sunny Southland.[4] While the Northern states were not saying much, it was the general impression that the North would attempt to force the South back into the Union at the point of the bayonet. Everybody seems to have gone wild. Nothing but war talk. War to the knife, and the knife to the hilt. At the same time our public speakers say, "I will drink all the bloodshed in this war. All we have to do is to secede from the Union and when the North sees that we are determined to leave them will say, 'Erring sisters depart in peace.'"

The Southern people are not going to be caught napping, but are preparing for war by capturing the [Federal government's] forts and arsenals in the South and organizing military companies. Being a firm believer in the doctrine of state's rights and secession, I considered it my duty to shoulder a musket in defense of my native state, which I put in execution by joining the Fort Gaines Guards, an infantry company organized at the fort. Capt. Brown[5] commanding, Lts. Turnipseed,[6] Webb,[7] and Tennille.[8] The Guards done gallant service in the Army of Northern Virginia in the 9th Regiment of Georgia Volunteers. Turnipseed and Webb both had the honor of commanding the regiment as colonel.

In February, Capt. F. T. Cullens[9] of the 1st Regiment of Georgia Regulars opened a recruiting office at the fort for the purpose of enlisting men to serve for three years, unless sooner discharged by competent authority. Thinking that it might be some time before the Guards would be ordered out, I decided to join the Regulars, and did so on the 26th day of February, 1861.

On the 7th day of March, I left Fort Gaines for Savannah, Ga., in company with O. W. Cone,[10] H. A. Morgan,[11] L. B. Wheeler,[12] John Boyle,[13] L. B. Standifer,[14] T. C. Beall,[15] Peter Lee,[16] W. L. Andrews,[17] James Lavin,[18] and Griffin Rowland,[19] all recruits for the Regulars. Fort Gaines Guards escorted us to the depot, where we took the cars on the Southwestern Railroad. Ate supper in Fort Valley, met 26 more recruits from North Georgia at Macon, leaving there at 9:00 P.M. with the understanding that we would breakfast next morning at the Pulaski House in Savannah, afterwards take in the sights of the city, and sometime late in the day report to the Oglethorpe Barracks for duty.

OGLETHORPE BARRACKS, GEORGIA

We arrived in Savannah at 8:00 A.M. on the 8th. But instead of going to the Pulaski House for breakfast, we were met at the depot by recruiting sergeant Ash[20] and marched to the barracks, where we were placed in line in front of the surgeon's quarters where we had to undergo a thorough examination by Dr. Charlton[21] before we could be received as soldiers. While waiting to be examined, our ardour was considerably dampened by the older recruits, some 300 in number, who made all manner of fun of us. Telling us we would think we were in Hades or the penitentiary instead of the army before night.

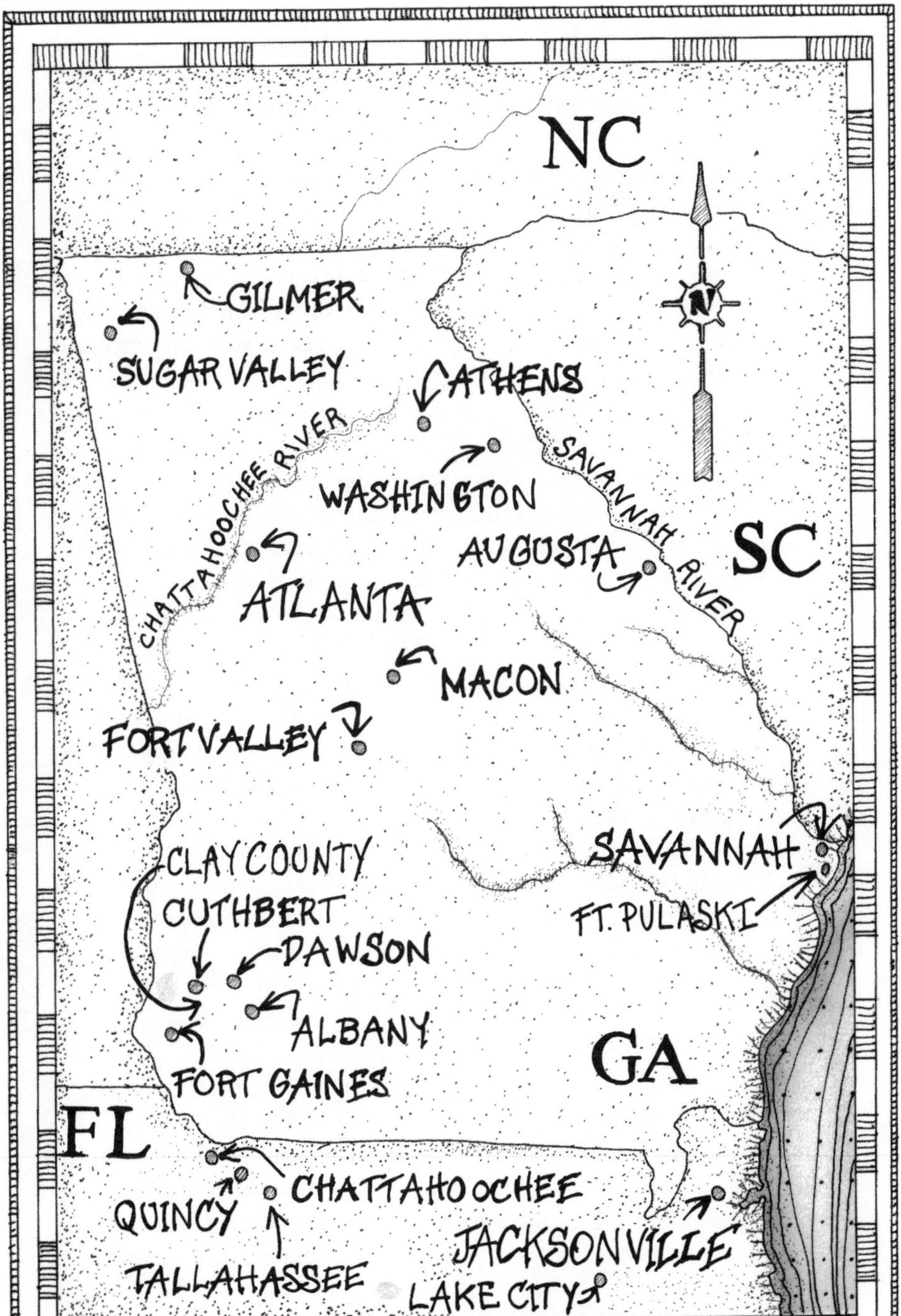
NC
SC
GA
FL
N
GILMER
SUGAR VALLEY
ATHENS
CHATTAHOOCHEE RIVER
WASHINGTON
SAVANNAH RIVER
ATLANTA
AUGUSTA
MACON
FORT VALLEY
CLAY COUNTY
CUTHBERT
DAWSON
ALBANY
FORT GAINES
SAVANNAH
FT. PULASKI
CHATTAHOOCHEE
QUINCY
TALLAHASSEE
JACKSONVILLE
LAKE CITY

About eleven o'clock Dr. Charlton got through with us, accepting all but Peter Lee, who had fits. I envied Peter his lot in being refused, as I thought at that time I would have been willing to have had fits or anything else just so I could have went back home. But as it was I was in for it, so had to grin and endure it.

At one o'clock the drum beat for dinner. We were marched to the mess hall where there were long tables with a plate, knife, and fork, tin cup and spoon for each man. In the plate was a piece of light bread and a slice of pickled pork, so fat you hold it up and see through it. The tin cup held yankee bean soup. What a dinner to commence our soldier life on. Shall never forget it. After forcing down a few mouths full, retired to the parade ground, thoroughly disgusted with what I had seen of a soldier's life.

Sometime in the evening we were ordered to go to the regimental barber and have our hair shingled. All men before the war wore long hair, with no beard or mustache on their faces. It went pretty hard with some of the boys to give up their glossy locks, but off they had to come. Saw an officer spoil a fellow's hair with his knife because he refused to have it cut off. In the way of uniforms we drew blue flannel shirts. And for bedding a blanket for each man.

What a change from an easy go as you please life to that of a soldier with no right to think, much less speak. You simply become a piece of machinery to have the steam turned on at someone else's will. There is no monkeying here. Our officers are mostly West Pointers and are capable of making soldiers out of us if such a thing can be done.

Later in the day we were assigned to different companies. Griffin Rowland and myself went to Company D, Capt. Gill's[22] company, who was afterwards chief ordnance officer on Gen. Bragg's[23] staff. We had for lieutenants, Branch,[24] Harrison,[25] and Berryon [?],[26] a well-drilled and clever set of officers. While they are strict, they are not haughty or overbearing. Lt. Branch was killed July 21st at Manassas, Va., while adjutant of the 8th Ga. Regiment. Lt. George P. Harrison surrendered at Greensboro, N.C., in 1865 with the rank of brigadier general.[27] Lt. Berryon resigned. Lt. Branch was ordered with his company to camp on the commons near the county jail, where we were drilled three hours each day, first in the green squad by a noncommissioned officer, and as we advanced we were placed in larger squads until capable of company drill.

When I enlisted, Capt. Cullens made me 1st corporal of his company, and gave me a recommendation to the commanding officer at Savannah, which was Capt. W. D. Smith, senior officer in command.[28] But I was told before the war that the duty of a corporal was to keep the dogs out of camp, so I decided I did not want it. But after we arrived in Savannah and had been assigned to different companies, the boys decided to try and get together in one company. So I carried my recommendation to Capt. Smith. Don't think I will forget what occurred soon. The captain had served 19 years in the regular army and was one of the strictest disciplinarians I saw during the war. He was a perfect soldier, every inch of him. I went walking into his office with my cap on, the captain was busy writing. He looked up and saw me. After sizing me up from my head to my heels, he remarked in a very commanding way, "Take off your cap sir, and place it under your left arm. Now take the position of a soldier and right hand salute. Pretty well done, you will make a good soldier when properly drilled. Now you can tell me your business." I had to think a while before I could recollect what I came for, he had me so badly scared. After hearing my request he stated that he would see Lt. Branch and if he would recommend me, it would be all right. So I left him, and I would not tackle him again in his office for a major general's commission.

I returned to my company fully satisfied to remain a high private in the rear rank. The biggest man I have seen here is Cpl. Pony Jones.[29] Gen. Scott's[30] overcoat would not make the flap to Pony's vest, provided Pony had a vest pocket. I hope to see Pony under fire some day.

While not on drill we get passes out in the city, the wharf being of the most interest, where the flags of all civilized nations are thrown to the breeze. All kind of sailing craft, from the magnificent *R. R. Cuyler* to the smallest of sailboats. Everybody seems to be in a hurry. The stevedores with their merry gangs loading and unloading vessels. The drays are almost impassable on the wharfs, hauling to and from the city. I like to listen to the merry "he-ho" of the gangs as they hoist away at their derricks, working with a will. Savannah's entire [water] front is full of crafts, and don't look like there is room for another.

My first Sunday in the army was rather a gloomy one, and especially in the evening, about the time I usually call on my best girl. Well, I guess the other fellow will have full sway now I am gone, but wouldn't I like to choke him just a little bit.

Some of the boys were quite merry, having succeeded in getting some tanglefoot through the back gate. One of them, Alvin Parr,[31] imbibed a little too much and was not as steady on his pins as he should have been. So he slipped up stairs to his bunk to sleep it off. Some of the officers found him out and sent a guard after him. As he made no effort to walk, the guard caught him by the feet and started to drag him. He said, "Hold on boys, you might stick splinters in Joe Dutton that way." His pleading might not have had much effect, but the name of Joe Dutton stuck to him until the end of the war.

Among the well-drilled officers are Lts. Branch, Kirkland,[32] Willis,[33] Harrison, and John Milledge.[34] The portly form of Col. John Milledge, state librarian, don't look much like the trim and handsome 1st lieutenant of '61. Nearly all of the officers appointed by Gov. J[oseph] E. Brown are still at their homes securing new recruits for the regiment. Numbers of them are arriving every day, 200 or 300 from Augusta in one squad, and the barracks are getting pretty full.

After being in Savannah one week, I was taken with pneumonia and placed in the hospital at the barracks. And for several days was quite sick. Hospital steward Mansfield[35] was very abrupt, and I think very unkind. At least he did not seem to have any sympathy for the sick. It learned me to appreciate my kind mother's nursing when I was at home, in a way I shall never forget. I owe all my kind treatment while sick to Mrs. Clower of Athens, Ga. When [her] son Pvt. Gus Clower[36] was sick in the same room, she brought me the same nourishment she did her son, for which I shall ever feel grateful. It was so kind of her to treat a stranger in such a way.

While I was sick, the regiment had been ordered to Fort Pulaski on the 15th of March. On the 31st, I was ordered by the surgeon to report to my company at the fort. Before leaving, I went to Capt. Smith and got a transfer to Company K, where my brother W. L. Andrews was.

Took passage on the steamer *Ida* for the fort. The *Ida* run a race with the *Cecil* from Charleston, S.C., and was badly beaten.

Fort Pulaski, Georgia

The fort was built by the U.S. Government on Cockspur Island about 18 miles below the city, and was considered a very strong fortress. When fully equipped it mounted 150 guns including [those in] casemates, ramparts, and [in] rear of the fort. When the Regulars entered the fort, there were no guns, only [except] in the casemates which were armed with 32-pound[er] smooth bored guns. The regiment mounted several Columbiads on the ramparts that throw a Colt shell.

On my arrival at the fort, I found Col. Charles J. Williams[37] in command, working day and night to have the fort in fighting trim. It certainly was no child's play mounting those guns. Weighing over 17,000 pounds, they would be dumped from the vessel onto the wharf. [They] were then suspended to a large cart on the order of a log cart, and pulled to the fort by about 200 men with ropes after putting down plank 2 x 12 lengthwise for the wheels to roll on to keep them from sinking in the ground. When we got them to the fort, they were hoisted upon the ramparts by sheers made of ship mast with heavy ropes, blocks, and tackles.

With mounting guns, infantry, and artillery drill, we are pretty well used up. Besides, the discipline is very strict, and we are nearly all new in regard to the duties of a soldier's life. Our rations are not enticing by any means, consisting of hard sea crackers, pickle pork, and yankee beans. Our breakfast consists of two crackers and a cup of coffee. At dinner we have two crackers, a slice of pickle pork, and a cup of soup. And at supper, two more crackers and a cup of coffee. And as there is nothing to be bought on the island, have to make out with it. Besides, the weather is extremely disagreeable. Either a dead calm or a small gale is blowing. Besides, we quarter in the casemates among the guns and have no fire.

The Regulars are getting well up in military tactics. At reveille the sunrise gun fires, and at the same time the large Confederate flag on the rear of the fort is thrown to the breeze. At sundown the regiment goes on dress parade. When the troop beats [drumbeats?] off, the gun is again discharged and the flag descends slowly to the ground. It is customary, when vessels are passing a fort, to salute by lowering the flag three times. Sometimes vessels pass without saluting the fort. A shot is then fired in front. If they fail then to salute, one is thrown in the rear. Should that fail, the third one is aimed at the vessel. The first or second one usually bring them to, or cause them to salute and pass on. The fort returns the salute by lowering her flag three times.

Sometime in April, the measles broke out in the regiment, over 100 being down at one time, myself among the number. I shall never forget the day I was hauled out of the fort on a mattress in a dump cart to the hospital on the island. I could not have felt more forsaken if I had been riding on my coffin to the gallows. Such treatment as we received will never be forgotten. Mattresses were placed in rows on the floor with a small space between them. A shovel of sand was used for a spittoon, where it remained all day covered in flies. Every morning it would be shoveled out and another one put in its place. In the way of nourishment, we had New Orleans molasses, rice, and sea crackers, a very tempting diet for anyone sick with measles. I must have been unconscious for several days, and was very sick for nearly two weeks.

When I began to improve a little, I was sent to convalescent quarters in the fort. While scarcely able to get up, Capt. Wallace[38] on his rounds as officer of the day made me get up and salute him. I thought to myself that if he was to pass through a graveyard, he would want the dead to rise and salute him. I was not able for duty in two months, sometimes trying to drill and fainting on the ground. [I] would have to be carried back to my quarters. It seems like I am in bad luck, first the pneumonia and then the measles. Might have fared better, but my brother was down with the mumps at the same time and could do nothing for me.

On May the 1st, the men were divided up into 12 companies, 10 infantry and 2 artillery. Sixty-six men to a company. Company K was changed to Company M. Capt. S. P. Hamilton,[39] Lts. Wise[40] and Bass.[41] First sergeant [was] John Ash, a kind-hearted son of Erin who did me many favors when I was sick by excusing me [from duty] when the surgeons would not. Regiment turned over to the Confederate States Authorities.

Capt. W. D. Smith was promoted to major of the Regulars, a position he is in every way competent to fill. He is feared by every man in the regiment. I heard him one day while on the ramparts order an officer on the parade ground to double-quick and do something. The officer started off in a brisk walk, the major halted him. "When I say double-quick, I mean run. Now do you run sir." And the officer moved accordingly. On going on dress parade one evening, Capt. Martin[42] had epaulets on his shoulders which the keen eyes of the major saw. "Capt. Martin return to your quarters and appear in your proper uniform." At another time when the companies were marching out on parade, Lt. W. W. Payne[43] was in command of a company that was behind time. Maj. Smith told him to double-quick his company into line. The lieutenant told his men to double-quick, but did not see a d——d bit of use in it. The boys claimed that the major could tell if a man's shoes were untied in the rear rank, on the right or left of the regiment. The major certainly was a daisy, but he did not exact anything more from his subordinates than he was willing to do to his superiors. His next-ranking officer had to toe the mark as though he was a private soldier. (The major soon left our regiment and was elected colonel of a North Carolina regiment. Afterwards he was promoted to brigadier general and died during the war.[44])

On May 31 the Regulars were relieved from duty at the fort and ordered to Tybee Island. In steaming past the fort on the *Ida*, it certainly had the appearance of a place that was almost impregnable. How silent and grim it looks with its dark portholes in the walls, and the muzzles of the Columbiads projecting over the ramparts. (But as formidable as it looked, in 1862 the Federals took it with a sand battery on Tybee Island opposite the magazine.[45]) I felt almost seasick as the waves dashed against the prow of the steamer, throwing a mist over it. I don't think I would like to be a sailor and get far from land. Our baggage was put in rice barges and towed by the *Ida*. As Tybee has no wharf, we had to wade out, landing near the Spanish Tower.

TYBEE ISLAND, GEORGIA

Tybee Island is opposite the mouth of the Savannah River and is about seven miles long and several miles in width. There is but few houses on it, the Tybee Light House and Spanish Tower being the objects of most interest. The lighthouse is said to be 120 feet high, with a 7,000 dollar lamp that can be seen 20 miles out to sea. The Spanish Tower is something of a curiosity, being built out of oyster shells and cement. It is about 40 feet high and 40 feet in diameter. The shape of it is round. The walls are said to be six feet thick, with a well in the center. Around the top were several openings resembling embrasures for cannon to shoot through. As to when, or by whom built, I have never seen any account of it in history. Suffice it to say, it is here and was probably built by the Spaniards prior to the settlement of Georgia.

The Regulars pitched their tents some 300 yards back of the tower in an open space. The balance of the island was covered in undergrowth. Where we camped might have been too poor for anything to grow, being all sand. Each company dug its own well in the sand, getting water at the depth of about six feet. Such water as it was, being brackish and almost unpalatable, but the best we could do.

Our rations have been changed from pickle pork to smoked bacon, but our cooking arrangements remain the same. One man is detailed to do the cooking for each company with the assistance of a supernumerary. Three-fourths of a pound of bacon and one pound of crackers is a day's rations for a soldier. The bacon for the company is all boiled in a large wash pot, which is certainly rich enough if plenty of grease will add anything to the flavor.

After we got straightened out, the boys would go swimming [sunning?] on the beach. But crabs, stingrays, and horseshoe turtles [crabs?] were about all they ever succeeded in catching, and the crabs were the only thing eatable. And according to my taste, a very poor diet.

While we are beyond the pale of civilization on the island, we are not so badly cramped as we were in the fort. Still it is bad enough, as we never see anyone scarcely from the outer world or hear but little news from other places. We are all more than anxious to be sent to the front, preferring an active campaign to remaining here doing coast duty and being ate up by the mosquitoes and sand flies. Besides, the heat of the noonday sun upon the sand is terribly distressing.

While the discipline is very strict, there is not much punishment inflicted on the men. I have seen but one man condemned by a court-martial. That was for sleeping on post. The penalty was wearing on the front of his cap a large pasteboard with the words SLEEPING ON POST inscribed on it. As the soldiers cannot get off the island or get any whiskey, I suppose that accounts for their good behavior.

The regiment is doing some pretty hard drilling every day besides guard and picket duty. A line of pickets are scattered along the beach, one post at the three palmettos, another at South Channel five miles down the beach, and several nearer the camp. What a lonesome vigil at the wee small hours of the night, tramping your lonely beat with nothing for company but the foamed capped waves as they break at your feet. You can imagine the waves capped with the enemy's small boats as they come rolling in, and how you wish to see again the light of day.

The yankees have blockaded the port of Savannah, a large man-of-war lying just outside the bar. And of course, we are expecting a visit from them at almost any time, and more especially at night in the way of a surprise. One night it fell to my lot to be stationed on top of the lighthouse. It is octagon shaped, the stairs being on the inside. And how weak my knees got before I reached the top. It seemed as though I never would get there, but did at last.

Sentinels are on duty two hours and off four. My last turn was just before day. The sentinel I relieved instructed me to keep a sharp lookout towards the South Carolina coast, as he had heard a steamer plying up and down while on duty. Should I hear or see anything unusual, make it known to the corporal of the guard who would notify the officer of the day. He then left me nearer heaven than I ever was since or before, perched on top of the lighthouse and apparently swinging in the breeze though it might have been only my head. It was not a great while before I could see the first bright streaks of day as they shot out upon the eastern sky. Brighter and brighter they got, until I could see the upper rim of the rising sun. As the sun emerged from its morning bath, could almost imagine I could see the water dripping from the lower edge. What a magnificent sunrise.

Armed with a four-foot telescope, I certainly was enjoying one of the most beautiful mornings I had ever seen, having almost forgotten that I was a soldier and stationed at the most important post on the island. But bringing the telescope to bear across the bar, I was speedily restored to my senses. Lying just beyond the bar was a large man-of-war. Between that and the island was a sailing vessel at anchor. Just above the man-of-war and steaming towards it, was a large sidewheel steamer which was but a short time in reaching the vessel. After getting alongside of the man-of-war, it did not look much larger than a lifeboat. The man-of-war then lowered her lifeboats and filled them with marines or infantry, as I could see the rays of the morning sun flash from their small arms in the boat. They then made for the sailing vessel next to the island. I called the attention of the corporal of the guard to it. He sent the officer of the day up, who viewed their movements for awhile and retired. Soon after I was relieved and have never been on the lighthouse since.

While not drilling, we mounted two 32 pounders at the Spanish Tower near the beach. Nothing of note happened until the 16th of July, when, on dress parade, orders were read ordering the regiment to report at Richmond, Va. And to say the boys went wild is putting it mild. Three cheers and a tiger was given for the front.

On the 17th we struck our tents, packed our knapsacks, and marched down to the beach at the Spanish Tower, where the *Ida* awaited our coming to carry us to Savannah. How the boys puffed and blowed marching over the hot sands of Tybee. What featherbed soldiers we are, but nothing better could be expected of us, as it takes hard training in the school of the soldier to become proficient.

SAVANNAH, GEORGIA

On arriving at Savannah we marched through the city and pitched our tents on the commons, where we drew new uniforms, shoes, caps, and overcoats. All having previously had their measures taken by a tailor. Our uniforms were of Confederate gray, single-breasted frock coats with Georgia buttons, black cords down the outer seams of the pants. Caps were gray. Overcoats extending to the knees, with large capes. Altogether we were nicely fitted up. Besides, we had a fatigue uniform consisting of jacket and pants. The Regulars were armed with muskets, and drilled in Hardee's tactics for heavy infantry.[46]

On the 18th after the drum beat for dress parade, one of the boys was drilling another in the manual of arms. He put him through the movements of loading, then ready, aim, and fire, and a musket ball and three buckshot went crashing through his head and he fell a corpse. He did not know the gun was loaded.

On the 19th the regiment was reviewed by Gen. Lawton.[47] After the review one of the handsomest state flags I have ever seen was presented to the regiment, the gift of Miss Howard of Columbus, Ga.,[48] Col. Charles J. Williams' sister-in-law. It certainly was a beauty, made of costly silk with the First Confederate colors on one side, and the state of Georgia on the other. Just below the coat of arms in large gilt letters is "First Regiment Georgia Regulars." It was a gift ever held sacred by the members of the regiment. At the same time, it was never unfurled to the breeze on a battlefield, but was used on dress parades and marching through towns and cities. (I am informed by Col. John Milledge that all of the flags used by the Regulars during the war are deposited with the Historical Society at Savannah, Ga.)

ALL ABOARD FOR RICHMOND, VIRGINIA

July 20, 1861. The 1st Ga. Regulars boarded a freight train for Charleston, S.C., having a passenger coach in the rear for the accommodation of the commissioned officers. Eleven companies were ordered to Virginia. Capt. Reed's company was left at Fort Jackson, four miles below Savannah.[49] To the best of my recollection will give the names of the captains who went to Virginia: W. J. Magill,[50] Martin, J. D. Walker,[51] R. A. Wayne,[52] John G. Patton,[53] Lewis Kenan,[54] F. T. Cullens,[55] Miller Grieve,[56] S. P. Hamilton, A. A. F. Hill.[57]

The regiment arrived at Charleston and marched through the city, making a handsome display in our new uniforms, the officers having dark blue, which looked extremely handsome with hats and plumes.

On arriving at the Northeastern Depot the citizens furnished the regiment with a splendid supper. The 21st Regiment took the cars for Florence. Every house and village the regiment has passed, the ladies and children wave their handkerchiefs and the boys have cheered themselves hoarse. At Florence the regiment was placed on flat cars with slats with legs in them for seats. Made the boys mad, so they would not cheer anyone at that place as they left for Wilmington, N.C., where we arrived after night. The citizens furnished the regiment with hot coffee.

Col. Williams received a dispatch stating that Gens. Johnston and Beauregard had defeated Gens. Scott and McDowell at the battle of Bull Run, Va., totally routing them.[58] Three cheers were given with a vim, for our victorious comrades on the plains of Manassas. On the 22nd from Wilmington to Weldon [N.C.], arrived after night. Hot coffee furnished by the good people of the city. Lt. Bass of Company M treated his company to something stronger which was most certainly appreciated by the boys.

[July] 23, on to Petersburg, Va., where the mayor and citizens had prepared for the regiment a splendid dinner which was highly enjoyed by all. On getting off the cars, I discovered that my cap was missing. Some drunken fellow had lost his and taken mine in the place of it. Felt pretty slim at the idea of marching through the city bareheaded, but Pvt. Brennan[59] loaned me one of his, he having retained his old one.

After dinner, proceeded to Richmond. Marched through the city with our beautiful flag thrown to the breeze and our splendid brass band at the head of the regiment. Went into quarters at Camp Winder. Pres. Jefferson Davis reviewed the Regulars, making a short speech.[60] The regiment certainly made a fine display in their new uniforms, besides they are nearly all young men from 18 to 25 years of age.

While in Richmond, Capt. W. J. Magill was appointed lieutenant colonel, Capt. John D. Walker major, George P. Harrison 1st lieutenant and adjutant, Fred B. Palmer[61] sergeant major, Capt. DeLaigle[62] quartermaster, Capt. McConnell[63] commissary. [July] 24, ordered to Manassas Junction. At Hannover Junction we met up with a good many poor soldiers who claimed to have been in the battle of Bull Run. Our sympathy was aroused to such an extent that the regiment made up a purse for them. We learned better afterwards when we learned something about an active campaign. We found out that all good soldiers remained with their companies, and not 100 miles in the rear. We then proceeded on to Manassas Junction, going into camps two miles beyond, on the railroad and near the famous Bull Run Creek.

SOME PRETTY HARD CASES IN THE ARMY

CAMP WALKER, NEAR BULL RUN, VIRGINIA

Our camps are named in honor of Gen. W. H. T. Walker,[1] brother of Maj. John D. Walker of the Regulars. Regiment assigned to Gen. Robert Toombs' Brigade composed of the 2nd, 15th, 17th, and 20th Ga. regiments, making a fine brigade.[2] Here it is all life and bustle as the hills and valleys are covered with the white tents of the different commands. We can mix and mingle with the various commands from different states, besides finding a number of relatives and friends among the Georgia regiments.

No trouble about something to eat here, as there is no better section in this country for beef, pork, mutton, kid, turkeys, chickens, and ducks. Scarcely anything raised in this country, only [except] to eat. We get three-fourths of a pound of fine beef each day for a ration. If that is not enough, you can buy all you can pay for from peddlers who visit the camps every day. So with all things considered we are having a jolly good time of it in the Old Dominion. Besides, we now have a sutler's store in the regiment which keeps all kinds of canned goods in stock.

On Friday the 26th day of July, with several of my comrades, I visited the battlefield of the 21st at Manassas. Crossed Bull Run where the battle of the 18th was fought.[3] Saw the famous Washington Artillery, Capt. Rosser's Company, drilling.[4] They certainly have the right name when called the Flying Artillery, for they certainly move in a hurry.

Words are inadequate to express my feelings as we strolled over the historic field of Manassas, ground that had so recently been the scene of a deadly conflict. I met on the field a captain of the 11th Ala. Regiment with several of his men, who took great delight in showing us over the battlefield. We first visited where the lamented Gens. Bee and Bartow fell while at the heads of their respective commands. A cedar post marks the spot where they yielded up their life's blood in behalf of their country's cause.[5] Next we went to the famous Henry House near the road running from Manassas to Sudley's Mills on the Bull Run above the stone bridge. The house is on a hill some half a mile from the brick house on Cub Run, and at the time of the battle was occupied by Mrs. [Judith C.] Henry, her daughter, and a Negro woman. Mrs. Henry was nearly 100 years old and was confined to her bed. Her daughter and the colored woman was under the bed. The enemy had driven our troops beyond the house, and had taken refuge behind it, when our batteries were ordered to open fire on it. The house was riddled with cannonballs, one knocking the head and foot board out of the bed. The old lady was struck with six minié balls, killing her instantly, while the two under the bed escaped unhurt.[6]

We next went to a strip of woods to the south of the Henry House and across the Manassas Road, where the 11th Ala. Regiment had been halted on the day of the fight by Col. Williams, who alighted from his horse and while hitching him to a limb, was shot and killed by a yankee sharpshooter who broke and run after shooting the colonel. Several companies of the regiment fired a volley at him. One of the captain's men said he believed he could find the yankee that shot him, and proceeded to hunt for him, while the rest of us went out into the field to pick blackberries. (Where we picked berries is where the right of Gen. Anderson's Brigade fought at the second battle of Bull Run.[7]) It was not long before he called us, and on going to him he had sure enough found his man. He was lying at full length on his back, minus his hat, coat, and shoes with six bullet holes in him that we could see. He was either a fool or a very brave man to shoot down the colonel in front of his regiment, for he certainly knew it would be instant death to him.[8]

Near the Henry House was a pit six feet wide and about 60 feet long where our soldiers had been buried. Poor boys, with a heave and a swing they were pitched to their last resting place unknown, unwept, and unsung. There to remain until the Judgement Day, far from home and loved ones, but such is war. Numbers of the dead have not dirt enough on them to keep the dogs from scratching them up. A number of dead horses are scattered over the field, and altogether forms a picture not soon to be forgotten.

Our visit, while nothing to compare with what I saw afterwards, made a lasting impression on my mind, and one that I will carry with me until I too shall join my comrades on the other shore, where we will rest under the shade of the trees. Towards night we returned to our camp, sadder if not wiser men. On September the 10th the Regulars moved from Camp Walker one mile beyond Centreville. On the 12th, went on a forced march near the Occaquon River with the 1st Md. and 13th Va. regiments. Come near being cut off and had to make a forced march back to camps. The 16th of September the regiment changed camps to Pine Creek, three miles towards Centreville.

CAMP PINE CREEK

On September 17 Regulars went to Munson's Hill, by way of Fairfax Court House, on picket duty. Munson's Hill is seven miles from Washington City. From the top of the hill we have a good view of the city, the national capitol, and fortifications around the city. Besides, we can see Alexandria, Arlington Heights, and the Potomac River. Col. J. E. B. Stuart[9] of the famous Black Horse Cavalry[10] is in command of the post, and Brig. Gen. James Longstreet[11] in command of the department. The hill is round or cone shaped, with a line of breastworks around near the top. On the Washington side there is some Quaker Guns made of logs about 10 feet long, with one end mounted on the front wheels of a wagon. I suppose they are called Quaker Guns because they are silent. [They were intended to deceive enemy observers as to the strength of a position.]

Down some three-fourths of a mile in the bottom is the Bailey House, which is on the yankee line. We can see the boys in blue as they stroll around and watch the hill. One day they advanced as skirmishers but our Quaker Guns were maneuvered in position and they retired. Our first picket duty was performed about one mile to the right of the Bailey House. The Regulars were stationed along the fence in the edge of a piece of woods, while the enemy's line was at a cross fence in the middle of the field.

It is quite amusing to look back at the capers we cut on performing our first picket duty. We certainly looked on the boys in blue as something more than human. Some of the boys claimed that they had horns, others said they had tails like monkeys. At any rate, we decided they were a natural curiosity and would have given anything to have captured a live one to start a museum with. The yankees had a line of rifle pits to protect themselves in while we were behind the fence. They would crawl out one at a time until there would be 8 or 10 of them watching us with the same curiosity that we did them. When our boys would spring up and bring their guns to bear on them, it would then be rats to your holes, as they would dive into their rifle pits. After awhile our boys would climb onto the fence until there would be a dozen or more. Then the yankees would jump out of their pits with their guns and the boys would fall off the fence like terrapins on a log. This would be kept up for hours without either side firing a gun. Just to our left was the 1st Md. Regiment, and from the sound of their rifles don't think there is any play on that part of the line.

On September 24 we were relieved by the 9th Ga. Regiment and went back about two miles to Falls Church, where we remained several days. This church is said to be one of the oldest in this country and was often visited by the illustrious Washington, the father of his country. It is built out of pressed brick, the first brought to this country, and is in a fine state of preservation.

One morning while at the church, a detail of 200 men was called for the purpose of going into Washington City. The number was soon made up, as everybody wanted to go. As luck would have it I succeeded in getting my name on the list. We struck out for Washington City as we supposed, and after going nearly to Munson's Hill, were halted and put to work throwing up a battery for the Washington Artillery from New Orleans. Done the hardest day's work I ever did in my life, and if God will forgive me this time, will never volunteer again.

September 25 while loitering around the church, everything apparently at peace with the world, the long roll was beat to arms. The regiment was quickly formed in the road. Couriers were dashing at breakneck speed in every direction. Gen. Longstreet, whose headquarters was not far from the church, was soon in the saddle. It was not long before the 9th Georgia, the 2nd South Carolina, 13th Virginia, Col. Stuart's Regiment of Black Horse Cavalry, and Capt. Rosser's battery of artillery was on the grounds, and away we went in the direction of Lewinsville. After going some distance, Company M (Capt. Frank Hill in command) and one section of the artillery was halted while the remainder of the command kept on. While with the artillery in the road, I saw a house about 150 yards up in the field. On top of the house were some of Stuart's men taking observations.

The enemy discovered them and opened on them with artillery which caused the lady living there to flee to the woods with her little children to escape the enemy's shells. She was a sister of Jackson, who killed Col. Ellsworth at Alexandria for tearing down his Confederate flag on his hotel and was killed by Ellsworth's men, being the first bloodshed in the Civil War.[12]

We were soon ordered forward, overtaking the rest of the command some half mile distant, who had halted. Just as we had overtaken the command in a piece of woods, the enemy's artillery opened on our command. My, but you ought to have seen some of the boys' eyes as the shells come crashing through the tops of the trees. Looked like you could have hung your hat on them, and it did seem like every shell was coming right at you as it seemed to say, "Where are you[?]" I had been itching for a long time to get in a fight, but don't believe there is any fun in it. At any rate, I would as soon be somewhere else.

The shelling soon ceased, and the enemy retired across Chain Bridge from where they had come. There were two men killed in the 2nd S.C. Regiment which was all the loss sustained in our first engagement. So we marched back to Falls Church feeling as proud as if we had really been in a battle of some consequence.[13]

On September 26 returned to Pine Creek. At Fairfax Court House our big-hearted captain, A. A. Franklin Hill, purchased a whole cheese and divided [it] among his company. There is nothing small about Capt. Hill except his little finger. His servant boy Tom, with his little wagon drawn by his horse Caliph of Baghdad, cuts something of a figure on our marches. We not only relished the cheese, but the captain's generosity that prompted the gift.

As we neared our camps tired and wearied out, what a change comes over us as our brass band strikes up some lively air, "Dixie" or "The Mockingbird." The order is given, quick-time. The ranks close up to their proper places and we march into camps as though we were just off dress parade. Music is the life of the army.

The boys are having a jolly time eating and drilling. Lt. King[14] puts us through in the double-quick. Sometimes the entire hour's drill will be on the double-quick. The boys puff and blow, but have to keep it up until the command "Halt" is given. Lt. Hudson[15] drills [us] more in the manual of arms, and the boys are certainly proficient with their muskets. Capt. Hill is not much on the drill and but few men make a good drill officer. They not only have to understand tactics, but have a good voice for giving commands. We did not see any use for the double-quick then, but did later on.

Some of the boys are having a pretty tough time of it for their wrongdoings. Some are bucked and gagged. Bucking is tying the wrists together, then sitting him on the ground with his knees drawn up. His arms are forced down over his knees and a stick run through between his arms and legs, and there you are. And there you will be likely to stay until you are turned loose. Should you have too much jaw, a bayonet will be placed between your teeth with a string passed around the head to hold it on, and mum you are. Some wear a ball and chain, others have to grub up stumps while some play with the cannonballs, having five of them, four being placed in a square about 10 feet apart. The fifth one is carried to the first corner, where you put it down and take up the other, which you have to change at each corner. While it looks like it might be funny, it is a considerable strain on the back, and by the time it is kept up two hours is very tiresome.

I would think that tying up by the thumbs was the worst punishment inflicted in the army. His thumbs are tied together over his head and up to something he can just reach by tip-toeing. If he stands there for two hours, he will be very apt to faint before he is cut down. Back at Camp Walker a fellow was tied up by the thumbs for refusing to go on inspection Sunday morning after he had come off guard. By some means he got hold of his gun and shot his left arm off at the wrist. That ended his soldiering. I expect most of them deserve all the punishment they get, for there is some pretty hard cases in the army, and without discipline the men had just as well be at home, for no army can be maintained without it.

We have a good many Irish in the regiment, and while they are good hardy soldiers, they are hard to control. [F]or they will have their dram if it is to be had, and they can find it where no one else will look for it, and after they get it, make the camps blue. Apple brandy can be found and bought at nearly every house in Virginia for 25 cents a quart, and as pure as the driven snow. I can't blame a fellow for getting happy on the way when it is from drinking applejack, as it is called.

The boys have fights in camps pretty often. The other day, Sgt. John Burns[16] and Sgt. M. L. Brantley[17] had a set to with fixed bayonets. Brantley, seeing that Burns was right onto him, threw his musket and broke Burns' thumb, but Burns, nothing daunted, bore down on him. Brantley was running backwards and struck his heel against something that threw him at full length on his back. Burns' bayonet went in the ground to the hilt, just beyond Brantley's head. His fall saved him, as the Irishman was bent on having his scalp.

The Georgia boys are no match for the Irish laddie with his fist, so have to resort to some kind of weapon to defend themselves. If two Irishmen fall out, they will go to the captain of their company and get permission to cross the guard line and fight it out with bare knucks. Whichever whips the other admits he is the best man, they make friends, and return to camps.

The regiment has had quite a gloom cast over it in the loss of our gallant colonel, Charles J. Williams, who left Virginia on sick leave and has since died. He was held in the highest esteem by his regiment, and no doubt if he had lived would have had the stars on his coat collar encircled by a wreath.[18] He was a man of commanding appearance, every movement denoting a perfect soldier. And while a strict disciplinarian, he was extremely courteous to all with whom he come in contact with. How I would have liked to have seen him leading his regiment in a charge, but such was not to be, as he was called to that bourne from whence no traveler returns, before we were even called into action. Peace to his ashes, a gallant soldier and a perfect gentleman has gone to his reward. We still have gallant officers left who will no doubt, when the time comes, display that bravery which all soldiers expect of their commanding officers. Lt. Col. W. J. Magill has been made colonel, and Capt. Martin lieutenant colonel, jumping Maj. John D. Walker, as Martin should have been major instead of Walker.

On October 6 the Regulars went to Accateek Creek on picket duty nine miles from Alexandria, the enemy's lines being four miles distant. Our picket line extended from the bridge up the run of the creek, with one company posted during the day at a farm house on the road and some half mile distant from the bridge. At night this company would fall back to the bridge where Company M was stationed.

One night while fast asleep on the bridge, I was awakened by men stepping over me, which excited my curiosity to know what was going on. So I stripped across the bridge where the excitement seemed mostly to be. Sgt. Burns ordered me with four others to get our muskets and go with him. We could hear what we supposed to be a company of the enemy's cavalry riding through the swamp in the direction of the bridge. Sgt. Burns ordered me to take two men and go out a little piece from the bridge and turn up the creek, while himself and the two others went up the creek bank. We had not proceeded far before both parties went head foremost into a ditch about four feet deep. What a surprise and a wetting we got. We pulled out and both parties got together and started up the creek bank. Our supposed enemy by that time was getting pretty close to the bridge. In the excitement the orderly sergeant had forgot to notify our pickets on the other side of the creek that we were going in front of them. When I called his attention to it, he sent me back across the bridge to notify them that we were in front and not to shoot. Pickets on the outposts have orders to halt anyone on or in rear of the line, but to fire on anything in front. About the time Sgt. Burns and his party arrived opposite the third sentinel, they fired. I never heard such a tearing through the swamp as the enemy made. We learned the next day that it was a lot of loose horses, but they were certainly scared.

On the 10th day of October the Regulars were relieved by the 16th Miss. Regiment. Numbering 1,600 hundred [sic] men, it looked like a young brigade and was the largest regiment I ever saw. We returned to our camps on Pine Creek where we remained until the 15th of October, when the army under Gen. J. E. Johnston fell back to Centreville, the Regulars going into camps at Rocky Run.

CAMP ROCKY RUN, VIRGINIA

The Regulars has drawn new tents, known as the bell or Sibley tent, mounted on a tripod in the center where we can have a fire in the middle of the tent, the smoke going out at the top. Fifteen men can occupy one tent.

The weather is getting rather chilly as the north wind sweeps down from the mountains. While on camp guard one day I saw every tent in camps blow down but one, and it certainly was cold. At every camp, each company builds a rock oven to cook bread in, and you ought to eat some of the delicious beef and mutton we bake in them. One day three out of four in my mess bought a quarter of mutton each. We ate so much mutton we ought to be excused for bloating.

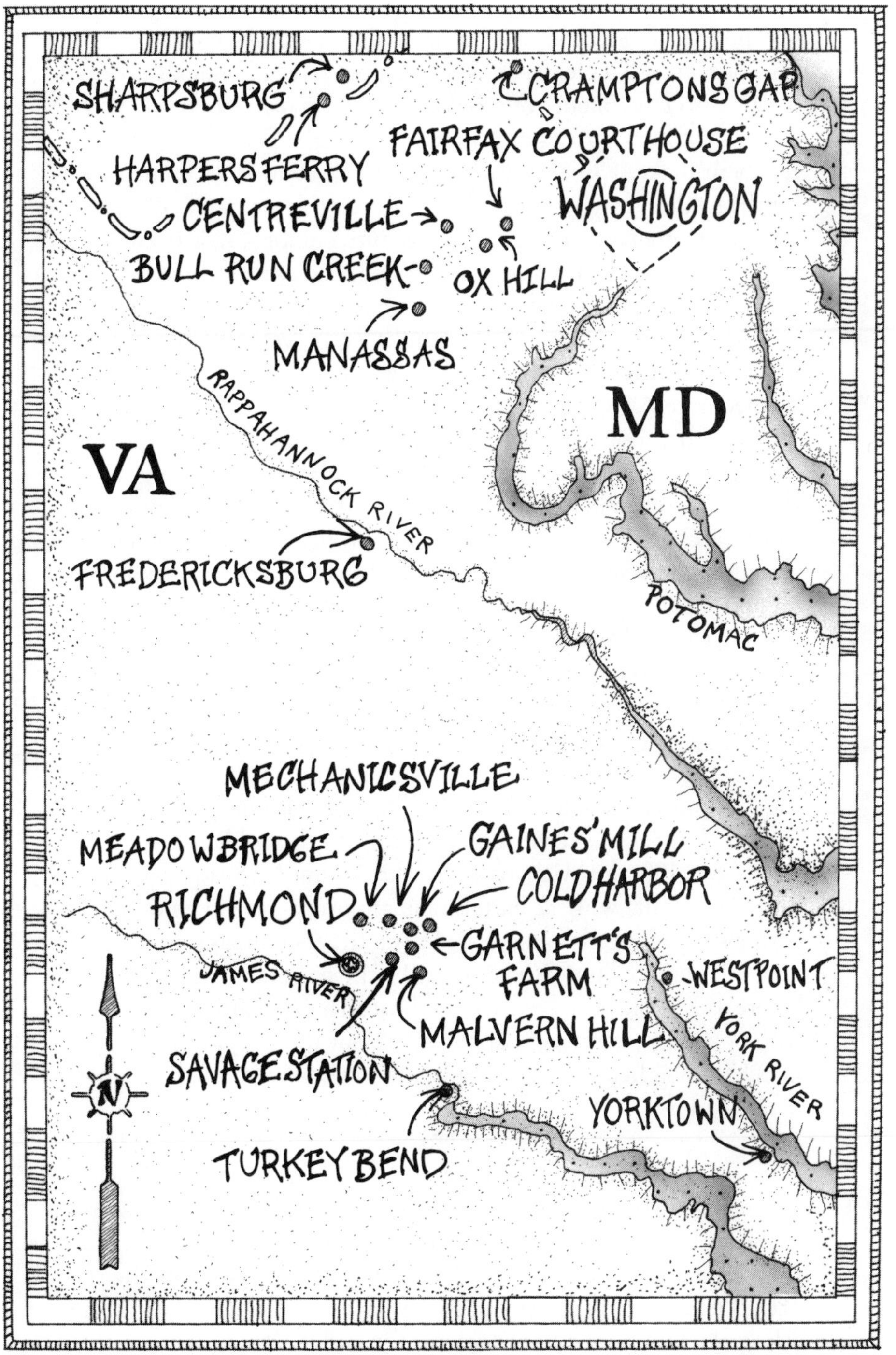

SHARPSBURG
CRAMPTONS GAP
HARPERS FERRY
FAIRFAX COURTHOUSE
WASHINGTON
CENTREVILLE
BULL RUN CREEK
OX HILL
MANASSAS
MD
VA
RAPPAHANNOCK RIVER
FREDERICKSBURG
POTOMAC
MECHANICSVILLE
MEADOWBRIDGE
GAINES' MILL
COLD HARBOR
RICHMOND
GARNETT'S FARM
JAMES RIVER
WESTPOINT
MALVERN HILL
YORK RIVER
SAVAGE STATION
N
YORKTOWN
TURKEY BEND

The army is building heavy fortifications around Centreville. The boys don't relish a pick or shovel much but have to knuckle down to it. We also have plenty of room for battalion drill, and Col. Magill certainly knows how to put the boys through. On dress parade the regiment makes a fine appearance, and [it] seems to be quite a treat for the soldiers camped around us to watch the regiment go through with the maneuvers. The boys have to turn out for parade in apple pie order, shoes blacked, brasses brightened, and white gloves on. The Regulars can go through the maneuvers on dress parade to perfection. Would interest anyone fond of military movements. Can't help making a fine display when the regiment is the best drilled in the Confederate Army.

We take turns in going on picket duty at Cub and Braid [?] runs. On the lookout for applejack more than anything else. Every hog trail in three miles of camp has a picket post on it. Every load of forage has to be searched by running our ramrods through it in search of bottles and jugs, and sometimes five-gallon kegs. The soldiers have a lot of mysterious ways to get into camp with it. For instance, push a stopper down in the neck of the jug, pour a little milk on it, and put in another stopper; or carry it in his gun barrel. With all the searching and watching, the boys will get it into camps sometimes in five-gallon kegs or in barrels. For instance, it is said one fellow had a barrel in his tent selling it, while another fellow was doing a thriving business back of the tent out of the same barrel. The boys are certainly up to snuff.

Gen. Johnston is death on drinking and the soldiers say he can smell it [at] 400 yards with the wind against him. A country man drove into Centreville with 12 barrels of apples in his wagon, and in each barrel was a five-gallon jug of apple brandy. As soon as it was known about the brandy, he sold his apples by the barrel like hot cakes. But before they could be moved, Gen. Johnston had a guard on the ground who opened the barrels of apples, took out the kegs of brandy, and knocked their heads in. The Louisiana Tigers drank it while running in the gullies.

The Tigers are a hard set, said to be wharf rats from New Orleans. They have the zouave, or bloomer, uniform, red pants extending full to the knee, where it is gathered to a band at the knee, the lower part of the leg being enclosed in leggings. Their jackets are of bright blue, their caps are in the shape of a sugarloaf and hang down by the side of the head. Around their waist is a belt in which there is a large knife. Altogether they are a hard-looking set, and if all accounts are true, they don't belie their looks. Could have seen two of them staked down and shot for striking an officer, but have no curiosity to see anything of the kind. They died game and wanted the bandages left off their eyes, but had to keep them on.[19]

On December 20, 1861, army reviewed by Gens. Johnston, Beauregard, and Smith.[20] Line of battle was formed. The generals rode around it, then placed themselves opposite the center and the army passed in review. The order was given for companies to right wheel and close column at half distance, which was done on the double-quick. Our regiment being near the left must have double-quicked at least two miles before catching up. Many a poor fellow dropped from exhaustion. It certainly was a hard review. The weather was extremely cold, the mountain tops being covered in snow.

On the 25th, Christmas day, I spent with my brothers E. M.[21] and J. D. Andrews[22] of the 9th Ga. Regiment, my brother W. L. Andrews of Company M [1st Ga. Regulars] being with us. We had quite a jovial time over our dinner and a bottle of brandy sent from home. Could we have seen in the future, it would have no doubt been a sad one, as it was our last Christmas together. Two out of the four were summoned to cross over the river and rest in the shade of the trees. But ignorance is bliss in some cases.

On the 26th the army was assigned to camps for the purpose of building winter quarters. Toombs' Brigade was located between Manassas Junction and the stone bridge on Bull Run near the battlefield of July 21, and being in a heavy-timbered piece of woods. One of Mrs. Henry's sons was at the camps the other day asking aid of the soldiers. He looked to be 65 or 70 years of age and made a pitiful plea. Col. Magill had the regiment formed and he made a speech, telling about his mother's death and how they had lost everything at the time of the battle. The boys went down in their pockets and assisted him liberally with money. No doubt the fellow was needy, his looks showed that.

January 1, 1862, found the Regulars busy building winter quarters. While labor and material is plentiful, tools are scarce. We go two and three miles from camp for material, and board timber especially. The weather is pretty tough, with the north wind sweeping down from the snow-capped mountains, besides a great deal of wet weather. All roads except turnpikes are almost impassable. The roads used by the army have to be causewayed with poles in order to keep out of the mud. Camps are not only dull but monstrous. The boys are wishing for a change, an active campaign, anything to be moving.

There has been a great deal of sickness in camps and many deaths, especially among the rank and file. A great many of them dying in camps and buried by their companies. What a sad thing, burying the dead with military honors. A private has a funeral escort of eight men commanded by a corporal, who march with arms reversed keeping time with the solemn strains of the dead march to the grave. The corpse being borne by six of his comrades, who lower his remains in a plain pine box to his last resting place which is usually near the camp. If a Catholic, a priest will officiate if he can be obtained. If not, some officer will read the burial service. His escort will then fire three volleys over his grave, wheel, and march off, the band playing some lively tune. The officers always manage to get home or to a hospital. Have never known one to die in camps.

The troops are not very jovial. Caused from homesickness and close confinement in camps. The Army of Northern Virginia of all arms is said to be 60,000 men. The Federal Army around Washington City is claimed to be 200,000 men who are being organized by Gen. George B. McClellan, who has the reputation of being a splendid soldier. Let that be as it may, the probability is that when the roads become passable that the fur is going to fly.

We are doing some picket duty near the camps, more to destroy applejack than anything else. I went with a detachment of 10 men under the command of Lt. James R. DuBose[23] beyond the Bull Run. Crossing at Sudley's Mills, wading the run with six inches of snow on the ground. My, but it was cold. We captured several barrels of apple brandy which was spilt on the ground. After three days, returned to camps. I saw icicles on the banks of Bull Run as large as my body and 10 or 15 feet in length.

On the 20th of January the Regulars completed and moved into their winter quarters. How warm and comfortable compared with our tents. Nothing unusual transpiring in camps. Nearly all of the boys have a nickname of some kind. For instance, in Company M we have Luney Burns, Father Kearnes,[24] Dad Slaven,[25] Pudge Reilly,[26] Polite Smith.[27] Alvin Parr is Joe Dutton. Brennan is Mary Ann, McCann[28] is Paddy Miles' boy, and so on through the company. Another year or two and the boys will forget their proper names. My younger brother, W. L. Andrews, has been detailed to drive Gen. Toombs' forage wagon. He selected and hitched up for the first time the six grays that pulled the general's baggage wagon. While his company loses a good soldier, Gen. Toombs secures a good teamster, a natural horseman who fears nothing on four feet.[29]

RETREAT FROM MANASSAS, VIRGINIA

March 7, 1862. Gen. Johnston ordered three days' rations issued to the army with instructions to hold themselves ready to move at a moment's notice. I was detailed on the Pioneer Corps of 60 men to go in advance of the army and repair the roads and bridges. So on the 8th of March, about one hour before day, the Pioneer Corps formed and marched to Gen. Toombs' headquarters where my brother with the forage wagon was waiting to carry our knapsacks for us. We deposited them in his wagon, but the horses having never been hitched together until the day before, refused to pull, so we had them to carry on our backs for that day's tramp. The next day, the horses were all right and our baggage was hauled for us.

On the 12th we arrived at Culpeper Court House after a pleasant march of four days. What a jolly time we have over our bright and cheerful campfires, boiling our bacon over the coals. The march giving us an appetite capable of eating anything. We crossed the Rappahannock and Hazel rivers by way of Warrenton. I have thought often of an incident that happened while marching through Warrenton. Virginia is noted for her handsome women with their bright eyes and rosy cheeks. On passing through Warrenton, the ladies in great numbers were out on the sidewalks waving their handkerchiefs at the soldiers, who of course cheered everything in sight. In passing a group of them on the sidewalk, one was heard to exclaim, "God bless the soldiers." An old commissary sergeant of Toombs' Brigade heard the remark and replied to her by saying, "God bless you some too." The old soldier looked like he meant just what he said. The lady blushed and remained silent.

On arriving at Culpeper the army went into camps, where we remained until the 16th when the march for Orange Court House was commenced. Arrived there on the 18th crossing the Rapidan River on a bridge made of wagons. Went into camps on the western side of the city. April 1st the army left Orange Court House marching on the plank road in the direction of Fredericksburg. It not only rained, but it come down in sheets all day long and late at night. What a march and such a wetting. After going 10 miles the order was counter-manded and we filed out by the roadside and went into bivouacs for the night. It was not long before we were drying ourselves by a comfortable fire and otherwise making the best of the situation. Early the next morning we went back to our camps at Orange Court House. The mud was just awful, and to make matters worse, we had burnt our camps before leaving them the day before.

On the 11th day of April the brigade took the cars at Orange for Richmond, arriving there in the evening and quartered at Camp Winder. When we reached the depot I was met by one of the 9th Ga. Regiment who informed me that my oldest brother, E. M. Andrews of the 9th, was lying at the point of death at the Chimborazo Hospital. So early the next morning I secured a pass for two hours to go and visit him. I soon found out that I could not get to the hospital before my time would be up, so I returned to camps and waited until the next morning when I secured a pass for eight hours. [A]gain [I] started for the hospital which I succeeded in finding after going several miles, it being on the opposite side of the city from Camp Winder. The house composing the hospital would make a good-sized little town. I succeeded in locating him in Ward H, where I finally found him, but all to no purpose as he had breathed his last the day before and at the time I saw him he was in the dead house on the cooling board. Poor boy, he had died a long way from home and friends, with no one to soothe his aching brow, or take his dying message to his kind mother, who will be heartbroken when she learns that her oldest boy is numbered among the dead. It was a sad sight to look upon his cold form shrouded in a sheet and ready to be borne to Chimborazo's burial ground, there to remain among strangers with no probability of his relatives or friends ever viewing the place where he sleeps. Fare thee well my brother, our loss is your eternal gain. Sleep sweetly in the bosom of old Virginia. I too may be buried in her historic soil.[30]

Having to return to camps, I left him with a heavy heart, as it would have been some consolation to have seen him laid away to rest. Have often thought since then, that he was lucky in dying in the early part of the war and thus escape the hardships that he would have had to underwent. (Life would be no inducement to me to go through what I did during the war. I would have considered myself blessed if I had died at the commencement of the war and escaped the hardships and sufferings through which I had to undergo.) My younger brother J. D. Andrews, of the same company, tried to get a permit to bring his remains home for burial, but failed in his undertaking. Should I die during the war, I hope it will be on some hard-fought battlefield, then bury me where I fall, as I have a perfect horror of being carried a thousand miles after I am dead to be buried. April 13 the brigade embarked on board the steamer *West Point* down the James River for the peninsula.

Such Is Life
and Such Is War

Siege of Yorktown, Virginia

About daylight on the morning of the 14th of April, '62, Toombs' Brigade landed near Yorktown and went into bivouacs within two miles of Dam No. 1. Assigned to Gen. Magruder's[1] Command, Gen. Johnston assuming command of the entire forces on his arrival. On the 15th heavy firing was heard in the direction of Dam No. 1 on the Warwick River. Our brigade was soon moving at double-quick in line of battle in the direction of the firing, but arrived too late to take an active part in the engagement. The enemy [had] been defeated and driven back across the Warwick River below Dam No. 1 by the 7th and 8th Ga. regiments. The enemy had crossed the stream 400 strong and attacked the 5th N.C. Regiment who had their arms stacked and were busy throwing up breastworks. The 5th was easily routed, but the 7th and 8th Ga. regiments being nearby, charged and put the enemy to flight, leaving 45 of their dead on the ground and God alone knows how many in the water.

In order to better understand, I will give a description of Dam No. 1 and vicinity. The James and York rivers form the peninsula, being several miles apart at Yorktown. The Warwick River heads around Yorktown and runs south to the James forming a line between the two armies, [under] Gens. Johnston and McClellan. At proper intervals along this stream the Confederates had thrown up dams to back the water over the swampland to keep the Federals from crossing it. Dam No. 1 is about two miles from Yorktown and the principal point I shall have to deal with. The stream is an ordinary creek, say 12 or 15 feet in width, but by the use of dams its width is increased to 75 or 100 yards. At Dam No. 1, outlet for the water is on the Rebel side where it passes around the dam. Opposite the end of the dam is a redoubt occupied by a 12-pound Napoleon gun double charged with canister.[2] On either side the breastworks continue in a solid line from Yorktown to the James River. In rear of the redoubt is a sand battery [behind sand fortifications] of four guns, and just in rear of that is a section of heavy works, say 100 or 200 yards in length and six or eight feet through, for the protection of infantry while not engaged. On either side of the dam for a space of 50 or 75 yards the timber has been cut down clear through the swamp to an open field. In that field, some 600 yards back from the dam, the yankees have three sand batteries containing four guns each, bearing directly on the dam. When our brigade arrived the enemy had been driven back across the stream, but the firing was pretty hot at Dam No. 1. The Regulars, under Col. W. J. Magill, were ordered behind the heavy works in rear of the dam, losing several in killed and wounded without returning the fire.

At night, soon after our arrival, Companies F and M were ordered to take position in the redoubt at the end of the dam. About nine o'clock, Sgt. James Copeland of Company F[3] was ordered to take four men [a]cross the dam and establish a picket post at the farther end. It fell to my lot to be one of the party to cross the dam. It would have been a moonlit night if it had not been cloudy. At the same time, the dam was visible from one end to the other. I could have seen a rabbit on any part of it. We slid down the bank, waded through the water where it passed around the dam. On reaching the dam we had to get on our hands and knees at the edge of the water, and make our way in that position to keep the enemy's pickets at the end from seeing us. What a trip that was as we drug ourselves through the mud and water, but after a long and hard struggle, we succeeded in reaching the other end crawling up within 20 steps of the enemy's picket post, close enough to hear them whisper. The hours of that night I shall never forget. Lying on my left side, half sunk in the mud, with my musket firmly grasped in my right hand. The least move would have brought the enemy's fire on our position, but everything passed off quietly.

Just before day, benumbed, cold, and stiff, we started back on our weary crawl. After an almost endless time, we succeeded in getting back to the waterway. As we waded through and were going to ascend the redoubt, the alarm was given. The soldiers, to a man, sprung to their feet. Their guns flashed over the works, and for the time being, I thought I was a dead man. But just in time to save us, someone spoke. The guns were withdrawn from over the works and we ascended safe, but badly scared. It certainly was a close call, and one I don't wish to go through with again.

During the morning, under a flag of truce, our men delivered to the enemy 45 of their men killed on the evening before. They claimed only a loss of 15 men, but 45 was what was carried to them. During the flag of truce, Sgt. Lyon[4] of the Regulars had a silver badge on his cap with the inscription of "God and our rights," which one of the boys in blue read and remarked, "I believe they will get them too."

The brigade remained near Dam No. 1, sometimes at there [the dam or?] above or below it. The works were occupied by lines of battle relieving each other every 34 hours,[5] and just after night as no movement of troops could be accomplished during the day, only under a heavy fire from the enemy. Under the fallen treetops above and below the dam, the enemy's sharpshooters would conceal themselves before day every morning, and it was worth a man's life to show his head above the works, five of the Regulars being killed by trying the experiment. In the first of the war, a soldier thought that he was not brave if he did not stand out and let a regiment shoot at him if they wanted to, but that finally played out and a soldier could hide behind almost anything he could find. It was certainly a very bad place, and one to be avoided if it could have been [done], but each regiment had to take its turn and the consequences with it.

Many nights while below the dam, we would sit with water up to our knees and sleep under the inspiring music of the frogs. Whoever thought there was music in the hollering and croaking of the frogs? Under certain circumstances there is. It is a well-known fact that frogs will not holler when the water is disturbed, and in that fact lay the music. As long as they kept up their music, we knew that the yankees were not crossing the swamp.

From some cause, I never knew what, there would be false alarms on the lines at night. Starting on the James River to our right, coming like a flash up the line, but when it would strike the Regulars would pass over and start on the other side. Don't think there was ever a gun fired in our regiment. The firing would usually draw the enemy's

artillery fire for a few rounds. Then quiet would again reign supreme
on the line. During the false alarm our pickets would have to get on
the opposite side of the trees. One night, during a false alarm, the
Regulars were stationed behind the heavy works. There was a large
force of Negroes throwing up works in our front. They worked by
details, one-half on duty, the others off. Sometime during the night
the relief off duty lay down among the soldiers and went to sleep, but
few soldiers being aware of their presence. During the night there was
a false alarm. The Negroes to a man broke to the rear, and most of the
soldiers with them, who on coming to their senses returned to the
works, but the darkies did not return until the next night. One of
them speaking to a soldier said, "Boss, I thought I could do some tall
running, but that white-headed man there left me out of sight." He
had reference to Pvt. Carolen[6] of Company M who run about two
miles before he could stop himself. Sgt. Garrett[7] run 75 yards before
he knew what he was doing and then made his way back faster than
he went off. Don't think he got over his run for six months or more.
The sergeant did not like the idea of acting the coward, even if he was
asleep.

The next day while we were lying behind the works, Sgt. Garrett,
Pvt. W. A. Bonds,[8] and myself were enjoying ourselves talking about
our best girls at home. Pvt. Bonds was in a jovial mood, and after
talking until he was tired, lay down with his back to the works and his
head against the stump on which I was leaning, and soon went to
sleep. Sometime afterwards, one of the Texan sharpshooters shot the
flagstaff in two on one of the yankee batteries beyond the dam. It
aroused the ire of the yankees and they opened fire on us: the first shell
exploding just as it passed through the works. Pvt. Boyle, lying at my
feet, was killed by a ball from the shell striking him in the heart. He
jumped to his feet, called Capt. Hill, told him he was a dead man, fell
back, and expired. A piece of the shell struck me just above the left
knee making a slight wound, and passed between Bonds' shoulders
killing him instantly. His head falling out of balance was all the move
he made. On examining him we found in his pocket an ambrotype of
a beautiful young lady whose face was all radiant with smiles. What
a contrast to her soldier sweetheart who was lying in the cold embrace
of death. But one short hour ago he was in the prime of life, no doubt
looking forward to the time when he could clasp to his heart one who
was dearer than life itself. But such is life and such is war.

After wrapping him in his soldier blanket, we lowered him into a soldier's grave. Sweet by your sleep my comrade, until the Judgement Day. Well done, good and faithful servant, you died at your post with no stain to cause the blush of shame to mantle the cheeks of your comrades [left] behind. Peace to your ashes, a genial companion and a gallant soldier. Rest in peace while your gallant comrades avenge your death. May my taking off be like his, like the bolt of lightning's flash. How I dread to be mangled up—death is preferable, so [if] I die on some hard-fought field with my face to the enemy.

One evening just at dark while the Regulars were posted above the dam, the enemy was very busy felling trees on the opposite side just above the dam. Lt. James Armstrong from Augusta, Ga., raised his head above the works to see what was going on. He had not more than straightened himself before a minié ball went crashing through his brain.[9] Another gallant soldier gone to his reward. He enlisted as a private, but for meritorious conduct was commissioned 2nd lieutenant. Dam No. 1 would be a good place for a man to commit suicide. Nothing to do but straighten himself up and shuffle off this mortal coil. We remained on duty in the vicinity of Dam No. 1 until the morning of the 3rd of May, when about one hour before day, the lines were withdrawn and we commenced to retreat to Richmond. Leaving Yorktown and vicinity with no regrets.

RETREAT FROM YORKTOWN, VIRGINIA

It was with a lively quick step we commenced our march, having no regrets at leaving a place surrounded with so much hardships and so many dangers. Sometime in the afternoon, Magruder's forces reached Williamsburg. How grim and silent the fortifications around that place looked, so soon to be the scene of a deadly conflict. After passing Williamsburg several miles, the heavy roar of musketry and the dull boom of the cannon told us that Gen. McClellan's forces had overtaken and attached our rear, commanded by Gen. Longstreet.[10] If anything, we quickened our march. The forts at Yorktown being vacated [evacuated], the enemy has nothing to do but steam [up the York River] past them and make an effort to cut off our retreat to Richmond. After nightfall the battle ceased, but our marching was continued with redoubled energy.

The Regulars were detailed to support a battery of artillery, or in other words, to pull it out of the mud. What a night we had of it, the horses to their knees in mud, with the axles of the artillery scraping the top of the road, the soldiers tugging at the wheels, the drivers cursing and beating their broke-down stock. All contributed to make it a night long to be remembered. After tugging at the wheels all night and just as the sun was rising, we hove in sight of the brigade which was just filing out into the road to resume the march. So without rest or refreshment we had to continue our march. What would I have not given could I have dropped down by the roadside and rested my weary limbs, besides snatching a few hours of sweet sleep so much needed, but alas no rest for the weary.

We managed that day to keep up with the command. At night we bivouacked by the roadside, but trouble never comes single handed. Our skillet wagons did not catch up, somewhere back in the mud. So we had to make all kinds of shifts to cook something to eat. I secured a piece of cloth, made out my flour dough on it, wrapped the dough around my ramrod, scooped out a small place on the ground, filled it with coals, and baked my bread. Rather a slow process, but succeeded in getting my supper after awhile. How blessed to stretch my weary limbs on the ground. How sweetly I slept, no doubt dreaming of home and loved ones far away in the sunny South.

Next morning the retreat was continued without molestation until West Point was reached. There the enemy landed and attempted to cut us off, but were defeated and driven into the river with heavy loss.[11] While our brigade was lying in reserve during the fight, I saw an incident that showed considerable pluck or nerve.

A horseman come dashing up the road at full speed. On arriving at our regiment he asked for our surgeon, Dr. Cherry.[12] The doctor being pointed out to him, he leaped from his horse, handed the bridle reins to a soldier, walked up to the doctor, and asked him to perform a surgical operation on him. He had been shot through the arm just below the elbow while resting his arm on his gun. The surgeon called four men to assist him. He stretched the poor fellow on his back and almost in the twinkling of an eye, had it off. He rose from the ground, thanked the surgeon, vaulted into the saddle, and away he went as though nothing had happened. He was what I call game. After defeating the enemy at West Point, continued the retreat to Richmond.

SIEGE OF RICHMOND

On the 17th of May the army arrived at Richmond and formed our lines about five miles north of the city, extending from the James River beyond Meadow's Bridge on the Chickahominy River. Gen. McClellan on his arrival formed his left on White Oak Swamp, crossing the Chickahominy at Meadow's Bridge then out to Mechanicsville, 15 miles in length. On our arrival at Richmond, our brigade was ordered to Meadow's Bridge on picket duty where we caught a heavy shelling from the enemy. Remained in that vicinity until June the 1st when we were ordered to Seven Pines, a heavy battle having been fought between Gens. Johnston and McClellan on May 31.

What a forced march we had, many soldiers fainting and falling by the roadside. How hot it was, the sun coming down with all vengeance and not a breath of air stirring. Arrived too late to take part in the engagement. The enemy had crossed White Oak Swamp in force. A rise in the creek cut them off, as Gen. Johnston supposed, and he decided to kill or capture them. But reinforcements were rapidly sent to their assistance, making a drawn fight with heavy losses on both sides, Gen. Johnston among the wounded. Gen. Robert E. Lee assigned to the command of Gen. Johnston's Army, known as the Army of Northern Virginia.[13]

June the 2nd our brigade went on picket on the York River Railroad where we remained two days. Nothing transpiring worthy of notice. June 4 [the] brigade went to Garnett's Farm, on the Nine Mile Road. Remained in that vicinity doing picket duty between the Nine Mile Road and Meadow's Bridge until June 20, when we were transferred from Toombs' to Anderson's Brigade. I shall never forget when Gen. Toombs ordered us to report to Gen. Anderson. We were on picket in the branch in front of the brick house on Garnett's Farm. He rode down to our line in a perfect rage, ordered Col. Magill to take his d——d regiment and get to the rear, as we were not worthy of facing the enemy, would send his regiment to the rear and make a wagon guard of it. We marched out, leaving our place vacant and exposed to the enemy some 200 yards distant, as he brought no relief to take our place. Now crestfallen the Regulars looked as they marched out with their heads hung in shame. Not worthy to face the enemy, to be made a wagon guard of, enough to make the men hang their heads in shame.

While Gen. Toombs acted very harshly, he believed he had sufficient grounds for his actions. The Regulars were his pets. Often had he told them the 1st Georgia shall always hold the post of honor.

That means, in military parlance, the post of danger. The Regulars were under the strictest military discipline. Gen. Toombs was a big-hearted man and could not bear for his men, as he put it, to be imposed upon. So when any of the Regulars were punished, whether rightly or not, they would report it to the general who would ride over to the regiment, curse out the officers, and return to his quarters. The officers of the regiment got tired of it and appealed to the secretary of war for a transfer, which resulted in our being turned over to Gen. George T. Anderson's Brigade.[14]

There has never been but one Gen. Robert Toombs. He would have taken sides with the poorest private in his command against President Davis if he thought he was trying to impose on him. He always defended the weak and helpless. He acknowledged no superiors, and but few equals. The Regulars loved and admired him. He afterwards stated to some of the men that his aspersions were not intended for the men, but for the officers of the regiment.[15]

The Regulars reported to Gen. Anderson in rear of Garnett's Farm, his brigade being composed of the 7th, 8th, 9th, and 11th Ga. regiments. A gallant brigade with a gallant commander. The next day after joining Anderson's Brigade, there was mutiny in Company M. The troops had been ordered paid off. Eight companies were paid off, leaving M and another company still to be paid. From some cause our company was not paid in one or two days, so one evening we returned from dress parade, after Capt. Hill had turned the company over to Sgt. Burns for dismissal on the company parade grounds, Sgt. Burns made a proposition to the company to not break[16] the stack of guns until we were paid off. Pvt. Craft[17] and myself told Sgt. Burns he could leave us out. As we never enlisted for money, we would never mutiny for it. The balance of the company remained silent, thereby giving their consent. Someone reported the matter to Capt. Hill in five minutes after it was done. He had the company formed, told them of what he had heard, and asking all that had formed that resolution to step two paces to the front. Sgt. Garrett stepped out, the rest of the company remained motionless. Capt. Hill ordered Sgt. Burns to take a file of men and arrest Sgt. Garrett, and take him to Col. Magill's headquarters. On arriving at the colonel's quarters, charges were made against him for mutiny, the penalty of which is death. As a gallant soldier, Sgt. Garrett stood as high as any man in the regiment, a fact well known by the colonel. After talking to Sgt. Garrett awhile, Col. Magill told him if he would acknowledge that he had done wrong and was sorry for it, he would return him to his company. Sgt. Garrett informed the colonel that he had done what he did with his eyes open and had no acknowledgements to make. Col. Magill had him placed under a guard and sent to Castle Thunder in Richmond to await his trial for mutiny, and confined in a dungeon.[18]

Now I will make this assertion, there was not 10 men in the Army of Northern Virginia who would not have accepted Col. Magill's proposition and returned to his company. Not so with the gallant Sgt. William Jasper Garrett, a worthy representative of his illustrious namesake, Sgt. William Jasper of Revolutionary fame.[19] Sgt. Garrett remained in prison two or three days and was then returned to his company. He had influential friends in Congress who would have made it hot for the officers who had been ordered to pay off but failed to obey orders. So they were glad to open the prison doors and return him to his company without so much as reducing him to the ranks.

It seems strange with plenty of money, and within five miles of Richmond, that the troops should go 10 or 12 months without their scanty wages. Three-fourths of the soldiers are wool hat boys, with families at home depending on them for support. But such is the case, being an everyday occurrence for men to get letters from home stating that their families are on the point of starvation. Many a poor soldier has deserted and gone home in answer to that appeal, to be brought back and shot for desertion. Hard it certainly is. Would desert myself under the same circumstances. Thank God I have no wife and children to suffer on account of an ungrateful government.[20]

Another cause for dissatisfaction is the substitute law. A man who has money can hire a man to take his place. The poor man has to take his own place. Another bad law is the 20 Negro law, a man owning that number [of slaves] being exempt from military duty if he chooses to stay out of the army. Another cause for complaint is the conscript law, forcing a man into service whether he wants to go or not, allowing him no say so about the company or command he serves in. But from the appearance of everything, we will soon have something of more importance to think about.[21]

Gen. McClellan is now confronting the capital of the Confederacy with 120,000 men. He has heavily lines fortified [sic] at many points on his lines. He has siege guns, wire fences, the trees felled in front of his line with the limbs sharpened and drove in the ground with points sharpened to the front. Almost impassable for a rabbit, much less a line of battle. Altogether, times are looking squally. We are having a hog-killing time comparing it with Yorktown. I have been under the fire of sharpshooters but one time, that was on Garnett's Farm just below Meadow's Bridge. Gen. McClellan's line crossed the Chickahominy River at Meadow's Bridge. His picket line being posted through the open field where they had rifle pits. The pits being full of water, the men walked their post as if on camp guard. While they were in range of our guns, we were not molesting them, something the Regulars never done if it could be avoided. If the enemy let us alone, we would them, but if they wanted a fight, we gave them the best in our shop.

Sometime during the day, Capt. H. D. D. Twiggs[22] come down on the line and ordered his company, G, to open fire on them. It was amusing to see the boys in blue strike the water in the rifle pits, but they soon turned the laugh on us by making us hug the trees and ground. The first shot cost Pvt. George Toole his arm,[23] and passed through Pvt. Parish's[24] body costing him his life. The firing was kept up until night.

A few days afterwards I was in charge of a picket post farther down the river, but still on Garnett's Farm. I could hear something like giving commands or someone making a speech, but could see nothing from where I was. So I left the three men I had, and crawled down a gully to the bottom of the hill where I had a good view of the enemy lines. Just to my right about 400 yards, the enemy was drawn up in front of their breastworks in line of battle, with their officers riding up and down the line. How blue these lines looked, and how bright their arms looked in the sunshine. Never knew what they were up to, reviewing or making a speech. Several times they cheered with that terrible "hip hurrah," all as one man. Enough to lift your hat if it don't lift your feet. I thought they might be going to advance, so I made my way back.

Inside of the enemy's lines, in front of Garnett's Farm, a balloon has been sent up for several days. The last time I saw it, Long Tom, a noted rifle[d] piece captured from Sherman's Battery at the First Battle of Manassas, was fired at it.[25] It come down in a hurry. I suppose the balloon was let up by a rope, and when at the proper height to see along our lines, was anchored out until the aeronaut wished to descend. The balloon would then be hauled down.[26]

Opposite the point of woods on Garnett's Farm the other day, I saw a yankee sharpshooter concealed behind an old chimney whip two pieces of artillery, they having to withdraw without knocking the chimney down. One of the yankee's bullets struck the tire of the wheel, split it open, and wounded two men.

In passing the 9th Georgia the other day, I saw something that certainly amused me. A soldier was lying at full length on his back, fast asleep. A calf was feeding nearby. I reckon the calf must have taken the soldier for a log, as he lay so still. The calf stepped over him with his front feet, still nibbling the grass. The soldier moved and scared the poor calf so bad that it jumped up and down on the soldier's breast, which scared the soldier as bad as it did the calf. The calf finally succeeded in getting from over the soldier, who then struck the calf on the side of the head with a brick bat, nearly killing it.

June 24 the Regulars joined the rest of the brigade above Meadow's Bridge on the hillside. The troops having honeycombed the hill [with rifle pits] to protect themselves from the enemy's shells on the north side of the Chickahominy River. After the Regulars were transferred from Toombs' to Anderson's Brigade, my brother W. L. Andrews had to report to his company for duty.

SEVEN DAYS' FIGHT AROUND RICHMOND

In order to understand the movements of the two armies in the Seven Days' Fight, I will try and explain the positions occupied before the fight opened. Gen. McClellan had established his base at the White House [Plantation] on the Pamunkey River, receiving his war supplies from Washington City by way of Alexandria and Fredericksburg, thus placing his army between the two capitals. Gen. Lee, with about 50,000 men, was between McClellan and Richmond. Gen. Stonewall Jackson[27] was beyond the Blue Ridge Mountains in the [Shenandoah] Valley, where he had just won a decided victory over Gens. Frémont,[28] Shields,[29] and Banks,[30] three commands which had been sent out to capture him from Washington City. But Jackson and his foot cavalry had out generaled them all, whipping them in detail before they could unite their forces.[31]

McClellan's lines around Richmond was impregnable in Gen. Lee's front; so Gen. Lee ordered Gen. Jackson from the valley with 30,000 men to strike and turn McClellan's right flank at Mechanicsville, which Jackson succeeded in doing on the 26th day of June, 1862. Jackson's turning of McClellan's right flank at Mechanicsville uncovered Gen. Lee's left on the Chickahominy, which he speedily taken advantage of by crossing the troops of Gens.

Longstreet and D. H. Hill to Jackson's assistance, leaving Gen. J. B. Magruder with 25,000 men between the enemy and Richmond. Gen. Lee's object was to turn McClellan's flank, fight him in rear of his works, and if possible, cut him off from his base of supplies at the White House. Gen. Magruder was to defend [against] any attack made on the city, and at the same time, harass the enemy's front by making feint attacks so as to draw his attention from his rear.[32]

On the evening of the 26th, Gen. Anderson with the 1st and 9th Ga. regiments attached the enemy's works on the Nine Mile Road. Gen. Anderson remarked to the Regulars as we started out, "Boys, I don't doubt your fighting qualities." He was correct in his opinions, and never had any cause afterwards to change them. We entered the woods to the right of the Nine Mile Road, where Gen. Howell Cobb's Brigade was in position, and halted. Skirmishers were then thrown out from the 1st and 9th, who charged and carried the enemy's rifle pits, driving them back to their main line of works, our men occupying the rifle pits.

As soon as the enemy entered their works, they opened on us with grape and canister from their siege guns. It was simply terrific. Seemed more like nail kegs loaded with spikes than anything else. What a crash it made coming through the trees. We certainly hugged close to old mother earth as she seemed very dear at that time. I could not help watching the boys to see if anybody else was as bad scared as I was. My eye finally rested on the worst scared piece of humanity it has ever been my lot to see. He was lying spread so flat on the ground, he did not look like anything but a jacket. His eyes looked like bursting from their sockets. Altogether he was the worse scared and most contemptible-looking creature I have ever seen. On looking a little closer, I discovered it to be no less a personage than Cpl. Pony Jones. How the mighty hath fallen. Not many months ago, the corporal was in his glory, arresting men and putting them in dungeons, going the grand round and getting the boys' guns away from them. But now where is he? Crouching under the enemy's guns and scared within one inch of his worthless life. A little more grape [shot] Mr. Yank, his eyes will come [out of their sockets] after awhile. Our loss in the two regiments amounted to 25 men killed and wounded. On retiring, we could hear the distant guns of Jackson, Hill, and Longstreet as they were gradually forcing back the enemy's right flank at Mechanicsville.

On the 27th the battle of Cold Harbor was fought, still turning Little Mac's right flank.[33] From the roar of musketry and booming of cannon, the conflict must be a desperate one. In the afternoon, the 7th and 8th Ga. regiments charged the enemy's works on Golding's Farm, between the brick house and the enemy's battery to the left of it. Col. Lamar of the 8th fell on the breastworks and was captured by the enemy.[34]

It was a desperate attempt, but failed with heavy loss to the 7th and 8th regiments. The 1st and 9th started in as reinforcements, but was halted by our division commander, Gen. D. R. Jones.[35] We got close enough for the bullets to be quite familiar, one passing between mine and Sgt. Burns' head. That peculiar zip a bullet has makes a fellow feel spotted. Returned to our position above Meadow's Bridge.

In going in, we passed one of our batteries. Just before we got to it, met two men bearing between them a wounded soldier with both legs shot off just above his ankles. A small piece of skin held his feet on. It was a sickening sight to see his feet as they twisted and dangled to his legs. Death would be preferable to such a wound as that.

On the 28th was fought the battle of Gaines' Mill.[36] The booming of cannon and roar of musketry tells us that the fighting is getting nearer each day, as our men are still driving the enemy back. Gaines' Mill is on the opposite side of the Chickahominy from us. While we listen to the awful roar of musketry and artillery on the other side, the yankees are not slighting our brigade by any means, as their artillery is shelling us for all we are worth while we grin and endure it.

At night we took a position on Garnett's Farm opposite the point of woods. We remained under arms all night expecting an attack from the enemy. But the night passed off quietly with nothing to disturb us. Towards sunrise, our scouts were ordered forward to ascertain the whereabouts of the enemy in our front, Sgt. W. J. Garrett being the first man to enter McClellan's lines, finding them deserted. The troops were then ordered forward, our brigade leading the advance.

BATTLE OF THE PEACH ORCHARD

We marched out by the brick house on Garnett's Farm, crossed the branch, and entered the enemy's lines at a fort on Golding's Farm. Just as we were entering the works, a courier come riding along the line in our front with a lady's garment tossed to the breeze. What a yell went up at the sight of it. If we could not cheer a woman, we could her wearing apparel. The soldier had secured it in the enemy's camps, which we soon entered and found all their tents standing just as they

had marched out and left them. We found quartermasters, commissaries, and sutlers supplies all intact. Our men broke ranks and began
pillaging, some one thing and some another. Most of them succeeded
in getting a turn. After a great deal of trouble, the officers succeeded
in forcing the men back into ranks. The brigade was halted and the
Regulars were ordered to the front.

After going some little distance, we were deployed as skirmishers
and moved forward through a piece of woods. The Regulars moved
forward quite jovial, having no idea of overtaking the yankees, as we
supposed they had left early the night before. Some were singing,
others whistling, and all in a jolly good humor. After going some
distance through the woods, and when least expecting it, we received
a volley from the enemy's line of skirmishers in ambush, who after
firing, rapidly retreated to a small branch. The Regulars were halted
until Col. W. J. Magill could receive orders from Gen. Anderson
whether to attack or not.

While we were halted, I was keeping a sharp lookout to the front.
I saw as I supposed, a yankee not far in advance making his retreat. I
placed my gun to my shoulder, took deliberate aim, and pressed the
trigger. Just as I was in the act of shooting, the yankee stooped down
to pass under a limb, and who should it be but Lt. Fred B. Palmer, who
had a yankee overcoat on his arm that he had picked up in the enemy
camps. The cold chills crept up my spine after I found out my mistake.
A close call for the lieutenant who was scouting in front. Had it been
my misfortune to have shot him, I would have always regretted it. The
lieutenant was a favorite with the regiment, having served a long time
as sergeant major, and he made a good one too.[37]

While we were all awaiting orders, we will take a peep in front and
see how the ground lies. A few yards in front of Company M is a small
strip of cleared ground. And just beyond that is a small branch with
a few trees growing on its edge, now occupied by the enemy skirmish
line. Just beyond in a large field you can see the enemy's line of battle,
5,000 men with eight pieces of artillery on the right. And directly in
front of Company M, the right of the yankee line is in a peach orchard,
while in the rear is some farm houses. Not an inviting picture for
Company M, especially as we will have to advance through the open
field in full view of the enemy. The rest of the line to our right being
woods down to the branch. Company M is the ninth company in line,
which throw us near the left of the regiment.

The order was soon given to forward skirmishers, and we moved briskly to the front. On entering the clearing you should have seen the charge of Company M through the clearing, with the enemy skirmishers in the branch popping away at us as we charged. We soon entered the branch and then someone else had to do some running. As I entered the timber, a big, broad-shouldered yankee with a large knapsack on his back run out on the opposite side. I drew a bead at the small of his back and fired, and with a spring and a bound, I landed behind a good-sized black gum tree. And none too soon, as the bullets rattled among the undergrowth like a summer shower of rain. At the same time, the artillery belched forth missiles of death and destruction. They certainly gave us a warm reception, and to make matters just a little bit warmer, a battery of ours took a position in the opening just in rear of Company M, thereby placing the company between the two batteries. How the shells and canister flew. What a place to be in, between two batteries of artillery and a line of infantry 60 yards in front. Our battery was soon silenced. Four pieces opposed to eight had no show whatever, and soon had to drag their pieces to the rear.

The fighting continued until sometime in the afternoon, when our line was flanked on the left and had to beat a hasty retreat. It certainly was a hot place. During the fight I had a ball lodged in my gun, and stepping back to drive the rammer against the tree, I was struck just above the elbow of my left arm with a spent ball. It never broke the skin, but deadened my arm so I could not move a finger in several hours.[38]

While I was rubbing and bathing my arm and hand in a little stream that run at the root of the tree behind which I was standing, my brother W. L. Andrews was at the next tree to my left. At one time he crawled to the little stream in front of him to get water. He then worked his way backwards on his stomach to his gun. We had a good laugh over his way of wiggling away from the water. (Poor boy, it was his last laugh on God's green earth. His time was fast drawing to a close.) After getting back to his gun, he again made it warm for the enemy, but only for a short time. He had gotten from behind his tree and was firing from his knee, when he was struck by a musket ball and a buckshot between the hip and short ribs on the left side. He fell over, but managed to get off his coat and accoutrements. How the poor boy suffered no one will ever know. Sgt. Garrett wanted to carry him out, but the firing was so heavy I decided to wait and take our chances of getting him out later. So when the order was given to retreat after we were flanked, he was still in the branch.

As the regiment retreated, two of my company, Pvts. David Gann[39] and —— Kelly,[40] come to my assistance. It certainly proved a daring undertaking, with a line of battle and eight pieces of artillery in our front, and a line of battle on our left. When ordered to retreat, our comrades were quickly out of sight, leaving us a target for everything in sight. Time and again we had dirt thrown over us by canister from the artillery. As to minié balls, the air was full of them. How we ever escaped, God only knows, but a kind providence must have been watching over us.

He weighed 185 pounds, and was as much as two men could carry, the other one carrying the guns. At least every 30 steps he would make us put him down and beg us to leave him before we were all killed, but my faithful comrades stuck to me until we carried him out of danger to a farm house that the yankees had used for a hospital, and the Confederates were putting it to the same purpose. There we found our assistant surgeon, Dr. Mayo,[41] who examined his wound and stated that it was not fatal. My gallant brother was then dying. Placing him on a mattress with his head in my lap, I watched his hard breathing with feelings I cannot find words to express. So young, so full of hope, with the best part of his life yet in front of him. It was hard to see him in the throes of death. What made it go harder with me, I was the cause of his being in the army. After I joined he would follow me. How our poor mother's heart will ache when she hears that another one of her soldier boys has gone to join the first.

Soon after our arrival at the hospital, he was placed in an ambulance with Lt. J. D. Anthony[42] and Pvts. Shields,[43] Smith,[44] and Watkins,[45] all members of Company M who had been wounded in the fight. As the ambulance started off, he called to me, and the last words I ever heard him say was, "Revenge that shot," which rang in my ears on many a hard-fought field afterwards. He was carried back to the brick house on Garnett's Farm and died in 15 minutes after his arrival. He was wrapped in his soldier's blanket, and filled a soldier's grave. After he had been placed in the ambulance, I again started for the front.

After the Regulars fell back, the Federals continued the retreat to Savage Station, where a heavy engagement took place that evening. In passing where we fought, I examined the tree my brother was behind and found 14 balls not over waist high. During the fight, a rabbit come hopping down the branch in front of our line. All of the boys wanted a shot as it passed. Pvt. Mahan[46] of Company G, in his eagerness to get a shot, stepped from behind his tree. As he did so, he received a ball through his heart. He was laughing at the time, and death was so sudden that the muscles of his face never relaxed. Looked to be laughing when I saw him several hours afterwards. First Sgt. Alex Clemency[47] of Company G received a very peculiar wound. He was struck by a ball between the corner of his eye and his nose, and passed out through his under jaw. His skull must have caused the ball to glance.

After crossing the branch, I looked for my yankee with the broad back and large knapsack that I shot at when entering the branch. I found two knapsacks near where I shot. One was shot centrally through and was bloody, while in the other the ball had passed through the knapsack to the back of it, where it has struck a small round looking glass, passing through the front, breaking the glass and lodged against the back. Did not know which was my shot, but think one or the other was.

After the enemy retreated, the Regulars again advanced as skir-mishers and continued in line until Savage Station was reached, but were not in the fight at that place. So I followed on after the regiment until night overtaken me, then dropped down exhausted by the roadside, where I remained for several hours until our brigade re-turned from Savage Station, marching back near the peach orchard where we bivouacked for the night. How it rained. Come down in torrents.

BATTLE OF FRAZIER'S FARM

Gens. Lee and Jackson having cut McClellan off from his base at the White House, all of his forces were concentrated on the south side of the Chickahominy River. His only way of escape was by the James River. On the next morning, the 30th day of June, we saw a portion of Jackson's Command, among them the bloody Louisiana Tigers, rank and file with one commissioned officer. Maj. Wheat, their commander, had fallen at Coal Harbor, where they charged the enemy's works the fifth time before they succeeded in gaining an entrance, the major falling in the last charge. On entering the works, it was told that some of them bayoneted as many as 11 of the enemy. The loss of their commander made them furious. After the fight [they] returned to where the major fell, and wept over him like so many children. Maj. Wheat was said to be a comrade of Gen. Walker in

Nicaragua.[48] The Tigers' flag, the Confederate battle cross, looked like it had been used to clean out chimneys, and afterwards drawn through a briar patch. It was simply torn into shreds by the enemy's bullets. How *proud* they bear it aloft, and well they may be, for it would be an honor to any command.

On the railroad was a large brass cannon mounted on a flat car, with an engine to maneuver it, which could only be used on the railroad track. Jackson's men marched to our left, Magruder's going to the right. Late in the evening we again heard the roar of musketry and the booming of cannon, telling us our forces were again engaged in a deadly conflict at Frazier's Farm.[49] We quickened our pace but night overtaken us when within three miles of the battlefield. What a roar of musketry. Thousands of men engaged in a game of life and death.

From some unaccountable cause, we were until three o'clock in the morning taking our position on the field. What a wearisome march. Tired and nearly dead for sleep, we would halt then move up a few steps, then halt again. Keeping it up until we reached the field. On the way we met two cavalrymen with Maj. Gen. McCall, U.S.A., walking between them [as] a prisoner of war. I think they might have let him ride as it was twelve miles to Richmond.[50]

When we arrived on the field [we] stacked arms and dropped down to sleep. I must have been fast asleep before I struck the ground. When I awoke the next morning the picture that met my eye will never be forgotten. Directly in our front, 42 horses were lying six and six, just as they had been shot down the night before. Our forces captured 20 pieces of artillery at that point, and had to shoot down the horses to keep them [the Federals] from carrying the artillery off. How pitiful they looked, all with the harnesses on, some with their heads thrown over the necks of their mates, in the dying struggles. Hard that it should be so, but horses have just about as bad a time in war as men do.

In our rear the ground was covered with the dead from the ranks of the blue and the gray. How desperate must have been that fight, but the Federals were again defeated. This war is something terrible. Thousands of men have fallen in the last five days on either side, and the end is not yet, but another heavy battle will likely be fought today.

BATTLE OF MALVERN HILL

About sunrise [July 1], Gen. Anderson gave the command "Attention First Brigade, take arms." The line was quickly formed, stacks of guns broken, and we were ready for any emergency. Old Tige rode up and down his line telling the boys, "We will whip them out today and be done with it," and he looked like he meant just what he said. The First Brigade is proud of its gallant commander and ready to follow him to the cannon's mouth or the point of the bayonet. He then gave the word "Forward march." We moved in line of battle to the front, passing over many of the yankee wounded who had fallen the night before. How pitiful they appealed to us as we marched over them to not step on them, which we had no idea of doing. We passed out of the field, then through a piece of woods, and entered another field, where we were halted.

While we were halted an officer was seen riding some 200 yards in front of us and going to our left. Such cheering I had never heard. The soldiers went wild as they tossed their caps in the air. The officer doffed his cap, spurred his horse, and was quickly out of sight. On asking who it was, I was told that it was Gen. T. J. Jackson, the hero of the valley. The first thing I looked at was his foot, having sometime before read in a newspaper where Gen. Jackson was the second man to mount the walls at Chapultepec, Mexico, and that his foot was 14 inches long and compared him to the Irishman's game chicken. Some of the Irishman's friends had given him some Muscovy duck eggs and told him they were from game chickens. After the ducks hatched out and were about grown, the Irishman invited his friend over to see his chickens. After explaining all of their splendid points he remarked, "And bejesus will you be, after looking at his feet all h-ll could not trip him up."[51]

From what I saw of Gen. Jackson, he is a very ordinary looking man of medium size, his uniform badly soiled as though it had seen hard service. He wore a cap pulled down nearly to his nose and was riding a poor rawboned horse that did not look much like a charger, unless it would be on hay or clover. He certainly made a poor figure on a horseback, with his stirrup leather six inches too short putting his knees nearly level with his horse's back, and his heels turned out with his toes sticking behind his horse's foreshoulder. A sorry description of our most famous general, but a correct one.

Our line was then ordered by the right flank. Being subject to spells of rheumatism in my left knee and being almost past traveling that morning, I got permission to fall out of ranks and follow after the command doing the best I could. The command marched in the direction of the James River, and after going about two miles, halted, about-faced, and marched back over the same ground. I then asked Dr. Mayo for a pass, but he declined to give it to me but told me to hobble along and do the best I could. When the command turned back, I was no longer able to keep up, and was left behind. I will now tell what befell myself and follow the brigade later.

I struggled along, I suppose, for about one and a half miles to where the roads forked, one going to Malvern Hill. There was a farm house at the fork of the road that was afterwards used as a field hospital.

On reaching that point I decided to stop, as I had just about given out. I dropped down by the roadside where I remained some little time, it being then in the afternoon. Pretty soon the enemy's guns from Malvern Hill commenced shelling the woods. The first shells not reaching the road, but every one seemed to come nearer and nearer.

About the time I had decided to change my position, Sgt. L. B. Wheeler of Company B[52] come staggering along the road with his head bound up, having been badly shocked by a shell. He proposed that we go down a steep bottom just back of the house, where we would be less exposed to the enemy's batteries. So we made for the bottom, he assisting me all he could, but the farther we went the farther the shells flew. When we got into the bottom, the shells got thicker if anything, so we decided to climb the hill. On getting to the top of that, the shells come faster than ever. In a field just beyond was several batteries of artillery feeding their horses. Pretty soon the shells reached them, and such a stampede as they had of it dashing to the rear.

About that time, Wheeler and myself was getting pretty badly scared as we could not outrun the shelling. We decided to move to our left and get out of range. I saw numbers of men running to the rear completely demoralized, and apparently scared half to death. Several regiments were marching in, and made efforts to stop the fleeing stragglers and carry them back, but nothing short of a bullet could stop them. We made our way to a piece of woods, crossed a small branch, and went to a farm house on the hill. By that time it was getting dark.

For some time we had heard the battle raging at Malvern Hill. The rattle of small arms and the booming of artillery was simply terrific. As the battle raged in all its fury, the deserters became thicker. Each one had a tale to tell worse than the other. Some claimed they were the only ones left of their regiment. While the yankees were driving Lee's

Army before them, literally cutting them to pieces, they would again make for the rear and I have no idea, stopped short of Richmond 12 miles distant. To say that Wheeler and myself was demoralized would be putting it mild. We were simply daft.

The waves of musketry seemed to be coming nearer and nearer, as though our men were being driven from the field. I could stand the suspense no longer, so I told Sgt. Wheeler we would make our way back to the battlefield. Any place being preferable to where we were at. So we started for the line. It was then pitch dark, and nothing to guide us but the roar of musketry. We soon found ourselves in the worst swamp I have ever crossed in the night. Briers, brush, mud, water, and looked like everything else that could make a swamp bad. After seemingly an endless time, we succeeded in getting across to find ourselves in a worse condition than we were before. When we got out of the swamp, we struck a piece of woods which was swarming with men who had run out of the fight. Every one of them must have been shooting, as the flash of their guns looked like fire bugs. The balls were flying in every direction. No use to get behind a tree, just as apt to be shot in the back as anywhere else. So we pulled along the best we could, expecting every moment to be our last. We finally found our regiment going into bivouacs for the night. No one will ever know how happy I felt on reaching my company. That evening and night was the worse that has ever been my lot to experience. A battlefield is nothing to compare to it, and God being my helper, [I] will never be left behind my regiment again if I am able to crawl. Will now follow on after the brigade, as they go into battle.

On leaving the road several hundred yards, and by the side of a small branch, the brigade changed front by on the right, by file into tine [line], and while the ranks were doubled a small six-pound shell from Malvern Hill passed through both ranks [of] the 1st and 11th regiments, killing three men, cutting one man's thigh in two, disemboweled another, and passed through the third from shoulder to hip, then entered a tree about 10 inches in diameter, burst, and tore it down. After changing front, the line moved forward.

Will now describe Malvern Hill as I saw it, the second day after the fight. The hill is a high bluff on the banks of the James River, say 100 feet from the water, Dr. Malvern's residence being built on top of it.[53] For a mile and a half from the house, the land is under cultivation and is badly broken by hills and bottoms, with deep ravines running through the fields. On top of the hill Gen. McClellan is said to have had 70 pieces of artillery parked and bearing on his front. In the James River in his rear were several gunboats which took an active part in the battle. Our lines, on entering the clearing, would be exposed to the artillery fire from the jump.[54] Our artillery, on entering the field, would be simply annihilated before they could hardly unlimber for action. Our brigade entered the field and advanced upon the enemy's batteries, but did not succeed in getting more than halfway before being ordered out. The fire from the artillery being more than mortal men could stand. When ordered back the color bearer, Sgt. Baldwin of the Regulars,[55] refused to turn back and was forced back at the point of an officer's sword. Sgt. Garrett, my gallant chum, refused to return with the regiment and advanced by himself, near enough to pick off the yankee gunners, when a sharpshooter picked him off by shooting him through just above the knee, which laid him up for six months. The brigade lost a number of men in killed and wounded, but were not actively engaged. Malvern's Hill was simply a scorcher, and resulted in heavy loss to both sides. That night after the battle was over, Gen. McClellan continued his retreat down the James River.[56]

Thus ended the bloody battles around Richmond, the enemy being driven from all points, losing thousands of men and munitions of war. At the same time, the Confederate loss has been heavy, having at all times to attack the enemy in positions of his own selection.[57] We certainly fought men worthy of our steel. While Gen. Lee has proved himself the greatest general of modern times, Gen. McClellan certainly deserves great credit for his masterly retreat to the James. It is said Gen. Lee had 80,000 men and McClellan 120,000. Quite an army to maneuver on one road, in a retreat, without losing any of his wagons or artillery except what was captured in battle.

TURKEY BEND

Army remained at Malvern Hill burying the dead until July 4, when the army started in pursuit of Gen. McClellan. Overtaken his army at Turkey Bend on the James River, 30 miles below Richmond. The James formed a bend shaped like a horseshoe. The Federal Army was massed within the shoe with his gunboats occupying the river in his rear. His position was impregnable and Gen. Lee decided not to attack him.

The Regulars were on pocket in front of the bend where I saw Jackson rambling around on the picket line without any of his staff or escort. He looks over the ground for himself, thereby becoming acquainted with all of its strong and weak points. While on picket, I heard some of the wildest cheering I have ever heard from the throats of men within the Union lines. I learned afterwards that President Lincoln was reviewing McClellan's Army.[58] They all cheer together as one man, which will make the cold chills run up your back. The Rebels cheer like a lot of school boys, every man for himself. Nothing of interest is transpiring at the bend.

Heard an amusing story on Gen. Jackson, who it is said sometimes takes cat naps while riding along the road. While passing Magruder's troops in the road the other day, the general was enjoying one of his short naps. One of the men, not knowing him, asked him where he got his whiskey. On hearing the remark, the general said he guessed he had better stay awake.

On the 9th of July, the Army of Northern Virginia again occupied their lines around Richmond. Anderson's Brigade bivouacked on the Darbytown Road two miles from the city. July 24 [the] brigade moved camps to New Market Heights, each regiment in turn doing picket duty at Malvern Hill. On the 5th of August, Gen. McClellan retaken Malvern Hill, our forces but few in number, retiring at his approach. Gen. Longstreet's forces were then moved forward, ready for battle.

While resting by the roadside, I saw, for the first time, the greatest general of modern times, no less a personage than Robert E. Lee. It is useless for me to try to describe him, having never seen anyone who could in any way compare with him. He was mounted on his famous horse Traveler, a very dark iron gray. The horse might have passed without much notice had it not been for his rider, who could have been picked out of his army at the first glance. He was tall and well formed, sitting his horse with a grace acquired by but few men. His bearing that of a man born to command. While I may have seen handsomer men, I have never seen anyone who could match him in appearance. His beard covers his face, is closely trimmed and of a dark gray color. His eyes, well an eagle's would flinch before them. Riding by his side was President Davis and the secretary of war.[59] In his rear was his afterwards famous right bower,[60] Gen. James Longstreet, and several other generals of less note, with their escorts, forming quite a procession. The soldiers resting by the roadside simply stared at them as they rode past. Not a cheer broke the stillness. What if it had been Stonewall Jackson. The boys would have made the welkin sing.

On the night of the 6th of August, McClellan again withdrew his forces from Malvern Hill, occupying it only as a feint to cover a move in some other direction. August 10 our brigade returned to camps on the Darbytown Road. I visited the city on several occasions. One day while in the city, Main Street was covered with officers in uniform as far down the street as I could see. The boys say there is going to be another fight, as all of the officers are going to the city.

THE DANGER AND MISERY
SURROUNDING ME

ADVANCE ON GENERAL POPE

On August 13 our division under Maj. Gen. D. R. Jones went by rail from Richmond to Gordonsville, where Gen. Lee was rapidly massing his forces in front of Gen. [John] Pope commanding the Federal Army. Gen. Jackson had fought and defeated him a few days before at Cedar Mountain, causing him to retire in the direction of Culpeper Court House.[1] August 17 [we] taken up the line of march in the direction of the Rapidan River to the right of Orange Court House, where we marched and counter-marched until the 22nd, crossing the Rapidan at Raccoon Ford.

While near Stevensburg, a small village near Culpeper Court House, I saw a spy who had just been hung to a tree and cut down. He was captured by Gen. J. E. B. Stuart's Cavalry that morning, after he had shot and killed one of Stuart's men. The day before, he had been seen inside of our lines in citizen's clothes on foot. When captured, he was mounted and had on the Federal uniform. He was given the benefit of a drumhead court-martial, and paid the penalty by dying the death of a spy at the end of a rope.

On entering Stevensburg, saw a deserter being carried with a horse for him to stand on, to a clump of trees at a farm house near the road-side where he was to stand on the horse's back until the rope was adjusted. Then the horse would be led from under him leaving him dangling at the end of a rope. I have always thought he ought to have been hung for the want of common sense if nothing else. He had deserted a Virginia battery and joined the yankee army. He was captured that morning by some of Stuart's Cavalry who carried him with several other prisoners to Stevensburg where they were placed for safe keeping in an old storehouse. While our forces were marching through Stevensburg, he recognized his old company and told them howdy, instead of staying in the background where they would not have seen him. It is doubtful whether anyone outside of his old company would have known him. His want of sense cost him his life, while if his company had not seen him, he might have been exchanged without our government knowing him to be a deserter.

After crossing the Rapidan River at Raccoon Ford, I saw Gen. Jackson riding his famous battle horse, Little Sorrel.[2] He was at the head of his column and crossed the river at a ford above us. On the night of the 22nd, we camped on the railroad between Brandy Station and the Rappahannock River.

BATTLE OF THE RAPPAHANNOCK, VIRGINIA

At five o'clock, on the morning of August 23, Gen. Anderson's Brigade was ordered to reinforce Gen. Evans'[3] South Carolina Brigade at the railroad bridge on the Rappahannock River. The river runs east and the railroad north and south, passing through a large plantation before getting to the bridge. Just above, and on the south side of the bridge, there were some earthworks thrown up by the Confederates on the retreat from Manassas [earlier in 1862]. The works were on a small ridge near the river, then a bottom running out from the river at an angle of 45 degrees, then another or second ridge. The works were occupied by the enemy's artillery. Gen. Evans was to charge the works with his brigade, while Anderson's would be in supporting distance.

Our brigade moved forward some distance, then formed line of battle above the railroad, and marched square down upon the works. When we first got in sight of the works the enemy's guns opened on our line but failed to throw shells and solid shot to our line, it being out of range. But when in one mile of them, they began to pepper us right along. On reaching a wattled cedar fence running across the field we were ordered to halt and lie down, where we remained for several minutes and was again ordered forward. While getting over the wattled fence a cannonball passed through the regiment, knocking five men out of ranks. From there on, the shells flew fast and furious.

⸱ While we were advancing, the enemy evacuated the old works, crossed the river on the railroad bridge, and blew it up, then planted their artillery on the north bank of the river and proceeded to give us Hail Columbia. As we advanced, the second ridge was directly in front of the 8th and 1st Ga. regiments, the 7th, 9th, and 11th being on open ground to our right. As the 1st and 8th was ascending the ridge, Gen. Evans' Brigade charged the works to find that the bird had flown, but at the same time found themselves exposed to the enemy's battery of 12 guns some 200 yards distant on the opposite bank of the river. The fire of the artillery at close range was something terrible, completely demoralizing Holcomb's Legion,[4] who made a break for the rear, but on reaching the crest of the second ridge halted, reformed, and returned to the rest of the brigade who had remained in the bottom between the two ridges, the enemy's fire passing over them.

Just about the time the legion returned to the bottom, a Virginia battery, known as the Spotted Horse Battery,[5] dashed upon the ridge. I don't think they took time to unlimber before they were out and gone with all the speed they could make, all of the enemy's guns concentrating on the battery. It certainly was a hot place. After the battery escaped, they again turned their attention to our brigade. My, but it was a hot place, under the fire of 12 pieces of artillery. Could neither advance nor retreat, but had to lie down and endure it.

Towards the middle of the day, old King Sol certainly come down with all vengeance, numbers of men fainting, while the rest looked like well diggers lying on the red dirt with the perspiration streaming off them. The hours seemed to pass on leaden wings. The sun seemed to be stationary in the heavens. Had they a Joshua in the enemy's camps would have thought he had commanded the sun to stand still.

Just in front of the Regulars, Gen. Anderson was standing holding his favorite charger, a large bay stallion. He had been lying down but I suppose had got tired and got up on his feet. The general was ordering him to lie down again when he was struck and killed by a piece of shell. Old Tige looked as unconcerned as if he was in camps. Don't think the explosion of a shell would cause him to bat his eyes unless it took his head off.

Just to my right I saw our Adjutant Lt. R. H. Atkinson[6] sleeping as sweetly as though he was miles away from the battlefield. Wish that I too could go to sleep, maybe I would not be aware of the danger and misery surrounding me. With the screeching of the bursting shell, the pitiful appeals of the wounded to be carried to the rear, make this place a regular Pandemonium [sic]. Could we charge the enemy's guns, that would be a relief to us. Anything would be preferable to this, the worst place we have ever been in.

About twelve o'clock the enemy moved their guns farther up the river so as to sweep the bottom between the two ridges, where Gen. Evans' South Carolina Brigade was concealed. It was simply heartrending to see the Palmetto boys as they retreated under the fire of those 12 pieces of artillery at close range. They passed over the second ridge and tried to reform in rear of the 1st and 8th Ga. regiments, but the enemy's fire was too hot for flesh and blood to stand. For a little while the line wavered, then about-faced and retreated to the rear in perfect order, with the shells from the enemy's guns thinning their ranks at every fire. It looked like every shell knocked out from 6 to 12. The ranks would close up as though nothing had happened. The Palmetto boys are made of the right material or they could never have retreated in good order under that fire. We watched and admired them until they were out of range of the artillery, and then our turn come next.

Glad the Palmetto boys were out in [of] sight when we made our retreat, for we got out the best way we could. The 11th Georgia was ordered out first, about-facing and retreating in line of battle, drawing the fire of the entire battery, which caused the ranks to break and every man take care of himself and the yankees to get the hindmost one. It certainly looked like a race for life, it being at least one mile to the cover of the woods. The 9th's turn come next with the same result, a race for the woods where they would halt and reform. When the 7th's turn come, a change was made. Each company was deployed as skirmishers and made for the rear. The yankees thinking the game too small, ceased firing at them. Then the 1st and 8th got out in the same manner. On reaching the woods it was 2:00 P.M. Nine hours under the enemy's fire without firing a gun, with a loss of between 300 and 500 men.

At the woods we met a number of pieces of artillery going in to attack the enemy, but too late to be of any service to us. The enemy had certainly had a picnic all to themselves, and all their own way. So when our guns went in to attack them, they fired all the buildings on that side of the river and retreated.[7] On the 24th, we crossed the Rappahannock River about six miles above the railroad bridge and marched to Jeffersonton on the north prong of the Rappahannock near Warrenton Springs. 26th, we crossed the north prong of the Rappahannock at an old mill, passing around to the west of the Bull Run Mountains. 27th, we passed through Orleans to White Plains. Regulars on picket duty.

BATTLE OF THOROUGHFARE GAP, VIRGINIA

Before leaving White Plains on the morning of August 28, the 9th Georgia had passed us going on in advance.[8] About sunrise the remainder of the brigade at the head of Longstreet's Corps arrived. The Regulars took their position in line and the columns moved on in the direction of Thoroughfare Gap. On arriving at the gap, the head of the column halted, the Regulars being at the iron spout [pump] on the left, where we were getting water. We could then hear the reports of small arms at the other end of the pass. Capt. John G. Patton of Company F told his men to look to their guns. We again moved forward, advancing to a large stone barn directly in the pass, where we halted.

Thoroughfare Gap is where the Manassas Gap Railroad passes through the Bull Run Mountains. In the gap is the railroad, creek, and wagon road. To the left of the pass is a large stone barn and just beyond is a mill house built of stone for grinding wheat. On either side the mountain rises between 100 and 150 feet. While not a precipice, it is difficult to ascend. Opposite the mill there is a trench that was dug in the rock, in order to get rock to build with, that run well up the mountain on the left. It was about seven feet wide and five or six feet deep. On the east side of that ditch was the enemy in heavy line of battle, with their artillery just beyond and bearing on the gap. Certainly one of the strongest natural positions I have ever seen.

The 9th Georgia had passed through the gap and encountered the enemy, who drove them back into the gap, where they were when we arrived on the scene. When we reached the barn, the enemy's sharpshooters occupied the mill and they certainly made it hot for us, having to take shelter behind the barn for protection. Capt. Patton was ordered to deploy his company as skirmishers and advance up the side of the mountain. It was not long before he encountered the enemy in line of battle on top of the mountain. The rattle of small arms soon become lively, and the rest of the regiment was ordered to his support.

Just at the foot of the mountain is a small branch covered up in briers. There was but one place in front of Company M that a man could pass through, and that was on the right, directly in front of myself, acting 1st sergeant of the company.[9] I filed through and the company followed me. We then started to climb up the side of the mountain by clinging to the rocks and bushes, the air being full of minié balls from the enemy's guns on top of the mountain. On reaching a break off in the side of the mountain about breast high, I halted, the bullets flying around my head as thick as a swarm of bees. I did not have much time for reflection before I heard Lt. Hudson,[10] in command of Company M, say, "Forward up Sergeant Andrews." Throwing my musket up on the rock I gave a spring and succeeded in mounting the rock. From some cause, felt as though I would be a dead man before I could straighten myself, but thanks to a kind providence, found myself unharmed. I did not wait to see who followed, but made a bee line for Company F.

When near the top, lay down and crawled to the ditch, placed my gun on the loose dirt at the edge, and fired into the enemy's line of battle standing on the opposite side close enough to have touched bayonets. What close quarters to be in, nearly close enough to be powder burnt from the enemy's guns. As our men arrived, each one crawled to the ditch, making it so warm for the enemy that they retreated down the side of the mountain. As it was like fighting on top of a house, they did not have far to go before being out of sight. They then rallied, dressed their lines, and charged the ditch. Our men would drop back a few yards behind the works, wait until they had charged up and delivered a volley across the ditch, when we would again crawl back to the ditch and heat them so hot they would again retreat, halt when out of range, dress their lines, and again charge with the same result as before. They charged the ditch the third time, each time our men retiring until they would charge up and fire. We would then crawl back and rout them again.

The Regulars were putting into practice what they had been taught in drill, to take advantage of everything when engaged with the enemy. While the Federals (the 10th and 11th Pa. regiments[11]) showed game by fighting us in exposed lines of battle, they did not show much science in the art of war. When driven from the ridge the third time, it was pitiful to hear them beg for quarter. They at first claimed to be the 8th Ga. Regiment (having heard the colonel of the 8th give the command "Forward up 8th Georgia" as the regiment advanced up the mountain on the left of the Regulars). When they found that had no effect, they claimed to be our friends, but the boys would yell back at them, "Damn all such friends."

After they were driven back the third time, the officers tried to rally the men for the fourth charge, but could never get them back to the scratch again and had to retreat down the side of the mountain with a loss of 300 killed and wounded. I counted 45 dead the next morning, lying along the edge of the trench. The Regulars' loss was one killed and three wounded, Sgt. James Copeland of Company F being among the wounded, receiving a ball through his thigh. Pretty good fighting, 200 hundred [sic] Regulars causing the enemy the loss of 300 men. The boys had a lot of buckshot cartridges. Thirteen buckshot in each cartridge, a terrible shot in close quarters.

While we were lying down at the edge of the ditch, Capt. John G. Patton and Lt. Benning (a son of [Brig.] Gen. Henry L. Benning[12]) walked our lines, stepping over the men and in 10 feet of the enemy's line of battle. Neither one received a scratch, but Capt. Patton killed a yankee captain (Hanks[13]) and two privates with his pistol. Game Capt. Patton certainly was, and must have escaped by a miracle. Why both of them were not killed, I have never been able to account for, walking up and down our line in front of a solid line of battle. It seems as though providence must have been watching over them. While others might have walked the lines, I never saw them, and I am well aware that I was not on my feet in front of them.

After the enemy retreated, we marched down about halfway the side of the mountain and remained there for the night, Old Tige remaining with us, who said every Regular in the regiment was worth his weight in gold. You are mistaken there general, for I know several of my own company who never reached the summit or fired a gun. Could call their names, but will leave them to their own reflections, hoping that will make them feel mean [small] enough without exposing them to the world. Can imagine they must feel very small when they hear their comrades fighting their battles over again around the campfires. It is hard to tell who will make a good soldier until he is tried on the battlefield. Men who will fight you in camps for the least provocation cannot face the music on the field. While others you might kick all over camps and would not resent it, don't know what fear is on the battlefield. Strange but true, which is the brave man.

Thoroughfare Gap was a point of great interest to Gen. Pope, who claims his headquarters in the saddle, having never seen the faces of the enemy where he has been fighting them in the West.[14] Guess he will have to get in our rear if he wishes to see our backs. He has Gen. Jackson's Command backed up against the Bull Run Mountains with no line of escape, until Longstreet opened Thoroughfare Gap. So Mr. Pope, when you go to gobble up Gen. Jackson's Command, you will have to take Longstreet in out of the wet with his 50,000 [about 30,000] men. The Confederates have an old score to settle with Gen. Pope. While he was advancing his army towards Richmond with no one to oppose him, he captured citizens and noncombatants and held them as hostages, issuing his orders that if any of his soldiers were shot he would hang a citizen for every one shot. Gen. Lee retaliated by ordering that a yankee officer would be shot for every citizen or noncombatant that Pope strung up. So the feeling against him and his army is very bitter, and he will have a chance to make war on men, instead of women and children.[15]

SECOND BATTLE OF MANASSAS

August 29, Gen. Longstreet's Corps moved rapidly to the front arriving at Manassas about noon, taking position on Gen. Jackson's right, Anderson's Brigade being on the extreme right of the line. Sometime in the afternoon, Gen. Pope attacked Gen. Jackson on our left. Anderson's Brigade was ordered to reinforce Gen. Jackson. We double-quicked about two miles to our left, passing in rear of our line of battle, and when within 400 yards of the fighting, halted. Some little distance to our left, one of Gen. Jackson's batteries was desperately engaged with a line of the enemy infantry, who were advancing to capture it. When the yankees were within 100 yards, the battery ceased firing, the artillery men flying in haste. The yankees gave three cheers and charged. For a few moments all was still, then a terrible volley of musketry with that hair-raising Rebel yell. Again the fight was renewed by the yankees, who were driven from the guns which were again turned on them by the artillery men resuming their places. The enemy was rapidly driven from the field.

We learned the next morning it was a trick Gen. Jackson was very fond of playing on the yankees. He would expose one of his batteries, instructing the artillery men to run and leave it when attacked. In rear of the battery he would ambush a line of infantry, so when the enemy charged the guns [they] would find themselves confronted by a line of battle who would give them a volley, charge, and drive them from the guns, which would be turned on them again. In this fight Hood's Texas brigade were in ambush, and when they charged it became a hand-to-hand fight with clubbed guns and rocks.[16] Gen. Jones remarked the next morning that there was over 500 men had their heads banged up, but the Texans got the best of it, and the boys in blue had to get up and get. Anderson's Brigade then returned to the right of the line.

The morning of August 30 found Gen. Lee's Army in line of battle, awaiting the movements of the enemy. Our line on the right was through a large open field, the stacks of guns forming a continuous line to our right and left as far as we could see. The men were mostly passing the time stretched on the ground fast asleep, having been tramping since the 17th instant, and were very much in need of rest and sleep. A report had circulated up and down the line that there would be no movements made that day. So everybody seemed to be taking a holiday and passing it off in sleep. Some of the staff officers were leisurely riding along the line seeking old friends and acquaintances to pass the time away. In the afternoon about three o'clock, a battery some 400 yards to our front and left was firing away, shelling a piece of woods in their front, and were taking their time about it as though they had all the week to finish the job in.

Along the lines quiet reigns supreme. Our brigade is mostly in the arms of Morpheus. The Regulars are between the gallant 7th and the bold 8th, two crack Georgia regiments who had achieved undying fame at the First Battle of Manassas. We certainly feel highly complimented being placed between those gallant regiments. While we are not jealous of their fame so dearly bought, it will be a cold day in August before they can advance their flag farther, or hold their ground longer than the 1st Regiment of Regulars. As to our flanks we feel perfectly safe while one of the 7th and 8th live to defend it.

About four o'clock our battery seemed to wake up. The pieces were fired as rapidly as they could be loaded. Staff officers came dashing at full speed down the line. The orders were given to forward, and in less time than it takes to tell, our lines were moving to the front in double-quick time. Our brigade must have gone at least two miles before we encountered the enemy. While moving to the front saw Gen.

Anderson's chief of staff riding hard to the rear with a ball through his thigh.[17] A little farther on, Gen. Anderson's horse, one of his grays, was shot behind the right foreshoulder. Near a farm house and not far from a branch, a staff officer ordered our brigade to left half wheel, which was promptly done as we passed down the branch. To the right of the branch, as we ascended a small hill, passed over a gully full of men supposed to be wounded. A captain was lying flat on his back, waving his sword over his head, saying as we passed over him, "Go in my brave boys." Capt. R. A. Wayne of Company E did not put much faith in his wounds and disarmed him, taking his sword away and threatened to have him court-martialed for cowardice. Whether he did or not I never knew.

On reaching the top of the ridge, the right of the line opened fire, flashing down to the left almost like a greased streak of lightning. Looking to the front some 60 yards distant and down in a bottom were two lines of battle, one firing from the knee and the other in the rear standing up. They received us in warm style from both lines. How the bullets flew. Our line was ordered to lie down and they were quick about it, not waiting to be told the second time. When we halted there was a line of battle in front of the 8th Georgia some 20 paces in front, who were soon obscured from sight by the smoke of our guns. I never knew what command it was, or where they went to, but suppose they fell back in rear of the 8th.

Some little time after the battle opened, Lt. G. B. Lamar[18] of Company F ordered the line to stop shooting, that we were shooting our own men. No one seemed to pay any attention to him as the bullets were flying as thick as hail. I stopped, but seeing that no one else stopped, commenced shooting again. I was in the line of file closers standing up. Lt. Lamar ordered me the second time to cease firing, catching me by the shoulder and jerking me around, saying he did not care to repeat his orders the second time. I then stopped firing, placed the butt of my gun on the ground, and proceeded to take in the situation. The scene that met my gaze will never be forgotten.

Our line was lying down, every man shooting for all he was worth, looking like a solid sheet of flame from their guns. The double line of yankees were certainly giving us the best they had to offer in the way of hot lead. Besides the batteries in rear of their line on the hills near the Henry House was giving us what Paddy give the drum. The screech of their bursting shells as they crashed through the trees would have caused the heart of the bravest to quake with fear. To be actively engaged in battle is bad enough, but to be a passive spectator is simply awful. My first thought was to run to a tree, but there was none, only in our rear, about 30 feet distant. To run back was something I would not do, so there was nothing for one to do but stand and take what come.

Some 15 feet in our rear, Lt. Hudson, commanding Company M, was sitting on a small sapling that had been cut down, seemingly indifferent to passing events. Just to my right was Capt. John G. Patton, commanding Company F. He had stepped over me at Thoroughfare Gap, while walking one [our] line in front of the enemy, which I considered the bravest act I had witnessed during the war. He certainly was my ideal of a brave soldier, so in admiring him I was lost for the time being in passing events. His picture is indelibly engraved on my memory. He was standing at parade rest, the point of his sword being on the ground, his right hand grasping his sword hilt, with the left resting on the right. He seemed to be in a deep reverie, not a muscle of his face moved. How like a statue he looked, so cool, so composed. What a soldier to admire. The spell was soon broken. The captain was looking directly to the front, intent on watching the enemy's lines. He suddenly turned his head, looking down our line to the right. As he did so, a minié ball struck him in the left temple. The blood gushed out in a stream the size of the ball hole in his head. His limbs gave way and he dropped to the ground, fell backwards, and was dead by the time he struck. A brave man and a gallant soldier had yielded up his life's blood in behalf of the sunny South. No braver spirits on the blood-stained field of Manassas wafted its flight to realms on high than that of Capt. John G. Patton of Company F, 1st Regiment, Georgia Regulars.

I have always believed he had a presentiment of death before he entered the battle. About two hours before the battle opened [I] saw him write a letter on a piece of wrapping paper, fold it, and direct it, then gave it to one of his company who was sick and told him, "If I am killed in this fight, mail this letter for me." After he fell I turned my attention again to the line.

To the right of me and walking down the line was our adjutant lieutenant R. H. Atkinson, with our flag in one hand and his sword in the other. Our colors had fallen the fourth time. Our gallant color bearer Sgt. Baldwin[19] had lost his life, besides two others who were killed who had lifted the colors up by the time they had struck the ground, the fourth man being wounded. Then Lt. Atkinson raised them up. He was certainly making a conspicuous target of himself, but fear was a stranger to him. There was not a sound on the line except the roaring of the musketry and the screeching of the bursting shells. A wave of grayish blue smoke hung over the lines, almost obscuring the men from view. The air was full of minié balls with that particular zip coming from the front. I heard one from the rear, and it made my cap rise on my head. It will demoralize a soldier quicker than anything on a line of battle.

Heard someone say, "Pass the word down the line boys, hold your position just ten minutes longer. Gen. Jackson is getting in the rear of them." From the rapid firing after that announcement the boys must have felt somewhat buoyed up. Not long afterwards heard some soldier sing out, "I will be d———d if Jackson has not cut off more than Longstreet can whip this time," and he spoke it in earnest.

About that time, Cpl. Joe Herndon[20] of Company M called to me to assist him to the rear. He had been shot through the knee, I raised him up, placed my left arm around his waist, he placing his right over my right shoulder, and started to the rear. It certainly was slow traveling, and before we had proceeded 10 steps a minié ball grazed my neck just above his arm. The cold chills run up my back, but it was no time for flinching. After carrying him about 40 yards, he gave out from loss of blood. I placed him behind a tree, and just as I was starting to return, Lt. Gus Rutherford[21] came along going to the rear. He told me he was wounded and asked me to examine him, which I did, finding on his left side a place about the size of the palm of my hand and as black as my hat where a piece of shell had struck him. Told him he was badly bruised but the skin was not broken. "Oh well," he says, "if that is all I am going back into the fight."

While I was examining him we were standing over one of the 8th Georgia who had a portion of his foot shot off. [I] have never heard anyone beg as pitiful as he did to be carried to the rear, being in as much danger where we were as he would have been on the line of battle. Lt. Rutherford told me to carry the poor fellow down under the hill where he would be in less danger, and he would return to the line. I got him up and carried him along like I did Cpl. Herndon for some distance down the hill. I then told him to get on my back, squatting down in front of him. He got on and mashed me flat on the ground. I could not get up with him so had to make him get off. I was completely exhausted, but did not feel it on account of the excitement. Told him he would have to do the best he could, as I had to get back to our line. I left him not far from the branch and decided to fill my canteen before I returned.

Just as I left him, Gen. Toombs passed me going in at full speed and calling on the Georgians at every jump his horse made. A little farther on met his brigade going in to reinforce our line. I certainly felt good all over, and for the first time since I had been in the army tossed my cap in the air for which I received a good sound cursing for being a d——d coward, running to the rear. I let them pass over me, then watched them as they rose the hill. They were moving rapidly to the front, but were dodging as fast as they could bob up and down. It was certainly a hot place, but I had been there long enough to get used to it, and if there is anything in this world I like better than another, it is to see a line of battle go into action.

I then made for the branch, the ground being covered with the blue and the gray. The groans of the wounded and dying was simply heart-rending, everyone begging for water. I filled my canteen five times and it was as quickly emptied by friend and foe. On going back the sixth time, met the second line of reinforcements going in. It was one of the prettiest sights I had ever seen, trail arms with fixed bayonets, moving at the double-quick, their guns looked like a wall of steel. As they approached the branch I stepped back some six or eight feet from the water, but not far enough to keep one of their bayonets from piercing my right leg, making a slight wound.

They passed over me and dashed on up the hill. I followed them, stopping long enough to pick up a Springfield rifle. The ground being covered with them, looked like a line of battle had thrown down their arms to a man. The one I picked up had not been fired, and was as bright as a silver dollar. After securing cartridges to suit it, again dashed up the hill. When about halfway up saw Capt. —— well, for the sake of his gallant brother will not divulge his name, but he was certainly making Nancy Hanks' time.[22] The enemy had just received another line of reinforcement, and these opening fire, had lent wings to the captain's feet. Just before he reached me, I jumped behind a tree and hailed him. He ran to me, crouched down at the root of the tree, asked me for a drink of water, which I gave him, then remarked, "Sergeant, it is too damned hot for me," and he again made for the rear. He certainly was badly scared. After watching him run until out of sight, I again dashed up the hill, and the higher I got, the thicker the bullets flew.

Just before I reached the place where I had left Cpl. Herndon, met what was left of our brigade retiring from the line having been relieved by the two lines I had met going in. We crossed the branch and went up the hill, where we bivouacked for the night. It was getting dark when the brigade retired from the line, but the battle continued until nine o'clock at night. There was some scattered firing until after midnight. Several wounded yankees kept firing at our men until they were killed. Guess they thought that was a good way to end their trouble and put an end to their sufferings.

After midnight, a slow drizzly rain commenced to fall and continued the most of the next day. We passed the night near a farm house which was used as a field hospital. The groans of the wounded and dying was awful to listen to, but nothing keeps the soldier from sleep after a hard-fought battle. He may stand the strain like a man while fighting, but after it is over he will be as limp as a dish rag. The loss in our regiment and brigade was something terrible. The brigade carried into action 1,260 men and lost 690. The Regulars carried in 194 men and lost 104, 27 being left dead on the line. Among the killed was Maj. John D. Walker (brother of Gen. W. H. T. Walker), Capt. John G. Patton, Lt. Porter,[23] Sgt. Baldwin, color bearer Sgt. Tucker,[24] 1st sergeant of Company F, Pvt. Robertson[25] of Company M. These are all that I can recollect at this late date having kept no list of casualties during the war. Col. W. J. Magill was in command of the Regulars.

The Second Manassas was the most desperate battle I was in during the war, and the largest. The Confederates under Gen. Lee numbered 80,000 [55,000] men, while Gen. Pope of the Federal Army commanded 120,000 [75,000]. Gen. Jackson routed Pope's right and center. His [Pope's] troops were then massed in front of Gen. Longstreet on his left. The double line Anderson encountered was reinforced by three other lines of battle. Late in the night after the fight was over, Gen. Pope withdrew his army in the direction of Centreville. In the wee small hours of the night heard the rumble of his artillery wheels as he withdrew over the turnpikes. Could not help feeling relieved and wishing him a speedy exit.

The next morning the brigade moved over about one mile in front of where we fought near the old Henry House. The old lady Henry who was killed at the first battle was buried in her garden, and at the second fight, three yankees fell across her grave. At one place saw where one of the enemy's batteries had been in position in an open field, where the grass was pretty thick. The grass caught fire and burnt the wounded to death. Horrible sights to look upon with their clothing burnt off and their flesh to a blackened crisp. Saw the dead in all conceivable positions. Some on their knees still grasping their guns, others died eating, with their hands and mouths full of crackers, how sickening. Did not think I could ever eat another cracker. Most of them had been robbed by someone. Some had nothing on but their underclothing. If they had on any pants the pockets had been turned. Strange that it should be so, but it is nevertheless. You can't find a [dead] man on the battlefield the next morning that has not been robbed. I can't stand the idea of handling a dead man. At the same time I am not afraid of ghosts. We spent most of the day near one of the enemy's field hospitals. Arms and legs were piled in heaps, while numbers of those who had their limbs amputated were lying around in the house and yard, dead. We are getting pretty well hardened to such sights, and can look on a dead man with the same feelings we would a hog at home, in hog-killing time.

Saw Gen. Lee today with his arm in a sling. Someone said he had been struck by a spent ball this morning by some cowardly devil who failed to shoot off his gun yesterday.[26] Gen. Lee has won the confidence of his men. They trust him with the same faith that a child does while in its parents' arms, with no thought of tomorrow. We have been victorious under his leadership in every battle, and expect to still win victory wherever he directs. Gen. Longstreet and Old Tige come in for a full share of our love and esteem. We trust them blindly, and will go to the jumping-off place if they so direct. Late in the evening Longstreet's Corps marched out to Sudley's Mills on the Bull Run, where we bivouacked for the night. Passed a portion of Gen. Jackson's command. Saw the 13th and 31st Ga. regiments of Gen. Lawton's Brigade.[27]

BATTLE OF OX HILL, VIRGINIA

September 1, Longstreet's Command moved forward in the direction of Fairfax Court House. About sunset filed out of the road to camp. After we stacked arms, the rain come down in torrents. Some 200 yards to the right of us there commenced a lively racket of small arms, said to be in Gen. Drayton's Brigade.[28] Gen. Anderson gave the order to fall in, take arms, double-quick, march, and we were off down the road like a flash, leaving our baggage behind. We soon heard in front of us the booming of cannon and rattle of musketry, and knew that the devil was to pay down the road apiece.

After going about one mile we were ordered by the right flank, jumping a fence by the roadside, marched down through a field some 400 yards to a piece of woods. It was then dark, but the enemy's batteries were still shelling, crashing through the tree tops over our heads. Long towards ten o'clock the firing ceased, and about eleven o'clock we went back to the road and built fires out of fence rails to dry ourselves with. The fight was between Gen. Jackson's forces and a portion of the enemy under Gen. Kearny, and known as the battle of Ox Hill.[29] After night the enemy again retired in the direction of Washington City.

After we had dried ourselves awhile, Lt. Hudson ordered me to take a detail of men and go back after the company's baggage where we had left it to go to the fight. On arriving at the baggage, we found some of the boys who had remained behind had built fires. While we were at the fire, a lieutenant with four men bearing a litter on their shoulders came up to the fire and put the litter on the ground. Lying at full length with his arms folded across his breast was a dead soldier, dressed in the uniform of a major general of the U.S. Army.

A little later some of our men brought in three yankee prisoners, a sergeant, and two privates, who had been captured while out foraging for their suppers. The sergeant told us the officer was Gen. Kearny, one of the bravest officers in the Federal Army, having lost one arm in the Mexican War. He also showed us a rent in his coatsleeve where a piece of shell had struck him on Saturday at Manassas. About dusk, him and his staff dashed up in front of Jackson's lines mistaking it for his own. On seeing his mistake had wheeled his horse and made a dash for the rear. As they did so the 44th Georgia fired a volley at them, killing Gen. Kearny, who fell from his horse. The rest made their escape. Gen. Kearny was taken up and carried to Gen. Lee's headquarters. The next day he was sent through the lines under a flag of truce.

The 2nd day of September we remained near Ox Hill, where we cooked up three days' rations. On the 3rd, marched in the direction of Leesburg up the Potomac River where we arrived on the 6th. Nothing worthy of note transpiring on the march.

MOVED FORWARD
INTO THE FIGHT

CROSSING INTO MARYLAND

On the 7th day of September, 1862, Gen. Longstreet's Corps crossed the Potomac River into Maryland, Gen. Jackson's having crossed on the 6th. Would like to have a picture of Longstreet's men fording the river, preparing to wade, wading through, and preparing to march, at the same time. Don't think the picture would be suitable for the parlor.[1] The river where we crossed is about 400 yards wide, and not over four feet deep at any place. Everyone had his own ideas about fixing himself up for wading and acted accordingly. On the north bank is the Baltimore and Ohio Canal, something new to me with its locks and canal boats.

On the 8th Longstreet's Corps arrived at Frederick City and went into bivouacs on the east side while Jackson's men are on the left, or west of the city. While staying in the city, Jackson's forces blew up the mammoth iron bridge over the Monocacy River belonging to the Baltimore and Ohio Railroad Company.[2] On the 9th Longstreet's Corps went in bathing in the Monacacy River. It was full [of troops] for *at least* one mile. What sport the boys had. Guess they needed a good scrubbing.

Don't look like wartimes in Maryland. Everything looks flush and prosperous. The men, if any has gone to the war, can't be missed on the streets. Numbers of them showed me their papers where they had been drafted for the army, but any men able to pay the government 300 dollars can keep out.[3] The women are handsome and true to their colors, as you can see by the little flags that adorn their breast. Saw aprons and window curtains of the Stars and Stripes. They all seem to be friendly disposed and have no reason to be afraid, as Gen. Lee's orders are very strict in regard to private property, with orders to shoot anyone who disobeys.[4]

On the 10th of September, Longstreet's Corps marched in the direction of the Blue Ridge Mountains. Passed through Middletown where I saw lying in the streets several dead horses. Gen. Jackson, with some of his cavalry, had entered the little town and were surprised by some of the enemy's cavalry. Gen. Jackson [was] pushed so close he lost his cap, but succeeded in making his escape.[5]

[We] passed through the Blue Ridge at Crampton's Gap, or South Mountain Pass, on through Boonsboro and on the 12th arrived at Hagerstown, Md. What a beautiful country we are passing through. Nature has certainly been lavish with her gifts, and not a mile have we passed over but there has been something to attract the eye. The houses and barns all have a thrifty appearance. The orchards are weighted down with the best of apples, with a richer flavor than any I have ever ate. The fences around the yards are lined with apple butter jars, washed and hung out to dry just before using them. Never found out the process by which the apples is made into butter, although it is very good.

Scattered along the road is flour mills busily grinding wheat, while every inch of space is filled with wheat or flour. Don't look much like starvation in this land of plenty. The corn is just in roasting ear and causes our boys to see trouble. There is a rear guard behind every brigade with instructions to arrest every man outside of the road. They capture a large number of roasting ear thieves, who are marched under guard until night, when they are required to place all of their corn in a pile. Each one will then have to shoulder a large fence rail and march around the corn pile in a circle for two hours. Don't know who gets the corn afterwards, but it is not the one who stole it. Poor boys, the way of the transgressor is hard, but guess they deserve all the punishment they get.

When Longstreet left Frederick City, Jackson's forces again crossed the Potomac into Virginia to capture Harpers Ferry, while Gen. D. H. Hill's Command remained between Frederick City and the Blue

Ridge Mountains. On the morning of the 13th, Longstreet's Corps drew two days rations. Sunday morning, September 14, Longstreet's Corps ordered back to Crampton's Gap in the Blue Ridge to reinforce Gen. D. H. Hill, who was being hard pressed by Gen. George B. McClellan, who had again been placed in command of the Union forces.[6]

What a march we had, a great deal of the time on the double-quick, the distance being about 25 miles. As we neared the mountains, we could hear the booming of artillery. As we drew nearer could hear the rattle of musketry. When Longstreet arrived, McClellan was forcing Hill into the gap, but with Longstreet's assistance, held his ground until late at night, when Gen. Lee evacuated the Blue Ridge and retreated to Sharpsburg, on the Antietam River and near the Potomac. Anderson's Brigade passed through the gap to Hill's assistance, but were not actively engaged; although losing several men in killed and wounded. While at Crampton's Gap, could hear Jackson's artillery at Harpers Ferry. From the rapidity of the firing, must have rained shell on that place.

Sometime after night and just before our forces started to retreat, Lt. F. B. Palmer was wounded through the hand. I went with him through the gap. When nearly through, we was held up by the rear guard, but as it happened Lt. Frank Myers of the Regulars[7] was in command of the guard and let us pass through. We went to Boonsboro where we found a surgeon who dressed the lieutenant's hand. We then went out from the main road near a garden and stretched ourselves under an apple tree and were soon in the land of dreams.

Sometime in the night we were roused up and told that our forces were retreating and we had better get away. On going out to the road we found numbers of soldiers moving in both directions, some towards the mountains and others towards Hagerstown, but none of them could give us any information. So the lieutenant and myself again sought a place to sleep near the roadside. When we awoke the next morning the sun was shining in our faces. We lost no time in getting away from there. We could not learn where the army was, or what direction it had gone in, but was told that the army had retreated during the night, and that the enemy was then entering the village, and if we desired to save our bacon we would have to make tracks in a hurry. Got the lieutenant and myself scared up, for being captured was one of the last things we wanted to take place. So getting on an elevated place where we could see the surrounding country, we looked to see if we could see anything of the army moving in any direction.

We decided that we would be governed by the movements of the stragglers. Whichever direction we saw the most of them marching we would follow. The stragglers were marching south and we followed suit. We had to cut through a plantation in order to reach the road leading to Sharpsburg. We had not proceeded far before we saw a man running as though he would cut us off. Told the lieutenant to wait a moment until I could load my rifle for we might have to fight our way out, but the man proved to be a Rebel sympathizer whose object was to assist us in getting away. We of course thanked him for his kindness and pushed on. We soon reached the road and crossed several burning bridges just in the nick of time. Don't think we could have crossed them five minutes later.

We saw a soldier who had shot himself through the hand. What a ghastly wound it was, with the leaders of hand jerked out three or four inches long and lying around on the back of his hand. Will bet my old cap that when I am shot somebody else will do the shooting. We offered him not even so much as our sympathy but passed on, soon after catching up with our command.

BATTLE OF SHARPSBURG, MARYLAND

On the 15th of September, Gen. Lee took his position on the ridge at the edge of Sharpsburg and south of the Antietam River, Longstreet on the right with D. H. Hill on the left. On the right of the road facing the river was Anderson's, Toombs', and then Drayton's Brigade on the extreme right. Gen. McClellan's forces soon arrived and took their position on the north bank of the river, his left against the Blue Ridge Mountains, his right extending up the river. Sharpsburg is a small town of some 1,300 inhabitants and is lower than the ridge, on which our artillery is posted just in front of it. There was considerable sharpshooting throughout the day. Sometime during the day, Harpers Ferry surrendered to Gen. Jackson, with 11,500 prisoners, 15,000 stand of small arms, and 70 pieces of artillery, with all of their supplies and munitions of war. Prisoners were paroled on the field and allowed to return home until exchanged.

Early on the morning of the 16th, we saw a signal flag posted on top of the Blue Ridge Mountains opposite McClellan's left. While we could not read the signals, knew that the devil would be to pay somewhere on our lines. We were not long in suspense, his batteries on his left opening on our extreme right, occupied by Gen. Drayton's Georgia Brigade, which was in full view of our position. Every shell seemed to explode right in their ranks, where they were lying down. What a stir it would make among them—we certainly knew how to sympathize with them in our sufferings. Gen. Lee's line of artillery only extended to the right of Anderson's Brigade and was posted along in our front, [the guns] about 20 steps apart. The artillery in our front opened on the enemy's artillery that was shelling Drayton's Brigade, which caused the enemy to turn their guns on our brigade. It certainly was one of the hottest artillery duels I have ever witnessed. Our brigade was lying some 40 yards in rear of the guns, and in rear of the hill.

Not many yards distant were the dwelling houses in Sharpsburg, which had been deserted by their occupants when we first formed line of battle. The enemy's shells would go crashing through them. At one time during the shelling some of our boys had entered a house in search of something to eat, as we had been two days without anything. They found a table with the meal all ready to sit down to, when the occupants were frightened away. The boys made themselves at home, took seats around the table, and proceeded to do justice to what was on it. About the time they had got in a good way, a cannonball came crashing through the wall, knocked the legs from under the table, and dropped it on the floor. It is needless to say that put an end to the feast.

During the shelling I saw the extremes of bravery and cowardice exhibited on the field. During the heaviest of the firing, Gen. Longstreet rode along the ridge in rear of our pieces, which were being fired for all they were worth, at the same time receiving more shots than they could return. Him and his horse both seemed to be perfectly indifferent in regard to the shells that was filling the air with death and destruction. He passed slowly down the hill as though he left the place with some regret. Not long after he passed, Gen. Pendleton,[8] chief of artillery on Gen. Lee's staff, rode the line in the same way, him and his horse seemingly indifferent to passing events. To cap the climax, Gen. Anderson, our gallant Old Tige, walked the line leisurely along, with his hands crossed behind his back watching the effect of our guns on the enemy's position. All three displayed the coolest and most daring bravery, which in a great measure accounts for the fighting qualities of our men. The officers lead and the men strive to emulate their example.

Just after the officers had thrilled the lines with their cool daring, our assistant surgeon of the 1st Ga. Regulars[9] gave an exhibition which caused no little amusement among the soldiers who witnessed the performance. The fire was so distressingly hot that the doctor was completely scared out of his wits and made a break to run. Some of the boys called to him, "Run here doctor, here is a safe place," and he wheeled and made for that part of the line. By the time he would get there a shell would explode close to him. Back where he come from, another fellow would call to him to run there, that he had a safe place, and away he would go to find a shell when he got there. The whole line was enjoying the poor fellow's antics and when a shell would explode near enough to him to almost lift him off his feet, would nearly bust their throats cheering at him. Poor fellow, he did not succeed in finding a safe place on the line, and made a dash for a small swamp to our right and rear. Then the boys rolled over and yelled themselves hoarse. What an exhibition for a man to make of himself. Death would have been preferable to a brave man. He must have been lost to all self-pride, as he could never have faced the regiment again. How will he feel when we get in camps again, to tell some of the brave boys who were laughing at him for his cowardice, to rub themselves down with a brick bat, a favorite prescription with some of the doctors.

The artillery duel continued for hours. Could not keep from watching the artillery horses which were near us. A horse soon becomes accustomed to an army life, and understands the commands nearly as well as the men. When a battery is engaged, the guns are posted on a ridge. The horses, with front wheels and ammunition chest, is carried under the hill so the horses will not be exposed to the enemy's guns. They are in that position here. Most of them look like they were enjoying a nap, with their heads and ears drooped down and their eyes shut. Saw one poor fellow who had been shot through the neck with a cannonball passing in front of the collar and between the neck bone and wind pipe. Was walking about the last I saw of him. To look at those horses in that sleepy condition don't look like a 10-foot pole would begin to move them, but wait and see. The enemy's fire proved more than our artillery could stand, so they had to limber to the rear. At the first command the captain give, "Riders prepare to mount," every horse's head and ears were erect. At the second command, "Mount," they were wide awake. And at the third, "Limber to the rear," they were simply wild, and it taken them but a few moments to dash from the field. After the artillery left, the enemy allowed us a resting spell.

About noon Gen. Lee was sitting on his horse in the road on our left, when Gen. Jackson rode up and saluted him. You ought to have seen the smile on the faces of Longstreet's men when they saw Stonewall Jackson. They knew his foot cavalry was not far behind. We certainly felt the need of help, with our ranks depleted to almost nothing, not over 600 in Anderson's Brigade, and not more than 50 in the Regulars. Where are our comrades, echo answers where. Company M is represented by myself and four others, making five without a commissioned officer in the company. Numbers were left straggling on the march after we left Manassas. Since we have been in Maryland, it was either keep up or be captured by the enemy. It is reported that there is 30,000 stragglers from Gen. Lee's army, and if the ranks of other commands have been thinned like ours, it certainly must be a fact. There was not a regiment in our brigade 12 months ago that could not muster more men than there is in our whole brigade today. Sad but true.[10]

We are now suffering from the pangs of hunger. Our rations were out Sunday. Monday and Tuesday we have had nothing but water. Guess we are getting in good fighting trim if hunger will produce it.

Gen. Jackson's command taken position on Gen. D. H. Hill's left, with the exception of Gen. A. P. Hill's Division, which was left at Harpers Ferry to parole the prisoners captured at that place. Sometime in the evening [September 16], McClellan's forces crossed the Antietam above Sharpsburg and attacked Jackson's left,[11] a considerable battle being fought. Just after dark saw a fine display of fireworks. Two of McClellan's batteries had an enfilading fire on one of Jackson's. Could see the movements of the shells by the lighted fuse until they would explode.

Just about sunset, a cow came feeding along in front of our lines. Gen. Anderson ordered her killed and divided among the brigade. Soon had my little piece broiled over the coals, and ate it with the blood running out, without either salt or bread. Just whetted my appetite but nothing more to be had. How long, oh how long will it be before we get something to eat? While we are all so hungry you don't hear any complaint among the men, all knowing that rations are not to be had, being so far from our line of communication, all of our supplies coming from Virginia. No foraging allowed by Gen. Lee on the enemy's country. What a contrast between our invasion and that of the enemy, who take everything as they go.[12]

No one could tell that Lee's Army had passed through Maryland, apples being the only thing we have made a raid on. And who could help it when the orchards are weighted down and look so tempting to a hungry soldier. No doubt a great many of our men have appeased their appetites on roasting ears, as the corn is in that stage at this time, but where our command is there is nothing but an old field. At night we stretch ourselves on the ground to try and sleep off the pangs of hunger. No one knows what a day may bring forth, but from the appearance of everything tonight, thousands of poor soldiers will have no use for rations by tomorrow night. For tomorrow no doubt will be another bloody day.

Lee's Army is greatly reduced, but what men he has is fighting men, as everyone so inclined has had the opportunity to fall out. Barefooted men are not compelled to keep up or go in battle, thousands being in that condition. I have seen numbers of poor soldiers who could have been tracked by their blood, trying to march over the rough turnpike roads, where a horse could not travel without being shod.

The gray streaks of dawn had just begun to mantle the eastern sky on the morning of September 17, 1862, when fighting was resumed in Jackson's front and soon became a general engagement along our entire front. Anderson's Brigade was ordered to Jackson's left. We moved out by the left flank, left in front. As we neared a bottom near the town, the ground was strewn with the dead and wounded. As we passed over them, some of the wounded would ask what brigade. On being told Anderson's Georgia Brigade would wave their caps and cheer us on. Poor boys. Stretched helpless on the ground, but their spirits unbroken. We inclined to the left through a strubble [stubble?] field, where we were ordered by Gen. Anderson to unsling knapsacks, each regiment forming a pile to themselves.

We must have went at least one mile to the southwest of Sharpsburg when the order was given by the right flank. We then marched in line of battle through a large field to a heavy timbered piece of woods that was occupied by the enemy. On reaching the woods the enemy's sharpshooters opened on us from behind trees. Gen. Anderson gave the order "Sharpshooters to the front," which was quickly obeyed by the men springing out of ranks and dashing to the front. The brigade reached the fence and tore it down and formed an obstruction by piling up the rails lengthwise so that we could lie down and shoot over them.

Soon after we arrived, Kershaw's South Carolina Brigade[13] marched up within 20 feet of us and halted. Just at the right of our brigade a regiment moved in by the right flank. (In front of us the enemy's line of battle was just over the ridge and not visible to us.) As their heads rose over the hill the enemy opened fire on them. The order was given right wheel into line, which was done on the run, engaging the enemy as they rose the crest of the hill. Gen. Kershaw's South Carolina boys were then ordered in, marching over us. As they moved over us, Gen. Kershaw asked what command, and on being told Anderson's Georgia Brigade, gave three cheers for the Georgians with a vim, and moved forward into the fight. It certainly does the heart of a soldier good to watch the brave Palmetto boys as they moved in under the enemy's fire. As the heads of the men become visible to the enemy over the ridge they opened fire on them, but not a man flinched, or a gun fired, until they rose the hill and the enemy was in full view. Then it seemed like every gun was brought down at the same time, and such a volley would have scared a weak-kneed soldier half to death, but time is up and we too have work to do.

Gen. Anderson ordered his brigade by the left flank at the double-quick, and away we went down the line with guns at the right shoulder shift. How steadfast the boys moved as though on drill. As we were well under way, the enemy opened on us, their line being on top of the ridge, and not more than 60 yards distant from the fence. What a hazardous move, under full fire of the enemy's line of battle, but not a bobble or a break until we gained our brigade distance to the left, so we could come in on the left of the Palmetto boys. Gen. Anderson gave the order "By the right flank," and we jumped the fence. It would have then done your heart good to have heard the rifles of the Georgia boys.

As I jumped over the fence and cast my eyes to the front, I saw directly in front of me the Stars and Stripes. How defiant they looked as they unfurled to the breeze and again fell back around the staff in the color bearer's hand. How I itched to drop those colors, thought it would be honor enough for one day at least. Bringing my rifle to bear on the color bearer, I pressed the trigger, and my gun snapped. To say I felt sold is putting it mild. I then had to pick the tube, put [fresh] powder in, and recap my gun.[14]

It seemed only a moment, but when I looked up, the line seemed to be all confusion. Saw Lt. Lamar in front of the line waving his sword and calling on the men to follow him. I rushed through the line to find

Capt. Wayne and several other officers holding up the almost lifeless form of Capt. Montgomery.[15] I soon passed them and saw but one of the Regulars afterwards during the fight and that was Sgt. B. B. Smith of Company B.[16] He was certainly making the air blue with his oaths, as some of the boys had burned his face with powder, shooting from behind him. Every time he shot he would yell worse than a Comanche Indian.

After the second volley our men fired, they charged. The enemy's line giving away, it then became almost a tree-to-tree fight. In passing over where the line of battle was, the ground was covered in blue. Gen. Anderson remarked afterwards he believed every man in his brigade killed a yankee the first shot. Let that be as it may, I have never seen as many dead men on one piece of ground. As we advanced, numbers of the enemy would throw down their guns and hold up their hands. The boys would tell them to run through our line to the rear, and they certainly lost no time in getting in the rear of us.

It was one of the prettiest fights I have ever been in. How brave a soldier can be when the enemy is on the run. Besides I fought tree to tree. Being in front of the line I could select my own position, and as our boys crowded up, would make for another tree in advance. It was some 400 yards through the woods with scarcely any undergrowth, but enough large trees to almost shade the ground.

We drove them out of the woods and over a ridge in a field. The largest squad I saw after they entered the field was three, so you may know they were pretty well routed. It did not seem like we were many minutes in driving them through the woods, but I had 45 shots at them during the fight. When the line was nearly through the woods, a staff officer come dashing down the line in our front and ordered the brigade to fall back. The South Carolinians, having failed to move the enemy, left our brigade liable to be cut off. So our line retired back to the fence where we first encountered the enemy. Several of us, I suppose being flushed with victory, followed up the enemy until they disappeared over the ridge in the field.

My next move was to refill my cartridge box as it was empty. While I was engaged hunting cartridges, the enemy moved a battery up somewhere in the field in our front and commenced shelling the woods, several bursting near me. I saw not far from me a wounded yankee. He was sitting on the ground with his back to a tree. He had been shot through the thigh. As I got within 15 feet of him a shell burst between us. I dodged, and he laughed at me. Told him I could not help dodging when the shells burst so near me. Walked up and squatted down by him. He had his pants ripped up to where he was shot, and was bathing his wound with water from his canteen. He says we are having a warm time of it this morning. Told him it looked so to a man up a tree. He then said, "You boys seem to be getting the best of it." Told him we come there for that purpose. He then told me he was the color bearer of the 1st Minn. Regiment, carried the colors at the First Manassas, and had been carrying them ever since. But said he, "Some of you boys have been too sharp for me this morning."[17]

Wondered to myself if he was the color bearer I was so anxious to shoot in the first of the fight. Have no desire to harm him now. He is wounded and would do anything in my power to aid or assist him. Strange that while he was on his feet I would have killed him if I could, but now he is down at my mercy, have no animosity towards him. We had a good long talk about what we were fighting for. He claimed to be fighting for the Union, while I told him he was fighting for the Negro. He said if he thought so, [he] would never soldier another day.[18]

He gave me a newspaper printed in the little town where he lived and invited me to go north. [He] thought if I would go, would not want to come back south anymore. Told him I was several hundred miles farther north then than I wished to be, and preferred going the other way. He was very anxious to know how we treated our prisoners of war. Told him that a brave soldier would be kind to him, but a cowardly one might impose on him, as they were too cowardly to face the enemy on the field, and showed their bravery when the enemy was helpless. Said he had got in trouble at Crampton's Gap by defending one of our men. The shells were still bursting around us, but he did not seem to mind them and acted as though he was used to them.

An officer, I did not know what command he belonged to, called and asked me if I would take position with several others, on our left. That we were on the extreme left of our line and were liable to be flanked by the enemy. Told him I was at his service as my regiment was back to our right and rear. So he posted us along behind the trees to our left. We had just about got posted behind the trees when a number of pieces of artillery was posted on the ridge just inside of the field and opened on us. My stars, how the shells flew. Looked like they were going to cut down every tree in the woods. To get from under the fire, we made for the left instead of going back to our line. The fire was so heavy that our jumped-up squad became demoralized and made for the rear, every man for himself.

I soon held up in an apple orchard, and while the shells were bursting all around me, gathered my haversack full of apples, hunger predominating over fear, Wednesday being the third day without something to eat. It was then getting late in the evening, so I tried to make my way back to where I had left the brigade. On arriving there, found they had moved to some other position on the line. Hunted them until ten o'clock at night, then gave up the search. Stowed myself away in a pile of straw near a threshing machine, and slept the remainder of the night.

Next morning early, resumed the search and found the brigade not far from where we threw our knapsacks when we went into action. Everything I had was gone. Overcoat, blanket, clothing, and all. Right there and then I swore by Jeff Davis, Abe Lincoln, and all the rest of them, that I would never drop my knapsack again. If I got where I could not carry it, I would lie down with it.

Was told by my comrades the brigade, after they fell back, had been ordered to the right and charged the enemy in an apple orchard. Our gallant Col. W. J. Magill lost his left arm, which was unjointed at the shoulder. How sad to think he should be taken from us at last, after being with us in all of our marches and battles. Don't think he has been absent a day since he has been with the regiment, and I am pretty certain not since he has been colonel. He has been a brave and gallant officer, and has the sympathies of his regiment in his loss and sufferings. God hasten the day when he can return to his command.

Found my comrades of Company M. Pvts. Ables,[19] Gann, Humphries,[20] and McMullen[21] all safe without a scratch. The loss of our brigade was small compared with the slaughter we inflicted on the enemy. Sharpsburg was a desperate battle, the loss on both sides amounting to thousands of men.[22] At night when the battle ended, Gen. Lee was still in possession of the ground he held in the morning.

The 18th opened up with comparative quiet along the lines, with the exception of the sharpshooters who were popping away at each other. Our artillery on one part of the line opened on the enemy but receiving no reply were soon silent. And thus passed the day; both sides seemed to have [had] enough fighting on the day before.

Soon after joining my comrades, I went to a pump in the road we had passed out [on] the day before just in the edge of the village, after water, which I procured, and started back. But the tempting fruit in an apple orchard on my left caused me to get into serious trouble. I scaled the fence, filled my haversack with sweet rosy apples, and had I then left the orchard would have been alright. But finding a new oil cloth knapsack, decided to make me a new haversack out of it. So seating myself under an apple tree with my command in full view and about 150 yards distant, went to work, keeping one eye on my regiment so that if they moved I could join them in quick-time, not wishing for them to get away from me again.

I was so intent on watching my comrades in front that I paid no attention to what was going on in my rear. Pretty soon I heard the tramping of a horse's feet and on looking around, I was completely dumfounded and so badly scared I must have trembled like a leaf. Within 10 feet of me was Gen. Lee sitting on his horse and near him was a guard of six or eight men. Holy moses, how I wished the ground would open and receive me, but the general did not give me many moments for reflection. "What command do you belong to sir?" asked Gen. Lee. "Anderson's Georgia Brigade" was my answer. His next word was, "Guard, arrest him and carry him to Gen. Anderson and tell him to put him out in front."

Under the same apple tree was a sick soldier who was barefooted, the blood running out of his lacerated feet. I never heard a poor devil beg like he did, but it availed him nothing. I have never heard worse abuse heaped on two mortals than Gen. Lee gave to us. He certainly could call a fellow more hard names and in the fewest words of any man I ever saw. He called us cowards, thieves, deserters, stragglers, and everything else but good soldiers.[23] I turned and walked off. The guard belonged to my regiment and never even halted me. So I left them with the barefooted soldier. Don't know what became of him. Gen. Lee was looking for stragglers, and while I was near my regiment, I could not deny being a straggler. So I said nothing in my own defense.

I am confident I have never had anything in the course of my existence that hurt me as bad as being reprimanded by Gen. Lee. While I don't try to clear my shirts, it certainly seemed hard, having had nothing to eat but a few apples going on the fourth day. And then to be reprimanded by the commander-in-chief for taking a few apples to appease my hunger was a little too bad [hard?].

When about halfway to the regiment, turned to the left and went to a small spring where I found three of my company, Pvts. Ables, Crawford,[24] and McMullen. Crawford had just arrived that morning from across the Potomac. He was barefooted and had been straggling in rear of the army. McMullen gave me two crackers and a small piece of bacon which he captured yesterday from the enemy, the first I have had since Sunday night.

McMullen was one of the best fighting men in the Regulars. Never failed to be in his place in a fight or out of it. Ables had a sick pass from our surgeon, so after my escapade with Gen. Lee in the apple orchard decided that I would take a day off, believing that a good soldier received no more credit than a straggler did at the same time risking his life. I copied Ables' sick pass for Crawford and myself and then made for the rear, swearing by all that was good, bad, or indifferent, that I would not fire a gun on that day if the Army of Northern Virginia and Gen. Lee with it was wiped out of existence.

Ables, Crawford, and myself went about one mile south of the city in the woods and camped under a large tree for the day. We were annoyed considerably by the cavalry looking at our passes which proved to be all OK. They were collecting up the stragglers and returning them to the lines. No doubt a great many were trying to keep out of the fighting, but there was numbers of good fighting soldiers trying to appease the pangs of hunger. At any rate the woods was full of them.

During the day, Pvt. Ables gave me an account of a battle he was in yesterday on our right. Will to the best of my recollection give it in his own words. He begun by saying, "When we charged and broke the enemy lines yesterday morning, Capt. Montgomery was wounded in the head. Myself and three others were ordered to carry him to the rear. We carried him south of Sharpsburg and left him at a field hospital. As the country was strange to us, we did not know how to find our way back to the regiment, the way we had rambled around in finding the hospital. So we decided to go into the city and go out the way we had went with the brigade in the morning.

"When we arrived in the upper part of the city, the enemy had just succeeded in crossing the Antietam on our right, and in front of the town, they were driving everything before them. Gens. Toombs' and Drayton's brigades had been routed with the loss of our artillery. At that time Gen. Lee did not have a regiment but what was engaged somewhere on the line. I saw him walking the streets with the tears rolling down his cheeks and the bullets flying as thick as hail. His staff was pleading with him to go to a place of safety, but he seemed indifferent to the dangers surrounding him. After awhile he mounted his horse and with his staff, galloped to the woods south of town where they soon succeeded in collecting a number of stragglers, somewhere between 1,000 and 2,000 as the woods seemed to be full of them. Every regiment in the army must have been represented in that band of stragglers.

"Gen. Lee formed his line in the edge of and to the right of town, then stepped in front of them with his hat off and gave the command 'Charge,' which was done with a yell as we charged a rock fence the enemy were behind. Our line was simply irresistible and the enemy retreated in disorder. We drove everything before us, recapturing our guns. Forced the enemy back across the river and held our lines as they were in the morning. Sgt. Andrews you ought to have seen Gen. Lee as he stepped in front and waved his hat. Don't believe there is a man in existence who could have withstood that appeal. Even a coward would have forgotten his scare and rushed to the front." Quite a compliment for the stragglers, but a story I fully believe. While Pvt. Ables is very excitable, he stands to his comrades on the field.

We remained in the woods until near night when I told the boys I had pouted long enough and was then willing to return to the regiment and do my duty as I had always done. Shall not attempt to justify my actions but leave it to others to pass judgement on me. We went back to where we had left the brigade in the morning but they had moved to some other portion of the line. After hunting them until ten o'clock at night, give it up and again sought the straw pile where I had remained the night before, where we stowed ourselves away for a comfortable night's sleep. But men proposes and God disposes.

RETREAT ACROSS THE POTOMAC

We were not more than sound asleep [on the night of September 18-19] before someone was shaking us up, telling us to get out of this. The army is on the retreat, and if daylight catches you here, you will find yourself in the hands of the enemy. Told him he could not bluff me in that way and dropped off to sleep again. Our slumbers were soon disturbed again by someone else telling the same story. Decided there might be something in it, so I roused up my companions and everybody else that I could find in that straw pile, and it was pretty full. The next question was where was our army, and in what direction were they moving.

It was so dark, could not see five feet from you, but we struck out, having an idea of the direction of the Potomac. We had not gone many yards before I stumped my foot and fell over a dead man. A bad beginning with the hope of a better ending. As we could not see, had to depend on our hearing. We soon heard the welcome rattle of a canteen against a bayonet, and moving forward found ourselves near a column of troops moving in fours, moving with that silent tread used only in retreating at night in front of the enemy. Not a sound above a whisper and an occasional clink of a canteen against a bayonet being the only sound heard. We did not know where our command was whether in front or in the rear, so we decided to keep up with the procession at least until we had placed the Potomac River between us and the enemy.

Troops while marching have a right to the roadway and no one is allowed in the ranks. Only those who belong there. So we had to march along in the edge of the woods to keep out of the way of the column marching in the road. Think when I reached the Potomac, I had the measure of every stump on the roadside on my shins. Never had so many falls in my life as I did on that night. It was pitch dark, could not see anything. So when I struck a stump would be down before I knew there was a stump anywhere about. But was determined to keep up with the procession.

On arriving at the river we went to a house down the river, in search of an apple orchard Crawford said he visited that morning when he crossed the Potomac. But we never succeeded in finding it, so we returned to the ford just as our brigade started to wade the river. Fell into ranks with our company and waded through. At that point the Potomac must be at least 300 yards wide, and we averaged about knee deep with a rock bottom covered in moss that was perfectly slick. Don't think many of the boys succeeded in crossing without getting from one to a dozen duckings, and each one done some tall cursing while the rest laughed at him. After we crossed, continued the retreat in the direction of Martinsburg, Va.

As the last of Jackson's forces crossed the river about sunrise, he placed a battery in position on the ridge not far from the river. And just behind, in ambush, a line of infantry instructing the gunners to run and leave the guns when attacked by the enemy. About sunrise, the advance guard of the enemy some 5,000 strong, under command of Gen. Featherston, reached the river, formed a line of battle, and advanced to the attack, crossing the river under fire of the artillery, then charged up the hill. The gunners deserted their pieces and fled, leaving the enemy in possession of the guns. The yankees gave three cheers and charged. When they reached the guns were met by the line of infantry, who gave them a volley and then charged them and recaptured the guns, which again opened on the retreating lines, driving them back across the river with great slaughter. What a place to retreat under fire of the infantry and artillery combined. It was reported that the river looked like it was running with blood, the division being totally routed and cut to pieces. Gen. Jackson is said to be a Christian and I have no right to doubt it, but he certainly plays some dirty tricks on our friends the enemy. That was the last and only attempt to follow on our trail.[25]

While marching along on the 19th, my mess mate W. G. Humphries grabbed some Irish potatoes in a patch by the roadside. We marched until eleven o'clock at night when the command was halted as we supposed for the night. Nearly everyone soon dropped off to sleep. Humphries and myself decided that we were more in need of something to eat than we were of sleep. He proposed that if I would go after water to cook with, we would cook our Irish potatoes. So I struck out in search of water, which I succeeded in finding at a spring nearby. When I got back he had procured some wood and started a fire. So putting the potatoes, chipped up fine, with my little piece of bacon McMullen had given me at Sharpsburg into a small tin can, we soon had them simmering over the fire. Can't say we waited for them to get entirely done before we ate them, but can assure you that it was the best meal I have ever enjoyed. A supper that Old Tige himself no doubt would have enjoyed, if he had been out of rations as long as we had. It is now twelve o'clock Friday night and we ate our last on Sunday for dinner. How is that for a fast with nothing to break it except what apples we eat.

After completing our repast, stretched ourselves for a nap. Had not more than straightened out good before the long rool [roll] beat, the columns were again formed, and the march continued until daylight, when we halted and drew rations. With what feelings of thankfulness we received our rations, tongues cannot tell. Five days without rations had begun to tell on us. And had it not been for roasting ears and apples, would have fared worse than we did.

September 21, the army bivouacked near Martinsburg. One day while there, heard cheering down the road in our front. Some of the boys said it was Stonewall Jackson or a rabbit. The cheering come nearer and nearer, and finally reached our brigade. Everyone made for the road, and sure enough, it was Gen. Jackson galloping along the road with his escort. He passed us with his cap off and the cheering continued down the line as far as we could hear. The boys claim that he is getting tired of the army because Longstreet's men keep him bareheaded so much. What an ovation he receives every time he passes Longstreet's Command. He certainly creates more enthusiasm than all of the rest of the officers put together. But you must not think that Gens. Lee and Longstreet are not admired by the men. If you do, you will be sadly mistaken. As to Gen. Lee, the feeling his men have for him is simply too deep for utterance, while Gen. Jackson causes them to bubble over and go wild. While the soldiers admire both as great generals, don't believe they could swap shoes. In other words, fill each other's places.

While in camps, Capt. Kenan made out a list of casualties in the regiment while in Maryland. Lt. Gus Rutherford, in his dry way, told Capt. Kenan that he must not forget to mention that the gallant assistant surgeon of the 1st Georgia Regulars, Dr. Bickers,[26] had his horse killed under him while gallantly leading the wounded to the rear. The lieutenant seemed to think that the gallantry of the doctor ought to go on record.

We remained near Martinsburg until the 27th, when we moved camps to within four miles of Bunker's Hill on the Winchester Turnpike. The camps are again getting lively. The absentees are rapidly returning and our ranks are filling up. The fall weather is bracing the boys up after our long summer's campaign. We have no duty to perform, guard or drill, but simply eat and rest. The boys are in fine spirits and ready for another move.

Lt. Col. Martin has taken command of the regiment since we got back into Virginia, Col. Magill being left in the hands of the enemy at Sharpsburg, where he lost his arm. We don't like our lieutenant colonel who has never been in a battle with us but always looms up when we don't happen to be fighting. The Regulars claim themselves old veterans of many hard-fought battles and have no use for anyone who has not shared their hardships and battles with them. Besides, he is the best example of a militia officer I have ever seen.[27]

October 16, Anderson's and Toombs' brigades ordered to Cedar Run under quarantine on account of small pox having broke out in the two commands. Passed through Winchester and Kearnstown. The boys don't seem to have any fear of the disease. The patients are placed in tents some 200 yards from camps where they receive proper attention.

Drilling has been resumed and especially skirmish drill. Gen. Anderson had a brigade drill. The boys said for the special benefit of some young ladies, six in number, each one escorted by a staff officer. They looked very nice on their fine horses with long flowing riding skirts and no doubt enjoyed the maneuvers, but I am pretty certain the men performing them did not. It was certainly the hardest drill we ever had, and the longest, not less than two hours. Old Tige certainly looked well on his black charger he got over in Maryland, and I guess felt so by the way he drilled us. A brigade changing front forward on first company, eight in front, is pretty tough on the left of the line. If those young ladies could have heard all the cursing they received during the drill, would not have wanted to attend another one.

While we were in camps at Cedar Run, there was but one tent in our regiment, and that was occupied by Col. Martin. Gus Clower, John Toddy,[28] Alvin Parr, and some more of the bad boys in the regiment decided one night to have some fun at the colonel's expense. Sometime after taps, when everything was quiet in camps, the boys secured some rocks and proceeded to rock his tent. When the first one struck, the boys heard the rattle of the colonel's sword as he drew it from the scabbard. The boys stopped throwing and listened awhile. They heard the colonel say, "Well, I believe they have ceased firing," and returned his sword to the scabbard. His sword was a very heavy artillery saber with a metal scabbard. The boys were too well tickled to continue the fight and retreated in good order leaving him in possession of the battlefield.

Our soldier boys are very fond of honey (or anything else that is to eat). The other day, some of the 15th Georgia boys[29] discovered a gum in a chimney corner and decided to lift it that night. Soon after taps, secured a blanket, some matches and rags and made for the gum in the chimney corner. After seeing that the coast was clear and everything was still about the house, they slipped up, wrapped the blanket around the gum to keep the bees in, and then made off with it. How they puffed and blowed under its weight, with now and then an exclamation of "boys she is rich, my but ain't it heavy," until they reached a place of safety. They then put it on the ground, fired the rags, and proceeded to smoke out the bees. "Blow boys, they will come directly," but they blowed until out of breath and still no bees. They then examined the gum and found that it was the old woman's ash hopper instead of a bee gum. Don't reckon the 15th ever heard the last of carry back the old woman's ash hopper.

The soldiers certainly enjoy a joke at anyone's expense. A beaver hat, umbrella, or duster makes them go wild. Would not put on a beaver hat and walk through camps for anything. It makes no difference how venerable or old a man is if he has on a churn[-shaped?] hat he certainly catches it from all sides.

CROSSING THE BLUE RIDGE MOUNTAINS

October 29, Anderson's and Toombs' brigades broke camp on Cedar Run and marched in the direction of Siegley's [Fisher's?] Gap in the Blue Ridge. On the first day passed through Strasburg and waded the Shenandoah River just at night. It was the coldest water I have ever felt. Ten thousand needles sticking through your flesh would not have hurt any worse. Numbers of the boys give out and had to be helped out of the river. Have often thought of a remark I heard Lt. Magill, a brother of our colonel,[30] made while wading the river. The adjutant Lt. R. H. Atkinson was riding the colonel's horse. "My God," the lieutenant exclaimed, "my brother's horse and I have to wade." On reaching the opposite bank we struck camps and built fires which we enjoyed after our cold wade. The river was four feet deep and about 100 yards in width.

On the 30th, marched to Luray Court House. Just before we entered the town we crossed a creek and just above the road was a pretty deep hole where the boys of the town had a spring board. Pvt. Crawford of Company M had got hold of some applejack and was feeling good on the strength of it. To show the boys how level his head was, walked out on the board and fell in. Guess he was sober when he got out, and the boys yelled themselves hoarse.

From Luray there is one of the most magnificent landscape views it has ever been my lot to witness. Luray is on a considerable elevation, enough to give a full view of the valley and the Blue Ridge Mountains. You can see up and down the valley until the farm houses dotted over it don't look larger than a chicken house. The mountain is covered in the colors of the rainbow. A patch of green pines, then clumps of other trees with their leaves either red or yellow with now and then a great gray rock looking for all the world like it was just ready to tumble down the side of the mountain. Could have looked at the scenery always and never got tired. It is eight miles across the valley, just far enough to make the trees look like shrubbery.

On the 31st [of] October, crossed the valley and camped at the foot of the Blue Ridge. Tired myself down hunting hazel nuts and walnuts on the mountain. The boys tell me that I will perish myself to death yet eating nuts.

We are having delightful weather, just cool enough to enjoy marching and our campfires at night where we cook our rations and fight our battles over again. What is more jovial than a group of old soldiers telling war stories and smoking their pipes around the campfires at night. The soldiers are more lively and mischievous than I have seen in a long time. At the same time numbers of them are barefooted and almost destitute of clothing, the rags on their backs being all they have, having lost their baggage in Maryland. It seems strange that the government can't furnish shoes to its soldiers when they need them so badly.

November 1, crossed the Blue Ridge at Siegley's Gap. Said to be 15 miles over the mountain. Guess it is as it took us all day to cross it. In ascending it is like going up steps, only you walk the full length of the step and turn back just above the other. We watched the boys one and a half miles in our rear, the steps or turns in the road being some three-fourths of a mile in length.

Coming down on the eastern side is very different. Some points we would pass around great boulders. On the other side were chasms hundreds of feet in depth where the sun never shone. My, how it makes my head swim to go near it. One point is an extremely dangerous place, the road making a short turn around a large rock just on the edge of one of those deep chasms. (I saw an account in a newspaper some time ago about an awful accident that happened at that point during the war. A wagon train was crossing the mountain and when they started down on the eastern side, the wagoners were ordered to scotch their hind wheels by running a rail underneath the wagon body and through the wheels, thus locking the hind wheels. One of the teamsters who was driving six fine mules said he had no need of a scotch as his wheel mules would hold his wagon on any ground be it be as steep as it would. But to carry out orders he would use one, and did so. But just as his lead mules had passed around the curve, the rail broke, precipitating wagon, mules, and driver into that awful chasm below. What an awful death, but the driver was to blame. He had so much confidence in his mules, that he picked up the first rail he come to instead of taking time to secure a good one. He would have fared better without any, as the sudden breaking of the scotch pitched the mules over before they could check the weight of the wagon.)

A little before night, the columns halted to rest. After we had rested some time, Col. Martin said, "Attention 1st Georgia: About-face, rest." The boys said he turned us around so we could rest on the other side. Guess he did not know himself what he done it for. Just as we reached the foot of the mountain, the column again halted. Looked in our front like there was a water course of some kind. Guess our gallant colonel thought so as he gave the order "Prepare to wade," which the men promptly obeyed, most of the boys taking off their shoes and pants. Again the column moved forward. We had not gone far before the order was given to the Regulars to file right, and we entered a small field. One of the rockiest places I ever saw. We were going into camps for the night, and the rest of the brigade yelled themselves hoarse at the Regulars wading the rock pile. Our colonel is certainly a daisy.

November 2, marched to Madison Court House where we camped for the night. While on the march that evening, my little chum Humphries and McCann were foraging along near our line of march, and just before night succeeded in getting a canteen of applejack, which they brought into camps. Pvts. Childers,[31] McMullen, Smith,[32] and myself made up a purse and got them to go back after three more canteens full, which they succeeded in getting after being fired on by the brigade guard as they crossed the guard line. In order to have a social time, we invited our 1st Sgt. W. J. Burns to join us. We certainly enjoyed ourselves as we passed the canteens around, fighting our battles over and telling how many yankees we could whip in our next battle. The applejack was good and mellow, but some of the boys got still mellower. Everything passed of[f] nicely until the last canteen had been emptied of its contents. To say the boys were mellow is putting it mild. Some two or three of them could not get up, and remained where they were all night.

On retiring, Sgt. Burns, Humphries, and Smith occupied the same blankets. Smith retired first, too full to get up, Humphries next, and Burns last. When Burns went to lie down, Humphries for mischief would get in his way, which made Burns mad. He placed his knee on Humphries' breast and commenced striking him in the face. Almost before you could think, McCann caught Burns and pitched him about 10 feet. By the time he straightened himself, Humphries was up and onto him. I made a lunge to get to Burns, but someone caught me. I have no recollection of what I said, but the boys told it on me that I said, "Give him h-ll Humphries. I will relieve you when you get tired."

If I did not say it, I certainly meant it, for I was certainly good and mad.

Our scuffle aroused the rest of the company from their slumbers, and seeing the orderly with everybody against him rushed in to take his part with anything they could lay hands on. Times looked squally for a company fight, but everything quieted down before the officers found it out, which might have gotten all of us in trouble. I thought it very mean of Burns to act as he did after being our guest. But there is no accounting for a man under the influence of stimulants. I would have fought for Humphries before I would for myself. The next morning we were all ready to laugh over our spree of the night before. Soldiers are like children; quarrel and fight, make up and forget it.

November 3, marched to Gordonsville. November 5, passed through Orange Court House, crossed the Rapidan River, and went into camps between Orange and Culpeper Court House. It is right amusing to be awake sometimes in the wee small hours of the night and listen to the different noises being made in camps by the soldiers. In one part of the camp you can hear a rooster crow. Over in another direction you will hear a turkey gobble. In some other direction, a dog barking or a cat squalling. The lowing of a cow, a mule braying, a horse whickering, and everything else you ever thought of seemed to be in camps. Anything for mischief to create a laugh. If it was not for the devilment going on in camps, we would all die with the blues. Just before we entered camps, my youngest brother, J. D. Andrews of the Fort Gaines Guards in the 9th Ga. Regiment, knocked one of his company senseless with the butt of his rifle. Thought he had killed him at first, but he soon came to, but remained speechless for several days and was finally sent to the hospital. Guess he did not try to impose on him again because he was the youngest and smallest in his company.

Our soldier boys are still without shoes. Gen. Lee has issued an order giving the green cow hides to the soldiers to make moccasins out of by turning the hair side in next to the foot. Have seen several soldiers with them on. Don't imagine they feel much like shoes, but they are better than going barefooted. Poor soldiers, they certainly deserve more than they receive from the government. What a contrast between our army and that of the enemy who have everything money can purchase. It has been several months since the troops have been paid off and our clothes are almost as scant as our shoes. Nothing unusual to see yankee clothing in our camps, which was stripped off the dead on the battlefield. Saw Sgt. Alex Clemency of Company G wearing an officer's cap with a slot of his brains sticking to it. Sgt. Bridges of Company M wears a frock coat with a ball hole in the waist of it, and the tails covered in blood where the fellow was shot in the back. Don't think the boys wear them from choice, but from necessity.

November 7, snow fell for the first time this winter. What a time the boys had snowballing each other. November 19, Anderson's and Toombs' brigades recrossed the Rapidan River, passed through Orange Court House, and taken the upper road to Fredericksburg. Heavy rains and the roads knee deep in mud. At night had to sleep on a fence rail to keep out of the mud and water. Rejoined Longstreet's Corps on the march. November 22, army encamped around Fredericksburg. Our division, Hood's, went into camps near Hamilton's Crossing, about five miles from the city on the railroad.[33]

THE FATTEST TIME I
HAD DURING THE WAR

BATTLE OF FREDERICKSBURG, VIRGINIA

The Army of Northern Virginia was just in time to save the city. As Gen. Burnside,[1] who had succeeded Gen. McClellan in the command of the Army of the Potomac, had demanded the surrender of the mayor of the city, Gen. Lee replied by telling him to come and take it. The weather is extremely cold. The ground is hard frozen and we are without tents, sleeping on the frozen ground. At night we build log heap fires and all lie around them in a circle with our feet to the fire. Since we have been here, the troops have been paid off and money is plentiful as long as it lasts. The majority of the soldiers will not have any in one week's time. It is a feast or a famine with most of them. Gambling of all kinds are being carried on. Seven up Poker, Keno, Chuckluck, and everything else that can be thought of to risk a dollar at.

Gen. Lee has issued an order putting all barefooted men on duty. No one excused on account of not having shoes. Three days after the order was issued you could not find a barefooted man in camps. Don't know where the shoes come from, but my honest belief is a great many were carrying them in their knapsacks instead of wearing them on their feet. What is it some men won't do to keep out of battle. I don't mean to say all had shoes that were barefooted, for no doubt many good soldiers were without them and could not get them. Besides, being paid off enabled them to buy them.

December 5, Regulars relieved the 11th Ga. Regiment on picket at Hood's Fort on the Rappahannock River below Fredericksburg. When we left camps, it was raining, then commenced sleeting, and afterwards went to snowing, covering the ground about six inches. Then went to sleeting again, freezing the snow over on top. How cold it was with the wind sweeping down from the north. We were on one bank of the river and the yankees on the other, with positive orders from Gen. Lee not to have any fire on the picket line. I was at a plank fence above the old fort that made[2] down to the river. We tore it down and built a blind between us and the yankees. Dug a hole in the ground and kept a fire of coals burning all night, which we crouched around shivering in the cold. Could not tell what our friends the enemy were up to, as everything was pitch dark on the other side of the river. What a night it was. Hope I may never pass such another. The next evening we were relieved by the 8th Ga. Regiment and marched out on the ridge in a field and camped for the night.

It never gets too cold or too wet for the boys to have their fun. Last night while we were sleeping in the snow, Gus Clower crawled out for some purpose or other, and decided he would see how his voice sounded on the frosty air. Gus is something of a mimic and can imitate anyone's voice to perfection and especially Col. Martin's. So Gus decided to have a brigade drill all to himself and give the command "By companies right wheel." The colonel being awake finished the command for him, and Gus crawled off to his blanket and remained quiet, but he never heard the last of the command "Right wheel."

The next morning, went back to camps. During the day, a peddler, driving a two-horse wagon loaded with gingerbread, drove into camps. In 10 minutes you could not have got in 50 feet of the wagon, as the boys all had their mouths set gingerbread fashion. The peddler had his bread in large cakes and had it to cut up, which taken up considerable of his time, besides having to make change. The boys got him pretty badly wearied and finally made him so mad, he drew an ax on one of the boys. That seeded his doom. Several of the boys jumped up in the wagon and distributed his bread for him, not waiting to take in any change. Others cut the horses loose, while some more of the boys taken the wheels off, letting his wagon on the ground. A dirty mean trick of the soldiers. All they wanted was an excuse to take it without paying for it. If the soldiers never got anything to eat until I carried it into camps to them, they would go hungry.

On the 10th of December, I mounted brigade guard and was given a detail of three men from the 11th Ga. Regiment and sent to Hamilton's Crossing to guard Gen. Longstreet's commissary stores which were issued at that point.[3] The day passed off with nothing unusual transpiring. On the morning of the 11th of December, just before day, as I was nodding over a little fire, three cannons fired in rapid succession towards the city. The echoes of the guns had not more than died away on the distant hills before every little drum in the army was beating the long roll up and down the river as far as I could hear. It certainly startled me, not knowing what was up. Again all was silent. Soon afterwards day broke and we learned that the guns fired were signal guns informing the army that the enemy were placing their pontoons across the river at Fredericksburg. Each regiment had been notified for more than a week to form and take position when the signal was given. So by daylight, Lee's Army was in position and ready for the enemy.

During the day the enemy shelled the city from the heights north of the river, doing considerable damage to the city, and placing the citizens under the fire of their guns. I remained at my position, but expected every moment to be relieved. But the day passed off and no relief came, for which I felt thankful, for I would not have swapped places with Gen. Anderson, considering my position much the safest if not the most honorable. But seeking a bubble reputation at the cannon's mouth is not what it is cracked up to be.

During the day, the troops were moving in and taking their positions. A. P. Hill's command marched past. How silent and solemn they looked. A funeral procession would not have looked more so. Poor boys, the distant boom of the cannon tells them trouble is ahead. Each one feels that numbers of them will be called upon to yield up their life's blood to their country's call, and no one knows but what he might be the one to go.

Just before battle is a serious time. The skirmish lines are popping away at each other with an occasional shell thrown in for good measure, the troops moving in that silent, solemn way. The staff officers and couriers dashing at full speed in every direction. Soon the rattle of musketry and the boom of artillery will tell you the battle is on. Every horseman that dashes in your direction is supposed to have orders for your command. As time passes, suspense deepens with dread you cannot express. Is it dreading the consequences, or is it fear?

Have often thought I could not have felt worse if I had been sentenced to be shot. A horseman is seen coming at full speed. He delivers his orders to the commanding officer. The word is given to forward. You are soon under the bursting shells. Farther on and the familiar zip of the minié ball reminds you that the infantry is not far distant. Soon you are in firing distance, and when a wave of musketry passes over the line, all fear and doubt has disappeared and you are as eager for a fight as you ever were for a fox chase.

Anyone who has never been a soldier might ask how can you kill your fellow man. Easy enough. There is an intense hatred between the two armies. You might ask how you could hate someone you had never seen. Each army blames the other with all of its trouble. If we have a hard march, or [are] exposed to the weather, it is damn the yankees. If it was not for them, I would be at home and out of this trouble, and the longer the war lasts, the more intense the hatred becomes. So when we have a chance to shoot and kill, we do it without any compulsion, and the boys in blue feel the same way about the boys in gray.

At night the commissaries were ordered loaded on the cars, and were carried back to a side track some three miles from Hamilton's Crossing. On the 12th there was considerable fighting on the lines, numbers of the wounded being brought out where we were, on the railroad. Gov. [John] Letcher of Virginia with a number of old men from Richmond were there as a relief committee to care for the wounded. Don't think I ever saw a jollier set of old men as they busied themselves waiting on the wounded soldiers and telling amusing anecdotes.

On the 13th of December, the big battle was fought. Could distinctly hear the rattle of musketry and booming of cannon. How sad one feels to listen to the awful roar of firearms, knowing that hundreds of human beings are being swept into eternity by each wave of musketry, there to face the judgement bar of God, and give an account of the deeds done in the body. Have seen but few pleasant-looking corpses on the battlefield, but have seen some of the most hideous faces that anyone could imagine. If they had been held over a precipice by the hair of the head, could not have looked any worse or their features worse distorted.[4]

As a rule, the soldiers are desperately wicked. Gambling, profanity, and obscenity rule the camps. As wicked as I am, I often have to leave my tent a[nd] the crowd I am in to get out of hearing the language used being too obscene for my ears. Have not come in contact with a private soldier who made any pretenses to religion. What then must be their feelings as the Messenger of Death strikes them. But it is then too late to pray after the devil comes.

The fighting continued throughout the day. How thankful I am not in it. At the same time, if I knew my comrades were in action, would like to be with them and share the honors and dangers in which they partake. At night the commissaries were again ordered some five miles farther back to Guinea Station, on account of the enemy having attempted to turn our right flank and secure the railroad depot.[5] Nothing more than picket firing on the line. During the night, Gen. Burnside withdrew his forces to the north bank of the Rappahannock River. It had been a terrible experience for the enemy, leaving thousands of their dead on the battlefield. I was told that some of their brigades lost over half of the men carried into action. Color bearers would advance alone until shot down by our men. They certainly fought with desperation, as the odds were against them, having to form on the river bank and advance on Gen. Lee's lines stationed on the ridge, at least one mile from the river under fire of our artillery.

The Confederates are now fighting the world, Burnside having German, Irish, and Italian brigades. Complete from the brigade commander to the last man in the rear rank. It seems hard that the Confederacy should be opposed by the combined world. Every foreigner who puts his foot on American soil joins the Northern Army, for the sake of the bounty paid, if anything else.[6]

On the 15th, trains loaded with commissaries continued on to Hamilton's Crossing, leaving what we had at Guinea Station still under guard. What a fat time I had with all that I could eat, and but little to do at night. Would build fires over the ground where the commissaries were scattered (nearly one acre of ground) so we could see all over it. Myself and one man would stay up until midnight, then the other two would relieve us until day. Remained there for about eight days, the fattest time I had during the war. I was then ordered by letter from Capt. Hill to report back to my company. I got on the first train that passed and went to Maj. [R. J.] Moses' headquarters, he being Longstreet's chief commissary. He ordered me back to Guinea Station, stating that Capt. Hill had no authority to order me to my company. Being near camps, I went to my company and reported to Capt. Hill, staying with my company all night.

The next morning, Capt. Hill went with me to Gen. Anderson's headquarters. The general was hot when he told him what he had done, and told the captain he had no right to remove me, as the guard was placed there by Gen. Longstreet's orders. Had the captain pretty badly scared. His excuse for ordering me back to my company was he did not know how to report me. Gen. Anderson told him he should have reported me [as being] on detached service. But as the Regulars had been relieved from duty with the Army of Northern Virginia and ordered back to Georgia, he would send another man in my place. So I remained with the company. Capt. Hill, while a kind officer, could not bear the idea of any of his men having a good job out of the company. The captain made it all right with me by promising me the first furlough granted to the company on our arrival in Macon, Ga.

My comrades informed me that our brigade was not engaged or under fire during the battle of Fredericksburg, and that our gallant Col. Martin set up corn stalks in front of the line to show them where they must let the yankees get to before they fired on them. In other words, wait until you see the whites of their eyes, which I reckon was thankfully received as the boys were not used to fighting. I drew a piece of carpet in lieu of a blanket, not having anything in that line since the battle of Sharpsburg, and had it not been for the kindness of Pvt. Jordan J. McMullen of Company M, would have suffered from the severe cold weather. He had a homemade blanket, overcoat, and oil cloth which he allowed me to share with him. We would stretch the oil cloth over some sticks, make us a bed of leaves or straw, and cover with the overcoat and blanket. How was that on frozen ground and the ice on the creek two feet through. While nothing to compare with a feather bed, we would sleep warm.

December 25, 1862. Christmas day was spent in camps. Several of the regiments having fantastic drills and dress parades. Was well amused at the 9th Ga. Regiment having a fantastic battalion drill. A private in a brown jeans suit of clothes, with three large yellow paper stars on each side of his coat collar and riding a very small mule, was acting colonel. His men had their coats turned wrongside out and disguised in every way they could think of, with a blanket for a flag. The colonel formed his line and marched to the front, then gave the command "Right about march," which was promptly executed. On looking in front of his line, discovered the line of file closers. He dashed through the line on his little mule and called out, "What in the hell are you fellows doing here in front?" which caused a yell from everybody in sight. The drill was a laughable farce all the way through.

In the evening the Regulars had a fantastic dress parade, Sgt. W. J. Burns of Company M as colonel and Sgt. Maj. C. J. Boggs[7] acting adjutant. The most amusing feature was the adjutant's batch of orders in his left [hand?], which was read out. His orders informed the regiment of the proceedings and findings of a general court-martial convened to try Col. Martin. It was gotten up in military style with charges and specifications. The colonel was charged with overloading his horse, giving the number of quilts and blankets the colonel carried, besides his feed basket with all of its contents, down to the number of spoons, knives, and forks. It was a laughable farce on the colonel, and one he took exceptions at, and [he] went to Gen. Anderson to know if he could not have the boys court-martialed for it. Gen. Anderson enjoyed it as much as the boys did, and told Col. Martin the boys treated him worse than that. So the colonel failed in punishing the boys for their Christmas frolic. If our colonel don't wish to be laughed at, he must be more like a soldier and quit putting so much baggage on his horse that he cannot mount only from a stump or the fence.

The Regulars had been relieved from duty with the Army of Northern Virginia on account of their small numbers, only 150 men in the regiment. One year ago, three companies would have made a larger regiment than we have today. How sad to look on our depleted ranks and think of our comrades who have passed in their checks. Maj. [John E.] Rylander's 10th Ga. Battalion took our position in Gen. Anderson's Brigade.

The year 1862 has been a memorable year with the Army of Northern Virginia in which the 1st Regiment of Georgia Regulars have taken an active part, as the names of battles inscribed on our battle flag will show. First we have Yorktown. Then comes Meadow Bridge, Nine Mile Road, Garnett's Farm, Peach Orchard, Savage Station, Malvern Hill, Rappahannock, Thoroughfare Gap, Second Manassas, Ox Hill, Crampton's Gap, Sharpsburg, and Fredericksburg. In all, 14. How is that for a lively campaign in which our colors have always been borne to the front. No stain or stigma rest on the escutcheon of the 1st Ga. Regulars. We have borne our part like men, and can point with pride to our bullet-riddled flag to bear us out in our assertion. We have shared the trials and hardships as well as the honors of the gallant First Brigade, composed of the 1st Ga. Regulars, 7th, 8th, 9th, and 11th Ga. Volunteer regiments. Our relations with the rest of the brigade has been that of a band of brothers. No word or hard feeling has ever come between us, and while we are anxious to once more place our feet on Georgia soil, we leave our old and tried comrades with a sad and heavy heart, and will ever watch the career of the gallant old 1st Brigade with the greatest pride, knowing the actions of the past to be a safe guarantee for the future.

Our brave and gallant commander, Gen. George T. Anderson, will ever hold the first place in our affections, not only as a brave and fearless officer, but as a kind and humane man. He loves his soldier boys and has ever been kind to them. He seems more like a father than a commanding officer, and his memory will ever be cherished by the boys who followed him in battle as long as memory lasts. May he reach that fame he so eminently deserves is my honest prayer.

I shall ever look back with pride at the service spent in the Army of Northern Virginia under such gallant leaders as Gens. Robert E. Lee, Joseph E. Johnston, G. T. Beauregard, James Longstreet, Robert Toombs, and last but not least, our own gallant brigade commander, George T. Anderson. (In 1891, at the reunion of Gen. Anderson's brigade in Marietta, Ga., I saw the gallant old hero for the first time since the war. What feelings pass over me, as I look at his once erect and manly form. Now being bent by the weight of years, his once dark locks now silvered with gray. As I look back into the dim and dusty past, the tears will well up in my eyes in spite of me. Call it what you may, weak, childish, or womanish. All the same, I saw the tears streaming down his furrowed cheeks, as the boys of Georgia, now bent, wrinkled, and gray alluded to his war record. He said, "Boys, I am not too old to lead you again." May long life and prosperity be his.) December 29, 1862, the Regulars were formed in line and Gen. Anderson bid us a last farewell in a short speech. His allusions to our past services was quite touching, saying that if he had gained any fame or distinction, it was largely due to the 1st Regiment of Georgia Regulars. So giving our own gallant commander three cheers, we boarded a train of cars for Richmond, Va.

RICHMOND, VIRGINIA

On arriving at Richmond, went into quarters at Camp Lee.[8] As we had been on a long campaign, the officers and men were all eager to get passes into the city. Sometime after night, Capt. Hill asked me to go with him to the Spotswood Hotel. More as an escort than anything else, as Richmond was a bad place to be out in after night on account of the thugs infesting the city. We had to pass the residence of Chief Justice Marshall.[9] Capt. Hill was acquainted with him and wished to stop and see him for a few minutes.

The justice lived in a large brown stonefront, the yard enclosed with a brick wall and a heavy arch over the gate. Told Capt. Hill he could go in and I would wait for him on the inside of the gate, to keep the provost guard from picking me up. Capt. Hill rang the door bell, which was answered by a servant coming to the door. The captain sent in his card, and Justice Marshall made his appearance.

By some means (I reckon Capt. Hill must have told him I was in the yard), he insisted on my going in the house. I begged to be excused, but he would not receive any excuse. So I had to go in. He carried Capt. Hill and myself into the parlor where there was five young ladies. Capt. Hill was acquainted with them, and after telling them howdy, turned and introduced them to me separately. How small and cheap I felt with my dirty and ragged uniform. My pants were burst out in the rear from my knees down, besides being soiled every other way. To make matters worse, there was a large mirror on each side of the room and one at the end, all sitting on the floor and must have been at least nine feet high, besides a large, fine glass on the mantel piece. I could not look in any direction without seeing myself, and I certainly looked as bad as I felt.

The floor was nicely carpeted, with lounges and chairs to suit. What would I have given to have been out from there. Wished the floor would open and let me through. Capt. Hill seemed perfectly at home, and could talk to all of the young ladies and Justice Marshall at the same time, which left me to my own reflections, which were not pleasant by any means, being in the wrong pew.

Pretty soon Justice Marshall invited Capt. Hill and myself to go down in the basement and sample some of his old brandy, the young ladies following us. On arriving at the basement, found Mrs. Marshall with several small children. After sampling the brandy, which Capt. Hill pronounced just splendid, some parched ground peas were passed around and everybody had a good time but me.

After remaining about three-fourths of an hour, we left. Told Capt. Hill he would not get me into another such a scrape, that I would prefer going on a skirmish line anytime to facing ladies in my predicament. The captain enjoyed the joke on me hugely. Went with him to the Spotswood Hotel, then split the middle of the streets back for camps.

My reason for going in the middle of the streets was on account of the robbers in the city who lurked behind dark corners. When you passed [one] would spring out, pass one arm over your right shoulder and under your chin, and give you a lift onto his hip. No. 2 would knock the breath out of you, rifle your pockets, drop you, and escape before you could get your breath to call for help. So by going [in] the middle of the streets had an opportunity of seeing them before they could get to me. My messmate, Jordan McMullen, was held up in that way and robbed.

The next day I remained near the camps, Pvt. McCann having discovered a blind tiger close by. (Whiskey was forbidden fruit, and was seized by the government whenever found. But where an Irishman can't find whiskey, there is no use of anyone else looking for it.) We enjoyed ourselves, sipping a little of the over-joyful until late in the evening, when we returned to camps. There I found my gallant chum Sgt. Garrett waiting for me. We were certainly glad to meet again and as he clasped my hand remarked, "Old boy, I have had a glorious account of you." He had recovered from his wound he received at Malvern Hill and had been promoted to hospital steward at the old hotel used as a hospital, he having taken one course of [medical] lectures before he entered the army. My first question was, "You are going back to Georgia with us, are you not?" He said that all of the company had been after him to go, but he had declined to do so. But if I would go with him down to the hospital and stay with him all night, he would return with me in the morning to the company and go back to Georgia with us. So I went with him to his quarters, first visiting the famous *Merrimack*, an ironclad vessel lying in the James River.[10]

The next morning we started for Camp Lee. Sgt. Garrett had a monthly pass from Gen. Smith[11] commanding the city, while I had none. We had not gone far before we were halted by the provost guard. Sgt. Garrett was allowed to pass, but I was arrested, the guard carrying me to that noted prison, Castle Thunder. On the way Pvt. Posey[12] of Company G was also arrested, but just as we reached the Market House, Posey asked the guard to let him see a man in the Market House and gave the guard the slip. I was so mad would have assisted the guard in recapturing him if I could because he was so much sharper than I was and made his escape.

On arriving at the prison, I certainly thought I was done for. The captain of the provost guard said he was going to put every one of our boys in the dungeon that was caught after that, but I might go that time, and told the guard to carry me beyond the guard line and turn me loose. Just as we were starting, Sgt. Garrett arrived with a guard of eight men to carry me back [to the regiment]. He had hurried on to camps and informed Capt. Hill of my whereabouts, and he ordered him to take a guard and go after me. A pretty close shave for me, and had me badly scared, being my first time under arrest with a dungeon staring me in the face. I kept pretty close to camps after that as no pass was recognized but [that of] Gen. Smith.

Thus ended the year 1862. The Regulars, after helping to defeat four of the best-equipped armies of modern times—to wit, McClellan at Richmond, Pope at Manassas, McClellan at Sharpsburg, and Burnside at Fredericksburg—will now leave the Old Dominion in the hands of her gallant defenders and return to our native state with the consciousness of duty well performed.

OFF FOR MACON, GEORGIA

January 1, 1863. The Regulars boarded the cars for Danville, Va., where we arrived on the morning of the 2nd and went into camps three miles from the city. On the 5th, started on the march for Greensboro, N.C., 50 miles distant. One night while camping out, some of the boys sheared Col. Martin's horse's mane and tail, making the horse look like a mule if he had been sheared right. But as it was, looked like he had been through a hackle trap. It was a mean trick to disfigure the horse to spite the rider. The boys were extremely anxious to get back to Georgia and the colonel was not in any hurry, stopping three days at Danville when we ought to have been on the march.[13] Never knew who done the shearing. Guess someone would have paid pretty dear for his whistle if he had been found out.

Arrived at Greensboro on the 8th. On entering the suburbs we met a Negro driving a pair of horses to a wagon, with a long coupling pole. Suppose he was hauling lumber. As the horses reached the center of the regiment, they became frightened at our state flag. Wheeled short 'round, breaking the coupling pole, and dashed back towards the city. Have never seen a regiment stampeded as quick in my life. There was a plank fence on either side of the street, with a row of shade trees on the edge of the sidewalk. I was near the head of the regiment and opposite one of the shade trees when I heard the racket in the rear. On seeing the horses rushing back, I made a break for the fence on my right, which I did not take time to climb, but went over head foremost and none too soon, as the horses with the front wheels of the wagon struck the shade tree, one going on either side, the tongue striking the tree. The horses cleared themselves of the wagon and went flying up the street. One of the men jumped behind the tree just as the horses struck it and was taken up for dead but afterwards revived and was left at the hospital in Greensboro, where he remained several months.

At night bivouacked near a tobacco factory, sleeping on the ground. Next morning when we opened our eyes found about six inches of snow on our blankets which had fallen during the night. It was not disagreeable, but made us that much warmer. January 9, took the car for Georgia, passing through Charlotte, N.C., and Columbia, S.C., arriving at Augusta, Ga., on the 12th. What a yell went up from the boys as the train rolled across the bridge onto Georgia soil. Home again. The mayor and citizens of Augusta furnished the Regulars with a splendid dinner, which was certainly enjoyed to the fullest extent. After dinner the Regulars proceeded on to Macon by way of Millen, arriving at one o'clock on the morning of the 13th of January, 1863.

Pine Woods, Wire
Grass, and Saw Palmetto

Macon, Georgia

During the day, the mayor delivered an address of welcome from the balcony of the Hotel Lanier. At one o'clock the Regulars were tendered a sumptuous dinner by the mayor and citizens of the city. It was by far the finest dinner I had ever seen, barbecued meats of all kinds, with cakes of all descriptions iced over with beautiful trimmings, syllabub, and nearly everything else that was good to eat. A feast for the Gods. The dinner was given at the Union Dep[o]t on the second floor. Hanging on the walls were large wreaths. Across the center of the wreath was a piece of pasteboard with the name of a battle on it. Overhead was wreathed in large letters: WELCOME YE HEROES OF MANY BATTLES. The boys enjoyed our welcome back to our native state. The dinner was well gotten up and the boys knew what to do with it, for when it comes to eating, the soldiers are hard to down, being seldom they get as much as they want to eat.

After dinner we marched out on the M & W [Macon & Western] Railroad and pitched our tents (in front of Col. Blount's residence on Tatnall Square). On the 16th day of January Capt. Hill made his promise good by securing me a 20 days' furlough to visit my home at Cuthbert, Ga. Just before I entered the cars on the Southwestern [Rail]Road, I was handed a note from Capt. Hill which read as follows:

Camps, 1st Ga. Regulars
Near Macon, Ga.
January 16, 1863
Sgt. W. H. Andrews, Company M

Dear Sir:

    In visiting your home on furlough it gives me the greatest pleasure to offer you a letter expressing my entire satisfaction with your conduct during the whole war. As a brave, ever-ready, and reliable soldier of your country, any commander may be proud to have you serve with him. I regret that your gallant brother, Washington L. Andrews, has fallen in battle but he was at his post & like yourself, had always done his duty. Wishing you a pleasant meeting with your friends and relatives.

    I am with great respect,

        Your obedient servant
        A. A. Franklin Hill,
        Capt. 1st Ga. Regulars
        Commanding Company M

I can truthfully
Endorse the above
Jas R. DuBose
1st Lt. Co. M 1st Ga. Regs
Afterwards Capt. Co. M

I certainly appreciated the compliment and kind wishes of my commanding officer, but am afraid the captain overestimates my services. At the same time, the captain is my best friend, and I shall always strive to retain his friendship and good wishes.

I remained in southwest Georgia during my furlough. Can't say I enjoyed myself like I thought I would. The young men are all in the army, and the girls, God bless them, have to put up with the little boys (shinplasters, as the girls call them) for escorts to parties and church.

My sweetheart looks as handsome as ever. Had a nice time when I went to see her. She carried me around to sewing parties in the neighborhood, where the ladies were making up clothing for the soldier boys in the army. The girls are true blue and are very proud of their soldier sweethearts. A young able-bodied man at home is looked on with contempt, and well he may be for this certainly is a time to try men's souls, and the women's too.

But all things end after awhile, and so did my furlough. It is hard for a fellow to leave his best girl when he can go to see her three times a week, but how much harder when nearly two years had passed without seeing her. And then to return to the army with 20 chances to one that he will never see her again. It certainly is like tearing your heart strings out to bid her farewell. Tried to tell her goodbye at the door, but still stayed on. Asked her then to accompany me as far as the front gate. Maybe if I got that far, would be able to keep on. At the gate was no better off. Told her then to set the dogs on me, probably that would give me a send off, but the whistle of the coming train made me more in a hurry to keep from being left.

I am jealous of my best girl, and have a right to be, for an old widower with a spanking pair of horses and a light buggy is paying too much attention to her to suit me. At the same time must admit he is a man of good taste for there is not a prettier girl in southwest Georgia. Her height is about five feet six inches, weight 140 pounds, complexion brunette, eyes black and sparkling. Teeth as white as pearl, and a mouth, well I won't tell you any more, but will leave you to guess at the rest. While times look desperate at the front, danger is lurking in my rear. Wish the old fellow had to go to the army where some kind yankee might pick him off. But I have one consolation, I have another sweetheart near the banks of the swift-running Chattahoochee. She is just entering her teens and wearing short dresses. She has pretty brown eyes and a merry laugh, and is the sweetheart of my boyhood days. Her bright merry face haunts me in my dreams. Often when wrapped in my soldier blanket in front of the enemy or on some hard-fought battlefield, my spirit returns again to the far sunny South and tarries again with the little sweetheart of my boyhood days. The pleasure of those dreams linger with me for days after, and now just before entering a battle, if I dream of her, consider it a good omen and enter the battle with the full belief that I will come out safe. Maybe it is the spirit of my wee little sweetheart that hovers over me in battle and protects me from death or injury. So if the old widower cuts me out, I have another string to my bow. Time will tell. One old man at home may be worth more than two young men in the army.

How pretty the girls look in their homespun dresses with homemade hats. Everything is made at home, all of the Southern ports being blockaded by the enemy. Even the salt people use has to be made on the coast. A number of citizens will band together, go to the coast, and make salt out of the seawater, where they are often disturbed by the enemy's gunboats that are prowling around the coast. So far as provisions goes, everything is plentiful and raised at home. Three acres of cotton to the mule is all that is allowed to be planted by the government. A tax in kind is levied by the government. One-tenth of everything raised belongs to the government, which the party delivers at the county site, where a building is used for that purpose.

I find conscript officers stationed everywhere I go, watching for some poor devil who is trying to keep out of the army. If he cannot be caught any other way, will run him down with Negro dogs, and then take him to the front in chains. I would rather be at the front and take my chances among the bullets than to stay at home in the swamps and be run down by dogs and then have to go.

One fellow was caught in Albany, Ga., with a woman's dress on and was chained and carried to the front in that condition. Would prefer death a dozen times to being carried before our soldiers in that plight, for there is nothing more contemptible in the eyes of a soldier than a coward. Besides, no able-bodied man with a spark of manhood in his breast can stay at home and see his country overrun by the vandal hordes of the enemy, who destroy everything in their reach.

I am getting anxious to get back to my company again, don't feel right away from camps. Besides, the small pox is pretty thick in Cuthbert. There is about 30 cases of it and still spreading. Just three days before I left home, my oldest sister, Amanda, was taken sick. The doctor said it was typhoid fever, and the morning I left home for the army she was unconscious, but my time was up, and I was compelled to return to my command at Macon, Ga., so I left on the nine o'clock train and I learned afterwards my sister broke out with small pox at 1:00 P.M A close shave for me. If I had been there when she broke out, would have been placed under quarantine, and of course would have had the disease. Besides, would have been detained from going to my regiment. The enemy is bad enough, but the small pox is worse.

Returned to my company at Macon on February 10. Found everything moving along smoothly in camps. Our gallant Col. William J. Magill has returned and is in command of his regiment. How sad to look at his empty sleeve hanging limp and empty by his side. He has earned his spurs, and the stars that adorn his collar at the head of his regiment. He is a brave soldier and a good officer and receives the respect and admiration of his men. Our ranks are gradually filling up with the absentees now numbering about 200 men. So far as recruiting is concerned, that is a dead letter, as everyone who has to go to the army prefers going into a company made up from their immediate section where they will be with relatives and friends. If we gain any in numbers it will be from conscription, something we do not want, as a conscript as a rule is a very poor soldier, having to be forced into the army against his will.

The boys are having a huge time in Macon, resting and frolicking with an occasional fight with the railroad boys at night, the party of the fewest number getting the worst of it. Sgt. Garrett has been appointed hospital steward for the regiment, which I dislike very much because it spoils one of the best fighting soldiers in the regiment. At the same time he will make a good steward. Hate to give up my chum, for his place will be hard to fill. He ought to belong to some dashing cavalry command, like Gen. Morgan's.[1] Wouldn't I like to see my chum in a hand-to-hand contest on horseback. Think he would enjoy it as he enjoys anything that is exciting or dangerous.

I have but one objection to my gallant friend; he is an infidel in belief. There I differ with him, for I believe stronger in a supreme being than I do in my own existence. At first I thought he talked that way for the sake of an argument, but he convinced me afterwards when he showed me a letter from his father saying he preferred never seeing him again unless he changed his belief. Also one from his affianced telling him he would have to denounce his belief or she would break the engagement, but he remained firm in his faith. He is as firm as a rock and as true as steel to his friends. We enjoy ourselves of evenings after dress parade strolling around the railroad beyond the Confederate Army and back to camps.

The boys are again getting anxious for a move in some direction, as camps soon become irksome for the want of a change. The night before we left Macon, the railroad boys challenged the soldiers for a pitched battle which was accepted by the Regulars and about 75 of the boys slipped out of camps after tattoo and made for the city. By some means, the officers found it out and Col. Magill sent Capt. Louis Kenan with 50 men after them. On arriving in the city, Capt. Kenan arrested every man he could find, which broke up the fight. No doubt if the officers had not found it out in time, there would have been a great many broken heads, as each side was determined to settle the question as to which side was the strongest.

OFF FOR JACKSONVILLE, FLORIDA

March 20, 1863, the Regulars were ordered to report to Gen. Finegan at Jacksonville, Fla., the enemy having taken possession of the city.[2] Went by the Southwestern Railroad to Fort Gaines, Ga. March 21, proceeded down the Chattahoochee River on board the steamer *Indian* to Chattahoochee, Fla. Remained all night at the arsenal.[3] 22nd, marched 10 miles in the direction of Quincy. 23rd, arrived at Quincy and was reviewed by Gen. Howell Cobb[4] and staff. 24th, took the cars for Gen. Finegan's Command three miles from the city, the enemy's picket line being two and one-half miles this side [west] of the city. March 25, the enemy fired and evacuated the city, but the troops put the fire out before much damage was done.[5]

April 3, Regulars ordered to report to Gen. Cobb back at Quincy. We took the cars and went to Lake City. While there tried to obtain something to eat, but every door in the place was barred against us as though we were cutthroats or something worse. Well, every dog has his day, and the citizens of Lake City may see the day they will be glad to see the 1st Ga. Regulars. So mote it be.

April 4, arrived at Quincy and bivouacked near the depot. While at Quincy some of the boys behaved very badly. The little paper published at Quincy came out in a card abusing the whole regiment for the actions of a few bad men. A committee from the regiment waited on the editor and notified him he could do one of two things, retract in his next paper, or have his office torn from over his head. It is needless to say the retraction was promptly made. We have as good law-abiding men in the Regulars as there is in any regiment in the service. At the same time, there are bad men in all commands. If the paper had scored the guilty ones, all would have been right, but it had no right to abuse the whole of the regiment. April 7, Regulars ordered to Chattahoochee Arsenal, Gen. Cobb making the regiment a short speech in front of his quarters. On the 8th arrived at the arsenal where we went into quarters.

CHATTAHOOCHEE ARSENAL, FLORIDA

The arsenal is near the junction of the Flint and Chattahoochee

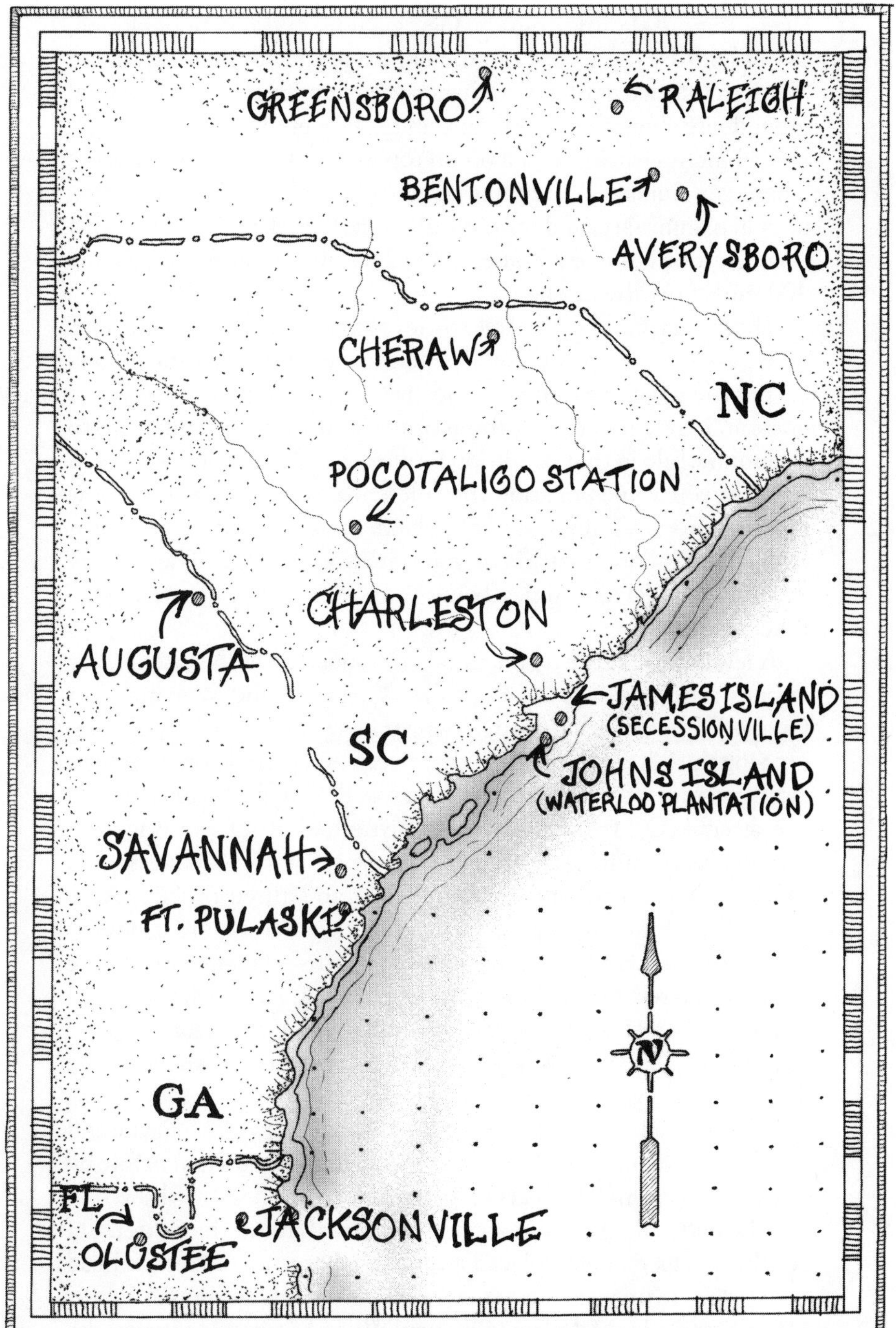
GREENSBORO
RALEIGH
BENTONVILLE
AVERYSBORO
CHERAW
NC
POCOTALIGO STATION
CHARLESTON
AUGUSTA
JAMES ISLAND
(SECESSIONVILLE)
SC
JOHNS ISLAND
(WATERLOO PLANTATION)
SAVANNAH
FT. PULASKI
N
GA
FL
JACKSONVILLE
OLUSTEE

rivers, some 200 yards from the Georgia line, in the state of Florida. It was built by the U.S. Government some time during the Indian Wars, as I notice graves of soldiers buried here in 1836. The arsenal grounds are about four acres, surrounded by a brick wall 12 feet high and 30 inches thick, capped off on top with a stone three feet wide. There is a number of buildings inside the walls: officers' quarters, arsenal commissary, and hospital, all built of brick and covered with slate. Outside is the pest houses and stables, the magazine being some 400 yards from the arsenal.

The arsenal building is three stories high with a seven-story tower. What a magnificent view could be had if there was anything to look at. But the upper portion of Florida is nothing but pine woods, wire grass, and saw palmetto. Nothing to attract the eye. You might go to sleep and while in that condition be moved 100 miles, and when you wake up, you would not know the difference. All of a sameness—how different from Virginia and Maryland. It is certainly God's own country, for it don't look like anyone else would have it. The country is thinly populated, Quincy being the nearest town of any importance.

A few days after the regiment taken up quarters at the arsenal, our wagon train, in charge of Capt. W. W. Payne and Wagonmaster George W. Eubanks,[6] arrived, having traveled by way of Fort Gaines, crossing the Chattahoochee at that point, and passed down through Alabama into west Florida, thence across the Apalachicola River to the arsenal. On his arrival Capt. Payne had all of the wagoners arrested and confined separately. The next day two commissioned officers, two noncommissioned officers, and three privates were ordered to report to Capt. Payne, in light marching order, myself among the number (Sgt. Wilf[7] and Pvt. Harris[8] of Company I being all that I can recollect). After reporting to Capt. Payne we proceeded to the landing at Chattahoochee and took passage on a steamer up the Chattahoochee River. When several miles up the river, landed on the west bank and marched out through the country.

After we had gone several miles we were halted by Capt. Payne and informed of our mission. He stated that on the second night before he reached the arsenal, he had camped where we then were. Showed us how he had parked his wagons in a circle, with his in the center. On retiring to sleep he had placed a small leather trunk under his head containing his papers, six or eight gold watches belonging to the officers, and 12,000 dollars in money. When he opened his eyes the next morning his trunk was missing, and on making his loss known to the wagoners, found that nearly all of them had been robbed during the night. Some lost their coats, while others lost their boots, hats, or blankets, all having suffered more or less from the midnight marauder. On looking around, the captain found his little trunk near a small sink or pond of water with his papers and the officers' watches all safe, but his money was gone, it having been placed in large envelopes, the same as his papers were. He secured some Negro dogs in the settlement, but failed in striking a trail going from the camps. Towards night his train hitched up and drove about two miles farther and camped for the night, and the next morning went to the arsenal.

"Now my object in bringing you here," said Capt. Payne, "is that I was robbed by the wagoners and that the money is buried somewhere in this vicinity. And what I ask of you is to make an exhaustive search in every direction around the camps to see if you can discover it." We started out on the search and kept it up until the next evening without making any discoveries in regard to the missing monies. We then gave up as lost for good and returned to the arsenal. A few days later, one of the wagoners was stricken with remorse and made a confession of his guilt. On being carried back to their last camp, he produced the money, having buried it in a two-gallon jug, twisting the envelopes until he could pass them into the mouth of the jug. After the money was recovered the wagoners were all released. Nothing of interest transpiring at the arsenal. One day about the same as the others.

May 27, 1863, the Confederate gunboat *Chattahoochee*, mounting four guns, was blown up while some distance down the Apalachicola River while getting upstream, killing 16 of the crew instantly and scalding several others so badly they died soon afterwards and was buried near the arsenal by the Regulars.[9] It was a sickening sight, portions of their flesh falling off. I saw the steward, William Tucker, a cousin of mine, rip the clothing from several of the crew who had been badly scalded. Poor boys, death would have been preferable. How they must have suffered. When my time comes, I hope I may go in the twinkling of an eye, as I have a perfect horror of being scalded or mangled up. But we all have to submit to what falls to our lot, good or bad.

There is a great deal of complaint among the men about something to eat. When we first come to the arsenal, Sgt. Wylly,[10] the commissary sergeant, procured a drove of beef cattle, and placed them in a brown hedge field, where there was not more than enough grass to last them two days. And there they remained getting poorer and poorer day after day, until towards the last they were so poor they reeled as they walked. Don't believe that a whole beef boiled would have produced three eyes of grease on top of the pot. It was so poor, the boys would throw their rations at the brick wall to see it stick. It was simply an outrage, and not fit to be eaten by anyone.

One night while the boys were yelling beef, Capt. Fort[11] was officer of the day and tried to put a stop to it, but while he was at one place, someone would yell beef at another. Thus keeping him going up and down in front of the men's quarters. At one time, when he was passing in front of the arsenal, a grape shot was thrown at him from the second story of the building, barely missing him. A discharge was offered to any man who would own throwing it, but it was never found out who threw it. Don't know whose fault it was in regard to the beef as Sgt. Wylly must have been carrying out someone else's orders, and therefore not responsible.

In June I visited Tallahassee, Fla., as a witness in a court-martial, and remained 10 days. This is the prettiest place I have seen in Florida, the country being broken. From here to Saint Mark's there is a signal line for the purpose of sending messages from one point to another. The signal stations are on elevated ground and in sight of one another and worked by two men. The flag is a red ground with a white ball in the middle. When the message is going to St. Mark's, the man working the flag faces the same way. The other man turns his back to the flag and faces the direction which the message is coming from. He calls out the movements of the next flag which is then made by the flagman at his back. For instance, he will call "right," "up," "left," "over," and so on. When he makes a mistake he will say "wipe out," the flag being carried around his head. Those in the secret understands the alphabet, but it is all dutch to me. I would call it a pretty expensive telegraph system, but the news have to be carried in some way and I guess that is the best way it can be done.

I saw in Tallahassee Capt. F. T. Cullens, the officer who enlisted me. He had resigned from the Regulars and returned to Fort Gaines, Ga., and raised a volunteer company, of which he was a captain, and Capt. Turnipseed of the 9th Georgia, who had resigned and returned home, was first lieutenant. After the court-martial got through with me, I returned to the arsenal.

On July 15, Companies E, G, H, and M went to Fort Gadsden on the Apalachicola River on picket duty. Being sick at the time, I did not go with my company. On July 20, I received 20 days' furlough to visit my home at Cuthbert, Ga. Being sick most of the time, did not enjoy my visit much, and to make bad matters worse, my best girl was married while I was at home.

When I reached home I called on her but found the old widower present. It being late in the evening he stated that he would go home. She insisted on his staying until after supper, which he did. After supper she insisted on his staying until bedtime. Not being hard to persuade, he very readily consented. I began to smell a mouse. Her object in having him to stay was to keep me from talking to her, in which she succeeded. The next morning I asked her for my letters and picture which had been in her possession for two and one-half years. We had a lovers' quarrel in the spring, and had never made up anymore. She gave me the picture, but my letters she would not give up. I then bade her a last farewell. So I lost my sweetheart just as I expected, but hope to live long enough to get over it. A few days afterwards they were married and I certainly wish them much happiness.

I have been considerably worried by the young ladies while sick, wanting to wait on me. They think it is quite an honor to wait on a sick soldier, but they worry me by fanning me half to death. Besides, they worry me with their presence. Would not object if I was well, but being sick would rather be by myself. My little sweetheart is all right, and it is to be hoped the war will end before she is old enough to marry an old widower.[12] Hang the old widowers. They ought to be sent to the front along with the rest of the boys instead of remaining at home and stealing the soldier boys' sweethearts away from then while they are at the front fighting the battles of the country. But I reckon my best girl thought an old man at home was worth three or four young men in the army, as it is not very healthy in the battle department.

August 11, 1863, returned to the arsenal at Chattahoochee, Fla. During my absence on furlough, the rest of the regiment had been sent down the Apalachicola River to Hammock's Landing, some 15 miles below the arsenal. At least two-thirds of the men had been sent off to Macon and Columbus hospitals, sick with chills and fever. What a country this is. Not fit for anything but alligators and mosquitoes, and I would not be surprised if they did not have the chills. I remained at the arsenal with a number of sick soldiers. What a time we had without any nourishment suitable for a sick man. We have rice, poor beef, and New Orleans molasses, enough to make a sick man heave at the idea of eating it. No medicine to be had except a little calomel or blue mass. Iodine is the most popular medicine for all ills, and if that fails [the doctor] will order you to scrub down with a brick bat.

September 3, I went down to Hammock's Landing where the left wing of the regiment was stationed, my company being still down the river at Fort Gadsden. September 10, the regiment from Fort Gadsden and Hammock's Landing returned to the arsenal on the Confederate States steamer *Swan*. About 60 men in the regiment, and most of them sick.

The celebrated steamer *Swan* is worthy of more than a passing notice. The boat is about 10 feet wide and 40 feet long. Has a captain, engineer, and pilot. The captain tells the pilot that all is ready. He reaches the Pilot House by climbing over the woodpile. The engineer takes his stand and the passengers remain on the bank and push the boat off, jumping on as the boat leaves the bank. The passengers then have to divide some on each side of the boat so as to balance it. If it screens too much to one side, the captain says, "Balance the boat boys," and they will shift from one side to the other. As for speed upstream, you have to get two trees in a line to see whether it is moving or not.

We remained at the arsenal two months, nearly everybody sick. November 10, the regiment, or what was left of it, again left the arsenal, five companies going to Hammock's Landing and the other five to Fort Cobb. November 11, white frost this morning for the first [time] this winter. A welcome guest, as the chills and fever will have to take a back seat.[13] Something to eat is getting pretty dear and Confederate money is getting almost worthless. Molasses, 500 per gallon, sugar 100 per pound, sweet potatoes 250 per bushel, chickens 175 each, eggs 150 per dozen, fresh pork 100 per pound, and corn meal 300 per bushel.[14] A private soldier's monthly pay, 11.00 dollars, will just about pay for his breakfast. Our meat rations have been reduced from three-quarters to three-eighths of a pound a day. Bread rations remain the same, one pound of flour and sometimes meal instead of flour, but a soldier don't want corn meal and especially if he has to march.

The sick are returning to camps. As the winter advances, the chills and fever disappear. Maj. Bonaud's[15] 28th Ga. Battalion is camped at the Landing, and just on the hill is a battery of several 32 pounders bearing on the river. Our men are drilled on them nearly every day.

The boys laugh at Maj. Bonaud, who is a Frenchman. Sometimes when he is drilling his men, they don't execute his orders to suit him. He will stop drilling and say, "Maybe you no understand me?" The boys would say they did, which seemed to nettle the major who would squall out, "Why in the hell you don't mind me then?" One day he was practicing with the artillery down the river. He said he give the gun three degrees and the ball went down in the water. He then give it four degrees and the ball went away hellwards over yonder.

December 25. Another dull Christmas in the army. The boys got up a fantastic dress parade, was the only difference in that and any other day. Caused some of the officers to have hard feelings against the men for making fun of them. Just across the river from the 28th camps is a large field planted in corn and pumpkins, which the boys have made good use of. And by crossing two sticks and sharpening the four ends, can carry on their shoulders four pumpkins at a time, which I would call some pumpkins.

Two brothers by the name of Norman[16] had an experience in that field they will never forget, let them live ever so long. They crossed the river one morning on a foraging expedition. About one-half mile from the river there is a low swampy place where the water backs when the river is up. There was some water backed that morning, but not enough to alarm them about getting back. In the evening when they returned, found the water rising rapidly. They made their way across the field to the river bank where they called themselves hoarse trying to get someone to carry them the batteau, but darkness settled around them with no prospects of aid coming to their relief. With the roar of the rising waters to keep them company, they resigned themselves to their fate. As the night advanced, the water rose. They kept giving back until they reached the highest point in the field. There the water surrounds them, first to their feet. They could go in no direction. The water was next up to their knees. Then as the night wore on, reached their waist. By that time they began to pray. No telling what promises they made the Lord if he would only deliver them from that awful death. What must have been the feelings of those two men as the wild waste of waters roared and surged around them, with not one ray of hope to sustain them through that trying ordeal. At daylight the water had reached their shoulders and [was] rapidly rising. They again yelled for help, which was heard on the other side of the river, and help went to their assistance as the water had reached their chins, but a little while longer and they would have succumbed to the raging waters. They were rescued more dead than alive.

HAMMOCK'S LANDING, FLORIDA, 1864

The Regulars commenced the new year at Hamilton's [*sic*] Landing. About all of the absentees have returned to camps and we are again in fighting trim. Rations are not very plentiful. By the way, our nearest neighbor, Rev. Joe Talley, a Methodist preacher, complains at headquarters about losing his hogs. The officers have the men's quarters searched, but find no meat. At the same time, the Rev. Mr. Talley finds his hogs' hides in the woods minus the meat. It may be that his hogs shed their hides like a snake. The officers don't search deep enough—the boys have plank floors in their tents and the meat box is under the floor, buried in the ground. When at home it was customary to scald hogs to get the hair off, but when a soldier kills one, he has to skin it like he would a beef. The scalding process would be the means of his being found out.

I don't believe every soldier who steals a hog does so from hunger. A great many of them are natural-born thieves and would steal out of one pocket and put it in the other. For instance, I saw [a soldier] marching up and down in front of the officer's quarters with what the boys call a Jeff Davis uniform, a barrel with one end out and a hole in the other just large enough to get his head through, pulled down over him with a card tacked on the barrel in large letters THIEF. He had to march up and down for two hours each day until his sentence expired. He had stolen a sack of salt weighing 200 pounds and hid it under his bunk. He had no earthly use for it, but took it just to keep his hand in.

Our term of three years' service will soon be up, and the boys all have some company in view, as they are anxious to get out of the Regulars so as to be with relatives and friends in other commands. So far as getting out of the army is concerned, it is not thought of, as the day has long-since passed that an able-bodied man can stay at home. As a rule, we have no objection to our officers who are brave and in every way competent to drill and fight us. Besides they are men of good standing, numbers of them belonging to the best families of the state, and it is not saying too much to say that the officers of the 1st Regiment of Georgia Regulars will rank with the officers of any regiment in the Confederate service. Besides, I will venture the assertion that more officers served with the 1st Georgia than any regiment in the South. Among those that have been promoted and left the regiment we find Gens. Smith, Sorrel,[17] Willis, Kirkland, and

Harrison, besides numbers of others of less rank, among them Maj. King, Capts. Milledge, Hamilton, Lane,[18] Lamar, and others too numerous to mention.

As to discipline, it is perfect and to the point. We don't have any of your "Gentlemen of the Banks County Guard, will you please come to attention." An order is given to be obeyed with promptness, and if it is not obeyed, someone will know the reason why. There is no familiarity between the officers and men, as familiarity breeds contempt. An officer who is familiar and social with his men is not respected in the Regulars, and the officers' quarters are not loafing places for every man off duty like it is in the volunteer companies.

It is reported in camps that the officers will have a conscript officer here to conscript us as our terms of service expire and retain us in the Regulars. It may be so or it may not, but I would hate to be the officer to undertake it, as we are too far from other troops to be coerced in that way, but time will tell.

January 23, regiment inspected by Capt. Rutherford of Gen. Gardner's staff.[19] He complimented my gun by ordering Capt. Hill to put me in the guard house with some brick bats and my gun, and keep me there three weeks. Capt. Hill laughed and told him, "That, sir, is the best soldier in this regiment," and that was the last of it. My gun, while not bright, was in good shooting order. I had sworn off bright guns on Tybee Island. At guard mount, the neatest-dressed man with the brightest gun would be excused from duty for 24 hours, the next would be orderly for the commanding officer, and the next best, orderly for the officer of the day. One day, I was orderly for the officer of the day and he came so near running me off my feet, decided I never wanted it again. So I got in a way of not keeping a bright gun.

On the night of the 31st of January, six noncommissioned officers—to wit, Sgt. Maj. C. T. Boggs; Commissary Sgt. Wylly; Ordnance Sgt. Weldon[20]; 1st Sgt. Company K, Morgan[21]; 1st Sgt. Company H, Camp[22]; and 1st Sgt. Andrews—decided to hang in effigy a conscript officer. A threat to the officers showing what we would do in the event one was sent into camps being the only way we could make our intentions known to them. After taps we met just below the camps and the first question we had to decide was where would we get the clothes to make the effigy out of. Sgt. Camp said, "Hold on boys, I will arrange that part of it" and returned to camps. (Camp was a daisy. He was shot in seven places at the Second Battle of Manassas and cannot handle his gun at the present time, but is doing his duty with his company. Sgt. Garrett tells a good one on Camp that happened before the war. He came from Gilmer or Murray County, Ga. There was a protracted [revival] meeting going on in Camp's settlement and on Sunday everybody for miles around went to church, and Camp among the rest. He was dressed in a copperas [colored] suit with his pants stuffed down in his boots and riding a steer with a saddle on him. On the saddle he had a pair of saddle bags filled with corn for his steer. In rear of the saddle he had two bundles of fodder. When the services were about half through, he left the church, went out and fed his ox, and then ate his dinner.)

Camp soon returned having a coat, pants, hat, and shoes. We never questioned him in regard to where he got them, but hurried off to the woods where we soon had a bright and cheerful fire burning. We then secured some moss from a tree and proceeded to make a man by first stuffing his pants, then sewed his jacket to his pants and stuffed that. We then shaped the head out of a piece of cloth and stuffed it, after sewing the head to the collar of his coat. So far so well. We then fastened on one shoe to his pants on one leg and a block of wood to the other leg with a card attached, on which was the word EXEMPT. We decided we had a pretty good imitation of a man.

We then proceeded to build the gallows by cutting down a small tree and nailing an arm on it for the beam to hang him to. After all arrangements had been made, we sent three of the boys back to camps to erect the gallows. Soon the other three followed with the effigy. By working with a vim we soon had the effigy hung, and put the hat on his head and a board over it with the words CONSCRIPT OFFICER in large letters. We viewed our work in the darkness and pronounced it good, then silently stole away to our tents to await proceedings.

About ten o'clock, one of the wagoners come riding into camp on a mule and had to go right by the effigy, at which his mule became frightened and liked to have thrown him. But he retained his seat in the saddle and made a bee line for the guard tent and informed the officer of the guard that a man had been hung in camps. The officer formed his guard and with the wagoner made for the corpse. On his arrival, the officer ordered his men to cut him down, but not a man could he get to take hold of him. After a great many threats, the officer succeeded in having him cut down, and they all felt badly sold after finding it to be an effigy. It was then placed by an officer's tent and camps were again quiet for the night.

Before good light the camps were in a stir going to see the murdered man, and the boys that hung him were as eager to see him as any of the rest. The poor fellow [whom] Camp took the clothes from was in a worse plight than anybody else, as he had no clothing to put on. It was never found out who done it and that was the last thing heard of a conscript officer coming to our camps.

February 8, orders came for the Regulars and 28th Battalion to move in the direction of Lake City, as the enemy had captured Jacksonville and was advancing on Tallahassee. The troops were soon on the march, leaving camps sometime during the night. As we marched by Rev. Brother Talley's, think every man must have been calling hogs. On passing his house, saw his yard fence lined with hog skins, so he must have been right about losing his hogs. But the boys swear they will kill any man's hog that tries to bite them.[23]

We marched 13 miles towards Quincy and bivouacked for the night. The boys amused themselves by singing "Maj. Bonaud," to the tune of "Billy Barlow." Don't expect the major likes it much, but says nothing. February 9 arrived at Quincy at about 1:00 P.M. and at 5:00 P.M. took the cars for Gen. Finegan's Command at Lake City. Between Madison and Lake City a serious accident happened. We were riding on flat cars which became uncoupled and ran into one another, badly injuring five men.

On the 10th, arrived at Lake City and was reviewed by Gen. Finegan. This time the citizens of Lake City was glad to see the Regulars and had a long table spread with a bountiful dinner for the boys. What a change. Before the doors were closed against us, now there is nothing too good for us. The near approach of the enemy has made the change, and a friend in need is a friend indeed. Well, for the sake of the good dinner we had, will love to forgive and forget old scores, for the Regulars could not help fighting if they get a chance. In the evening, the 1st and 28th marched out three miles east of the city and formed a line of battle.

February 11 about 9:00 A.M., the enemy's cavalry dismounted and attacked our skirmish line. Our line of battle was in the woods where a lot of rails had lately been split, and while our skirmish line was being driven back, busied ourselves piling up the rails for a breastwork to shoot from behind. We could see our boys and the yankees as they fought from tree to tree, flanking first on one side and then on the other. The zip of the minié balls sounded very familiar to the old soldiers who paid but little attention to them, but we had some new recruits who had never smelt powder before. One fellow in my company by the name of Walker,[24] a tall gawky-looking man, was the worst-scared fellow I had seen in a long time. At one time as I walked up with a turn of rails on my shoulder, he was lying at full length on the ground with his rifle cocked and pointing over the rails and trembling like a leaf. The first thing I knew, I was looking down the barrel of his gun. I told him to get up from there or I would break his cowardly back with a rail. The poor devil was so badly scared I was afraid he would shoot me for a yankee.

When within 300 yards of us, the enemy retreated, carrying their wounded with them. No one hurt on our side. Lt. John P. Fort[25] had a bullet shot through the rim of his hat. At night [Companies] F and M went on picket on the railroad. Reinforced by the 64th Ga. Regiment, 1st Fla. Special Battalion, and three pieces of artillery. February 12, the command entrenched on the railroad two and one-half miles from the city. The yankee cavalry yesterday retreated back towards St. Marys River.

February 13, the troops marched out of the works and formed by the side of the railroad where we waited for the arrival of a train to carry us to Olustee Station some 15 miles towards Jacksonville. While we were standing in line resting, a courier come dashing down in front of the Regulars with a stovepipe hat on his head. Everybody yelled at him to come out of that hat. "No use to say you are not up there, [we] see your feet hanging down" and everything else they could think of. Pvt. Dan McDuffie[26] of Company K jumped out of ranks and took after him demanding the churn. The courier wheeled his horse and dashed back to McDuffie, pulled off the beaver, taking his own hat out of it and presented the churn to McDuffie, wheeled his horse, and galloped away, leaving McDuffie standing in front of his regiment holding his hat and looking as much like a fool as anyone I have ever seen. The boys certainly made the welkin ring as they tossed their caps in the air.

McDuffie, while a good soldier, was a hard case. He taken life easy and many is the merry laugh he has caused around the campfires. McDuffie was very fond of his toddy and when he would get full called himself the widow woman's child. While at the arsenal, McDuffie went out into the country one day foraging for eggs and buttermilk. At one house where he stopped four or five women were busy carding and spinning thread, as all the cloth for clothing used in the Confederacy was made by hand. McDuffie acted the fool to perfection, and made the women believe that he had never seen anything of the kind before. When he got back to camps, it was worth a ticket to a monkey show to see him go through with the spinning performance as he imitated the women in dancing up to the wheel and back.

But about the worst sell out McDuffie ever had was before a Macon audience at Ralston's Hall. There was a ventriloquist and sleight of hand performance at the hall one night while the regiment was stationed there. The performer called for someone from the audience to assist him. McDuffie, always ready for anything, stepped on the stage. One of the acts performed and the one that suited McDuffie the best was furnishing out of one bottle any kind of a drink you could call for, and McDuffie must have exhausted the vocabulary of drinks by the number he called for. The next performance was the ribbon act, where he chewed cotton and blew fire out of his mouth, then pulled out any quantity of ribbon. The performer had McDuffie going through with him. Each one had a wad of lint cotton which they would cram in their mouths, the proprietor using a small stick to force it down with. First using it in his mouth and then Dan's. After packing the cotton in Dan's mouth until he was nearly suffocated, he commenced blowing fire out of his own, then went through with the ribbon performance while poor Dan looked the fool to perfection, pulling small bits of cotton out of his mouth causing the audience to go wild. After the performer got through with his ribbon, he turned to help Daniel out of his dilemma. He forced Dan's head back and pulled a roll of cotton out of his mouth that nearly reached the ceiling. Dan looked like he was relieved and I expect felt so. All such is the makeup of a soldier's life and is the only green spot in it, a good hearty laugh being a splendid remedy for the blues.

The cars soon arrived and the troops boarded them for Olustee or Ocean Pond. On our arrival, formed line of battle, our left opposite Ocean Pond, the right extending across the railroad. Worked all night throwing up breastworks. During the night we were reinforced by the 32nd Ga. Regiment, 6th Florida, and Chatham's Artillery.[27] February 14, finished our line of works. If the enemy should ever get close enough to see our features, they will think they are fighting colored troops, as we are smoked as black as Negroes over our pine knot fires. No use to try and keep out of the smoke for the wind blows in every direction.

Ocean Pond is a formidable lake of water, must be several miles in width and empties into the great Okefenokee Swamps. The waves roll like hogsheads and looks as blue as the ocean. During the day, Gen.

Colquitt's Brigade, composed of the 6th, 19th, 23rd, 27th, and 28th Ga. regiments arrived and took their position on the right.[28]

The officers of the Regulars applied to and received permission from Gen. Beauregard commanding [the Department of] South Carolina, Georgia, and Florida[29] to give the men 30 days' furlough, provided they reenlisted in the same regiment. This was done by the officers of the regiment to keep up its organization and thereby hold their commissions. About 80 of the men took advantage of the offer, reenlisted, and left for home.

I decided not to reenlist, but when my term of service expired to leave the regiment and join some volunteer company where I would stand some chance for promotion, as there was but a slim chance in the Regulars. Only six ever have been promoted from the ranks, all of the officers in the Regulars being appointed by the government. As the government has so many pets, it is a hard matter for an enlisted man to rise, let him be ever so worthy of promotion. A soldier has as much ambition to advance himself as men do in any other occupation of life, and why should not I as well as anyone else?

When the enemy landed at Jacksonville, they dispatched a force of cavalry and surprised in their camps a battery of artillery, capturing the guns and killing and wounding numbers of the men, the rest making their escape in the darkness.[30] Two or three days afterwards, about 80 of them were formed into an infantry company and placed in the 1st Ga. Regulars. They said they had never done any fighting, but if we got into one would stick as long as the Regulars did, which was all we could ask of them.

February 19, 1864. Some of the Regulars who returned to camps today reported that they saw on the bulletin board at Tallahassee where the Confederate States Congress had passed an act conscribing [conscripting] all companies and regiments as they now stand. That was simply a clincher, so I decided to make the best of the situation by reenlisting and secure the thirty days' furlough. Some 10 or 12 more of the boys joined me, and we all reenlisted. Our papers were carried to Gen. Finegan's for his approval. He stated that the conscript law had been passed, but as long as the boys had reenlisted without knowing it, he would have to let them go, and signed our furloughs. When they were returned to our commanding officer, Capt. Cannon,[31] he had heard of the act being passed and did not want us to have our furloughs. But as Gen. Finegan had signed them, he could not keep us from going. So we pocketed our papers and about twelve o'clock at night we struck out for Lake City on foot, the nearest place to board the cars, which left at 4:00 A.M.

I tried to get Pvt. J. J. McMullen to reenlist. He was a good soldier and a good fighter. I told him he would have to remain with the Regulars anyhow and had just as well take a furlough and go home while he had the chance of it. He told me he would not reenlist if he knew he would be riddled with bullets from his head to his heels, so I gave it up knowing him to be a man that when he made up his mind to do a thing, there was no turning him from his purpose.

BATTLE OF OLUSTEE, FLORIDA

On the morning of February 20, 1864, I boarded the cars at Lake City for Quincy, Fla. I will give an account of the battle of Olustee as it was afterwards given to me. On the 20th, Gen. Finegan ordered Gen. Colquitt to take two regiments of his brigade and reconnoiter in his front, if he encountered the enemy to gradually fall back and draw the enemy on the works. Gen. Colquitt advanced some two miles in front of the works where he encountered the enemy in strong force, resting by the roadside. Gen. Colquitt moved forward his two regiments to the attack and ordered the rest of the troops to move rapidly to the front. The battle soon raged in all its fury, but the enemy was driven from all points, and after a hard day's fight, deserted the field leaving their dead and wounded in the hands of the Confederates.

The Confederate forces were commanded by Gen. Finegan and was composed of two brigades of infantry, commanded by Gens. Colquitt and Harrison.[32] Besides the cavalry and artillery, all told numbering to 4,500 men, while the Federals numbered 13,000 men and was commanded by Gen. Seymour.[33] Among the Federal troops were several regiments of Negro troops which were badly cut to pieces in the fight, being placed in front with white troops in the rear of them. And when driven back by the Confederates, would be fired on by the yankees thus placing them between two fires. At one place there was between 200 and 300 of them dead on one acre of ground. When the enemy was driven from the field, they became panic stricken and fled in disorder, being another Bull Run retreat, and was kept up until they reached Jacksonville.

The Regulars under Capt. Cannon took a conspicuous part in the fight being a portion of Gen. George P. Harrison's Brigade. Capt.

Cannon commanding the Regulars was killed, also Lt. Dancy, acting adjutant.[34] The color bearer, Sgt. Bennett,[35] was shot down and seriously wounded some 50 yards in front of his regiment while waving his flag and calling on his comrades to keep up with him. There was five or six daring comrades with him when he fell. J. J. McMullen of Company M, my old chum and mess mate, was by his side when he fell. As the colors struck the ground, they were quickly raised by one of the boys and again thrown to the breeze and advanced to the front. The boys who were with the flag shot away all of their ammunition, and crowded around the one bearing the colors to get the ammunition out of his cartridge box.

While McMullen was standing with his gun on the ground and resting [it] in the crook of his left arm, with the arm extending across the body placing some cartridges in his box, he was struck by two balls, both passing through his arm and body, killing him instantly. No braver or better soldier died on the field of Olustee than Pvt. Jordan J. McMullen of Company M, 1st Regiment Georgia Regulars. Don't think he had ever been absent from any battle his company had been engaged in. He was a good soldier in every sense of the word, always at his post in camps or on the battlefield. A man of few words but considerable nerve. He had two balls shot through his clothing at the Second Battle of Manassas. He might have lived longer if he had taken my advice and applied for a furlough. Pvt. S. M. Hunter[36] of Company M had a portion of his foot shot off, making him a cripple for life. Poor Sam, he was unlucky, having served in the hospital department until this battle and then get crippled for life in the first one. As to casualties in the rest of the regiment, never took any note of it.

The Florida Artillery Company placed in the Regulars fought like veterans and was highly complimented by the Regulars for their gallantry. The battle was in a great measure won by Gen. Colquitt ordering the troops out of the works to attack the enemy when first discovered. Had he drawn them on the works the enemy could have faced them with an equal number of men and still had an army larger than Gen. Finegan's to have flanked him on his right, his left being protected by Ocean Pond and thus flanked him out of his position without a fight. Olustee was a hard-fought battle and numbers were killed and wounded on both sides. After the battle, Finegan's Command followed up the vanquished Federals to Jacksonville, where they were protected by their gunboats.[37]

When I left camps on furlough was just in the nick of time to catch the cars at Lake City, which left there at 4:00 A.M. When we arrived at Tallahassee we saw on the telegraph bulletin board where they were fighting like blue blazes back at Olustee, and that numbers had been killed. Late in the evening we arrived at Quincy where we bivouacked for the night and taken a soon start the next morning to march to the arsenal. On arriving at the arsenal, I visited the family of my cousin Ivey Andrews, who was a member of the Florida Artillery Company that had been placed with the Regulars.[38] When I left camps, he asked me to call and see his family and carry a message to them for him, which I promised to do.

On arriving at his home I found his wife almost heartbroken. Had neither slept or ate any in three days and nights. On the night the artillery lost their guns, one of the men that made his escape, returned home and told Mrs. Andrews that her husband had been killed, as he saw him when he was cut down by a cavalry man. The poor woman could do nothing but believe it and give way to the most intense sorrow. When I brought her the good news she was crazed with joy, and I had to visit her neighbors with her and tell them of the glad tidings. At first she refused to believe my story as the man who brought her the news was so positive about his death. So while the men are fighting their country's battles, the women are at home suffering the tortures of the damned, expecting every day to hear that they are widows and their children orphans. Terrible must be the suspense.

After remaining several days in the vicinity of the arsenal to get my pay, proceeded on to Cuthbert, Ga. Nothing transpired while at home worthy of note. March 24, returned to my regiment at Camp Milton, six miles below Baldwin [Florida]. In my absence, the Regulars had been transferred from Harrison's to Colquitt's Brigade. Capt. Wayne had been promoted to major, was in command of the regiment, Col. Magill and Lt. Col. Martin having left the regiment and probably retired from the service. The boys are in fine spirits and ready for another brush with the enemy. Gen. Colquitt has a fine brigade of men. They look stout and healthy and all nearer of one size than is often seen in companies. Gen. Colquitt is the hero of Olustee and certainly deserves it, while he is idolized by his men.

CAMP MILTON, FLORIDA

I saw the other day several prisoners belonging to Colquitt's

Brigade, being marched around to the headquarters of each regiment, preceded by the drum corps beating the Rogue's March. On each one was pinned a large piece of pasteboard with the words HOG THIEF in large letters on their backs. In passing one of the regiments, some of the soldiers charged them and tore the cards off. That put an end to the parade. The boys had become hungry and killed a hog and that was the punishment put on them. It must have been pretty hard on the boys to be thus exposed before the whole army, but they no doubt would have had the largest end of the command if all had been in the procession who had stolen a hog since being in the army.

We are drilling every day by way of recreation if nothing else. Was well amused the other day while drilling near Gen. Colquitt's headquarters. Sgt. Copeland of Company F is the tallest man in the regiment, and by the way is a jolly good soldier. The boys are always teasing him about being so tall, they speak to him as though he was up among the trees. They will say, "Jim, is it cold up where you are?" or "Jim, hand me down a chew of tobacco," and a great many other questions that would annoy anyone but the good-humored sergeant who takes it all in a joke. While we were resting, a lieutenant of the 19th Ga. Regiment walked up pretty close to Sgt. Copeland and stopped. Copeland looked up at him and his face assumed a sickly smile; the boys done the yelling. Copeland had found one man he had to look up to. The lieutenant was several inches the tallest, and must have been at least six feet and six inches high.

One day the 6th Ga. Regiment challenged the 1st Ga. Regulars for a battle with lighted pine burrs to take place at night. The Regulars accepted and both regiments went to gathering ammunition. We are camped in the piney woods, and the ground is covered with pine burrs which are very dry and will catch [fire] from a blaze almost like tinder. After dark each regiment formed its line of battle, each man having an arm full of burrs and a lighted one in his hand. The 6th Georgia boys charged the Regulars, and after a hard fight the Regulars surrendered, the 6th outnumbering them. The two regiments then joined forces and attacked the 19th, who had been interested spectators of the battle just ended. When they saw the two regiments marching down on them, they turned out to a man, from the colonel down, and formed a line of battle in front of their camps with a skirmish line deployed in front of that. The 1st and 6th formed line of battle with skirmishers thrown forward and advanced to the attack. The skirmish lines become engaged, the lines of battle then moved forward and such fireworks I have never witnessed. First one line and then the other would gain the advantage, but only temporarily, as the other side would rally and again charge the enemy, which was kept up for some time. The 1st and 6th found themselves outnumbered and out generaled and had to retire from the field. It was certainly a great sight to see hundreds of lighted burrs thrown from one line at the other. Each side had a squad of men collecting burrs, which they called their ordnance trains, and such charges as would be made to capture them. While numbers of them had their hands and faces burned, it passed off without any hard feelings.

Our camps were on the ridge and in full view of Gen. Harrison's Brigade, which was in the bottom near the railroad. The next day, Gen. Harrison's Brigade challenged Gen. Colquitt's for a pine burr battle, which was eagerly accepted and each side went to work gathering up ammunition. The night was an extremely dark one, just right for the lights to show off to perfection. After night, both brigades formed lines of battle with their skirmish lines deployed in front. The camps were some 400 yards apart. Each brigade formed line in front of their respective camps and both advanced at the same time. How the torches glistened in the darkness. The skirmish lines first moved forward, each one trying to take advantage of the other by flanking, which would be met by the other side. Then an effort would be made on the other end of the line with the same result. Pretty soon the skirmish line was hard at it and the lines of battle moved forward to the attack. There was between 1,000 and 1,500 men on either side and each one with a lighted burr in his hand, or probably 1,000 burrs flying through the air at one time. The lines of battle would sway first forward and then backwards as they moved first to the right and then to the left, trying to take the advantage by flanking each other. Finally Colquitt's Brigade drove Harrison's across the railroad. Here the fighting became desperate. Light wood knots were freely used in place of burrs. Finally Colquitt's Brigade made a wild charge and swept the field, driving Harrison's men through their camps and completely routing them. Colquitt's men then retired back to their own camps. A good many of the boys were badly bruised up. The next day, Gen. Colquitt issued an order prohibiting anymore fights with burrs.[39]

April 1, the Regulars, with two pieces of Gamble's artillery,[40] left Camp Milton at dark and marched 20 miles up the St. Johns River, where we arrived just at daylight and found the U.S. steamer *Maple Leaf* that had run onto a torpedo the day before and blew up.[41] A boat was secured and an officer and several men boarded her, finding nothing but some mattresses besides the machinery. The men fired the boat and returned to the shore. The artillery then fired several shots at the boat. We then about-faced and made back as fast as we could, leaving two men from each company to kill some goats we found near a deserted farm house. We left camps without anything to eat and was trying to appease our hunger. The boys who were left to kill the goats were told that the wagons would wait for them and haul the goats, but they must have become frightened and kept going, as there was a landing five miles below us where the enemy could land and cut us off. Most of the boys got tired carrying the goats and left them, some of them brought them on to camps. The steamer we burnt was a side wheeler and a splendid vessel, and was about 15 miles above Jacksonville. Capt. Miller Grieve was in command of the expedition. We made back eight miles towards camps and bivouacked for the night, Company M on picket duty. Some of the boys secured some sweet potatoes and we had quite a feast on baked goat and roasted potatoes.[42]

April 3. Arrived at Camp Milton at 12:00 midnight, pretty well fagged out after our long march. A big revival is going on in Gen. Colquitt's Brigade, numbers are joining the church. We have a regular old-fashioned campground. An harbor [arbor] is built out of poles and covered with palmetto leaves. Logs are cut and arranged for seats. The boys shout and go on just like they do at camp meetings. Hope they may be spiritually benefited, but have little faith in religion in the army, as his Satanic Majesty has full sweep in camps. And the more marching and fighting we have, the worse the men seem to get. Have been in many battles where you could have traced the different lines going in by the decks of cards being thrown away. From some cause or other, the boys don't like the idea of cards being found in their pockets after they are dead, so they throw them away before they get in battle.[43]

April 19, Gen. Colquitt's Brigade left Camp Milton for Savannah, Ga., and the Regulars were transferred back to Gen. Harrison's Brigade. When the yankees landed at Jacksonville, numbers of the citizens fled to the country and were soon in a desperate condition for something to eat. And while a soldier will steal the sweetening out of your coffee, he is at the same time very liberal when he finds anyone in distress. So the boys appointed committees to get up rations among the soldiers for the benefit of the citizens who were in distress. And while we did not have much, we divided what little we had with them and relieved them all we could.

Pvt. Posey of Company G,[44] while visiting some of the refugees, stole a ring from a young lady. Her father and mother come to camps and reported it to the officers and pointed out the thief. Posey was a noted thief and had been punished numbers of times for various offenses. The officers turned him over to the men to do with him as they saw proper. We soon had him mounted on a rail and marching through the camp with the drums beating the Rogue's March. When we mounted him on a rail he had a small stick in his hand to which he fastened his handkerchief, making him a flag. He seemed to enjoy the ride as a huge joke, waving his flag over his head as we marched through the camps. The boys soon decided that it was a one-sided affair and decided to change the program by taking him to the woods some 200 yards from camps, where he was blindfolded and strapped to a log and given about 75 lashes with wagon whips. He was then released and told that if he went back to camps, he would be killed. But he got back to camps by the time the rest of us did. He was a hard case, and was destitute of honor or remorse either.

April 22. Sixty men from the Regulars were detailed to hunt up deserters in Taylor County, Fla. May 1, Regulars marched from Camp Milton to Camp Finegan to relieve a portion of the 6th Florida from picket duty near Jacksonville. May 3, 40 of the Regulars joined the Confederate States Navy, some going to Savannah and the rest to Chattahoochee, Fla.[45] No navy for me; I had as soon be in the penitentiary so far as enjoying life is concerned. It is about like jumping out of the frying pan into the fire.

May 5. Regulars marched from Camp Finegan to the Double Bridges six miles from Jacksonville, where we were on picket duty. Captured several yankee prisoners. May 7, Regulars received orders to report in Savannah, Ga. Marched to Camp Milton and boarded the cars for Lake City. May 8, went through Lake City to Madison, left the cars, and marched 10 miles toward Quitman, Ga. May 9, marched to Quitman on the Atlantic and Gulf Railroad. May 10, Regulars left Quitman at 2:00 A.M. and arrived at Savannah, Ga., at 4:00 P.M. Went into camps near the park.

No Rest
for the Weary

SAVANNAH, GEORGIA

May 16, Regulars marched from Savannah to Greenwich Point, five miles below the city on the St. Augustine River where we went into camps. Sand flies and mosquitoes world without end, no rest for the weary. May 20, the detachment of 60 men that was left in Florida rejoined the regiment at Greenwich Point. May 26, 1st Ga. Regulars relieved the 1st Regiment of Georgia Volunteers on Whitmarsh Island.[1]

We had a hard time of it on Whitmarsh Island doing picket duty. The weather on the coast is extremely disagreeable. The wind is blowing a small gale or it is a dead calm, then the insects get in their work. It is right amusing some evenings while on dress parade to hear Maj. Wayne say, "Hands down in the ranks." But it is no use, for the sand flies are so bad they cover your face and you are just obliged to knock them off. Nothing of interest transpiring on the island.

Fort Pulaski being in the hands of the enemy with his blockading fleet across the bar, we never know when the yankees will pay us a visit. Hence, we are all the time on lookout for them. The boys catch a great many crabs and oysters to help out on short rations. Sometimes we draw Sturgeon fish in place of meat rations. As we do not know how to prepare it to eat, makes rather a poor dish, but when properly cooked, I like Sturgeon splendidly.

For some time my heart has been sad and heavy. When we arrived at Savannah from Florida, Sgt. Garrett secured a furlough to visit his home in North Georgia. Before his furlough expired, he wrote back to Dr. Cherry that he had joined a squad of mountain scouts and would not return to his command. He claimed that he was not deserting but was entering a branch of the service where he would be of more service to his country. The officers did not take the same view as Garrett did, and I was ordered to make out his descriptive list to be sent to a conscript officer near his home for his arrest. That was about the toughest piece of writing I have ever had to do, and I don't think I would have felt worse if I had been writing his death warrant.[2]

No one will ever know how much I loved my gallant friend. We were more than brothers, the hardships we had to pass through, binding us in the closest bonds of friendship. The papers were made out and sent off, then I expected every day when my best friend would be returned to his company branded as a deserter. How I hoped he might elude the officers and never be brought back. At the same time I did not look on him as a deserter, for I knew there was not a braver or truer Confederate living. Sometime later, news was received of his death. What a sad blow. The death of a brother would not be worse. To think my gallant friend and companion had crossed over the river and was resting under the shade of the trees. Sweet be his slumbers, for a truer friend or better soldier never donned the gray. May I, when my course is run here below, pass over the river and rest with my devoted friend under the shade of the trees. (Have always hoped and I am still hoping that the report of his death was a ruse to throw the officers off his track and that I may yet live to see the day that I will come face to face with the dearest friend it has ever been my lot to possess. It is now 30 years since I saw him last and I am still searching for him, while his memory is ever held dear.)

JOHNS ISLAND, SOUTH CAROLINA

July 3, 1864, the Regulars were ordered to Charleston, South Carolina. Marched from Camp Williams on Whitmarsh Island to Savannah where we boarded a train of box cars for Charleston. Arrived at the second station from Charleston, where we disembarked and marched from there across the Stono River on to Johns Island where we went into bivouacs about an hour before day. July 4, marched three miles down the road on the right side of the island. Johns Island lies north and south, being a long strip of land about three miles wide and several in length with roads running on both sides of the island. Camped the rest of the day and night as the rain was coming down in torrents. The Stono Scouts captured a yankee surgeon.[3]

The Regulars under Maj. Wayne were reinforced by two companies of the 32nd Ga. Regiment, two companies of South Carolina Cavalry, and two pieces of the Marion Artillery from Charleston. Heavy firing on Battery Pringle from the monitors and gunboats belonging to the enemy. July 5, advanced about three miles down the road, having a company on either side of the road as flankers, the undergrowth being so thick you could not see 10 paces from you. Sgt. Maj. John T. Cheshire[4] was sent forward by Maj. Wayne with an order for the companies in front, and by some means he missed our men and walked right into the enemy's line, composed of Negro troops with white officers. As soon as he approached the line, the Negroes fired on him. One ball passing through his lungs, from which he fell. The Negroes then charged him and would have dispatched him with the bayonet if one of their officers had not interfered and saved his life. About that time our skirmish line arrived on the scene and the Negroes beat a hasty retreat. Sgt. Cheshire was rescued and sent to the hospital at Charleston.

About the time Sgt. Cheshire was shot, one piece of the Marion Artillery fired several shots beheading several Negroes. The Negroes then beat a hasty retreat and we were in hot pursuit of three companies of the 26th N.Y. Colored Troops commanded by Maj. Dye.[5] Then a courier arrived and informed Maj. Wayne that the main portion of the enemy were advancing on the upper road and would be likely to cut us off. So we beat a hasty retreat. Pvt. David Gann of Company M captured Maj. Dye's blankets and satchel, with his toilet articles in it. We marched back to the upper road, then marched down that to within one mile of the main body of the enemy, where we remained during the night, Companies F and M on picket.

July 6 at sunrise, Companies F and M were ordered forward as skirmishers. We advanced some distances through the woods and then entered a large field. When about halfway through that, we come to a cross ditch running through the field. We were told that the enemy had possession of the ditch the evening before, but had retired to the woods some 700 yards distant, at night.

THE BATTLE OF WATERLOO ON JOHNS ISLAND

On arriving at the cross ditch, we halted and had time to look around us. We were then on the Waterloo Plantation. A public road passes through, running north and south. On either side of the road the bushes had grown up so thick you could not see across the road from one field to the other. On the left there was some Negro houses, on the right the field extended some three quarters of a mile. The ditch, or dirt fence, extended the entire distance, and was a splendid breastwork covered in undergrowth and trees, some of the trees 10 or 12 inches in diameter. Some 700 yards in our front at the woods was another dirt fence, which was occupied by the enemy.

Companies F and M were on the right of the road, where we had not been long halted before we heard over in the woods the command given to forward skirmishes. Our boys quickly concealed themselves behind the works and awaited developments. Pretty soon we saw a line of Negro skirmishers advancing through the open field. Orders were given our boys to lie low and let the Negroes get in close range. Capt. Hill was in command of company M with Lts. DuBose and Reese.[6] The Negroes did not advance far before they halted and dropped down in the weeds which were about waist high. The regiment with the artillery was in the road just in rear of us and were making a good deal of noise talking and laughing. When the Negroes heard them, they halted. Two rifle pieces belonging to the Washington Artillery[7] was just in rear of Company M some 300 yards back in the field. They opened on the enemy, but their shells exploded where our skirmish line was. They were then ordered up with us. By that time, the Negroes had become frightened, and all made for a tree, a large live oak in front of Company M and about 100 yards from the woods where their line of battle was. The two rifle pieces opened on the tree, bursting every shell under it. The poor devils cut some awful antics in getting away from there and back to their lines. You could see them make a break for the woods, going half bent with one eye to the rear watching the artillery. When they saw the flash of the gun, would fall flat until the shell exploded or passed over them. Then up and gone again until they reached their lines.

Some officer was killed or wounded under the tree, as desperate efforts were made during the remainder of the day to get him away.[8] At one time, carried an ambulance to the tree, but every time they made for the tree, the artillery would warm them up. I have seen considerable artillery firing, but nothing to compare with the two rifle pieces used by the Washington Artillery. You could not find one of the Regulars who was watching the fight, but what would be willing to bet you two to one, that the gunners could hit the head of a barrel 800 yards distant nine times out of ten.

Maj. Wayne of the Regulars was in command of the troops on the island and had altogether 350 small arms and four pieces of artillery, and by deploying his men five paces apart had only enough to hold his line in front of the enemy. It was ascertained afterwards by an officer's order book found under the large oak that the enemy numbered three brigades and had 4,500 men. On the left of the road the Marion [S.C.] Artillery had two 12-pound Napoleon guns, and on the right, two 6-pound rifle pieces belonging to the Washington Artillery. Our infantry line continued onto the right at least three-fourths of a mile. A company of Stono Scouts 20 strong were dismounted and occupied the extreme right of the line. The day passed off without any farther movements of the enemy. Remained under arms during the night, everything being quiet.

July 7. This morning the enemy's sharpshooters opened on our left from some Negro houses, but the artillery quickly routed them. The day seemed to be passing away without a fight. We were acting on the defensive and it seemed as though the yankees were playing the same game. Our forces were too small to assume the offensive and charge their works.

About 4:00 P.M., our suspense was quickly brought to a focus by the enemy attacking our right, center, and left with three heavy regiments of colored troops all at the same time. One regiment charged the two Napoleons on our left. Another charged the two rifle pieces on the right of the road, and the third charged our extreme right where the Stono Scouts were stationed. Companies F and M were on the line between our right and two rifle pieces and was accordingly ordered to the assistance of the scouts.

The regiment that charged our right was the 26th N.Y. Colored Troops,[9] about 1,000 strong. They advanced under cover of the woods until within 200 yards of our line when they entered the field and charged square down on our line, defended by the 20 men of the Stono Scouts. Before F and M could reach the right by several hundred yards, the Negroes had charged and taken the works, killing and wounding 14 out of the 20 scouts. They stood their ground like veterans, but the odds was against them and what was left had to fall back.

As we double-quicked to the right of the line, could see what was going on. After the Negroes carried the right, Companies F and M right obliqued from the works so as to front them in the open field. Just as we left the line, I saw a big mulatto in advance of his line. He was in the act of loading. I placed my rifle to my shoulder, took deliberate aim, and fired. The Negro jumped about three feet in the air and dropped to the ground. We continued some 250 yards out in the field so as to front them, they having two lines of battle. Seven companies had charged square down on the works, and the other three companies charged in column of twos, thus forming a flanking column. As 1st sergeant of the company, I was on the extreme right of the line with one line of the enemy in front of me and the other on my flank. We saw the Negroes when they mounted our works and saw them as they jumped down (horror of horrors) and put the bayonet to the wounded of the Stono Scouts. It certainly caused my blood to run cold. I had faced death on many hard-fought fields, but had never faced the black flag before, where quarter would not be asked for or given. I[t] certainly was enough to cause the heart of the bravest to quake with fear.

Our line deployed as skirmishers five paces apart, facing at least 20 times our number with no prospects of aid from any quarter as the left and center had their hands full at the same time and might be in need of help as bad as we were. But nothing daunted. Our gallant boys faced the music like men, and soon the cracking of our rifles made music in the air. The Negroes, made bold by carrying our works, still advanced pouring volley after volley into our scattering line, which gradually give back, but stubbornly contended for, every inch of ground.

Just as we commenced falling back, I saw one of the scouts throw up his hand and fall to the ground. It was heartrending to hear him beg to be taken out, but it was every man for himself and the devil for all. I had always thought that the dread of shells and minié balls was bad enough, but nothing to compare with the dread of the bayonets. Could almost realize that I could feel one crashing through my ribs. But it was no time to shrink from the consequences but fight like grim death.

The Negroes looked to be as thick as black birds and were pressing us hard from front and flank. One time I noticed the weeds around me seemed to be dancing a jig, and on looking to my left down the line, discovered that our line had retreated and left me a target for the whole line. You can bet I done some of my best running, our line having been ordered to retreat and had about 60 yards the start of me.

After running about 100 yards I overtaken Lt. J. R. DuBose who was then in command of the company, Capt. Hill having been wounded early in the engagement. The lieutenant was crossing a ditch as I overtaken him, his men some 20 steps in advance of him. He halted them and resumed the fight. I remained in the ditch where I could drop down and load and then get up and fire without being exposed all the time. While in the ditch got a ball about halfway down my rifle, where it lodged and refused to be forced any farther. It was an awful risk to run in shooting it in that condition, but worse to remain without a gun. So I blazed away without bursting my gun. The boys were firing away in rear of me, so I had to get back on the line with them to keep from being shot by them.

When we halted and commenced firing, we checked the onward rush of the Negroes, who remained stationary as they seemed to be afraid to charge us. We fought in that position for some time, barely holding our ground, and not strong enough to drive them from the field. What is it we would not have given for help but where was it to come from? We could tell from the firing on our left that our boys had their hands full if not in need of help themselves. The sun was slowly sinking behind the western hills and night was drawing on a pace. What would be the upshot of it, God alone knew.

The flanking columns of Negroes were still making for our rear and times certainly looked desperate enough to cause the heart of the bravest to fear for the result, but as long as there is life there is hope. Many times during that fight did I cast my eye to the left in hopes that I would see relief coming to our assistance, but failed to see anything in the way of help. Just about the time I had given up all hope, I looked again. And God be praised, saw two companies coming on the double-quick down the line. How thankful I felt, can never tell. As they come nearer and nearer, saw that the company in front was gallant old Company G of the Regulars, commanded by Capt. Charley Wylly, as brave an officer as ever drew sword.[10] They were moving at the double-quick at right shoulder shift, how like veterans they moved with 1st Sgt. Clemency in the lead. They quickly passed us and struck the flanking column at least 300 strong, Company G numbering 20 men. The company in rear of Company G belonged to the 32nd Ga. Regiment, 40 strong and commanded by a lieutenant who was a foreigner, and as he reached the right of Company M., brought his company by the left flank and ordered them to charge. But instead of charging, his company stopped stock still. He again ordered them to charge, but it was no use for the Negroes in front was as thick as black birds. By that time, the lieutenant seemed to be getting desperate and threatened his men with his sword, but still could not move them. All at once he rushed in front of his company, waved his sword in one hand and his hat in the other, and said, "Boys follow me." You would have felt proud of the 32nd Georgia boys, as they gave a yell and charged to the front. That yell was taken up by the Regulars right and left, and such a charge I have seldom seen with the odds to contend with, 100 men charging 1,000, but we moved them and moved them with a rush. When we were falling back, some of the Negroes, braver than the rest, got considerably in advance of the rest. And when we charged them, they found themselves some piece in rear of their retreating comrades, and in rather close proximity to the Rebel bayonets.

When we charged, Cpl. T. J. Musgrove[11] and myself were together and got within 20 feet of one, each calling on the other to shoot him. I was reloading my gun on the run. As I rammed the ball home, placed my rammer under my arm and after capping, brought my gun to my shoulder to shoot him. But as I did so, dropped my rammer and stooped to pick it up. That act no doubt saved my life, for as I stooped down, the Negro sent a ball whizzing over my head. Musgrove then shot and killed him. Will never forget how that poor Negro looked running half bent, looking back with his eyes ready to pop out. He was badly scared, and had a right to be.

When the charge was well under way, our gallant Maj. R. A. Wayne with his orderly (one of the Stono Scouts) dashed in front of us. Above the yell of the soldier and the report of our rifles, could hear the commanding voice of Maj. Wayne, "Give them hell my Regulars." A few moments later his favorite charger got into a yellow jacket nest and done some tall charging on her own account, but the major retained his seat and was again charging up and down in front of his line. His orderly was equally as conspicuous as his commanding officer. Both were conspicuous targets and well mounted and escaped on account of the poor marksmanship of the Negroes. As we charged over the Negro wounded, our men would make an effort to bayonet them, but our officers would keep them off with their swords.

We soon recaptured our works, driving the Negroes over them, the Negroes being too badly frightened to take advantage of the works and fight us from behind them. Their only object seemed to be their own works. As I jumped upon the works, a Negro was some 20 feet beyond. He was ordered to surrender and walked back near the works. When some of the boys said shoot him and he made a dash for liberty, a volley was fired at him and he fell with six balls through him. In the charge, Sgt. Watson of Company F,[12] as brave a soldier as there is in the Regulars, encountered a Negro corporal and ordered him to surrender. The corporal inverted his Enfield rifle and struck the sergeant with the butt of it in his forehead. Had it struck centrally in his head, would have broke his skull but it struck to one side and glanced, knocking him backwards. Before he could recover himself, the Negro had dropped his gun and grabbed him by the throat. It was but the work of a moment to choke the sergeant to the ground. As the Negro seized him, he hollered for help and Sgt. Copeland some five paces from him heard him and run to his assistance. He found the Negro on top of him and placed the muzzle of his rifle to the Negro's side and pressed the trigger sending a ball through him. He then pulled him off Sgt. Watson who sprang to his feet, clubbed his rifle, and struck the Negro four or five times over the head and then left him for dead. In the scuffle, the Negro had got one of Watson's forefingers in his mouth and tried to bite it off. With the exception of the bite and the choking he received, Watson was not otherwise hurt, but it was a close call for Sgt. Watson and one he will never forget. Sgt. Watson weighed about 160 pounds while the Negro weighed at least 180 was over six feet high and powerfully built. Watson was nothing more than a child in his hands. I saw the Negro just at dark, could not tell that he was alive, but he was possuming. He created quite a stir among the soldiers, as everybody wanted to see Sgt. Watson's Negro. He was sent through to Charleston the next day.

Our little army, under its gallant commander Maj. R. A. Wayne, had put up a gallant fight, defeating the enemy on our left, center, and right. The left and center was defended mostly by the artillery. I was told by men that witnessed the charge of the enemy on the Washington Artillery, that they did not get more than halfway through the field before the artillery had the air full of them. Every shell exploded right in the ranks and it did not take many to start them back the other way. Our loss was but few, Capts. Hill and Kennen were wounded and our adjutant Lt. Horace P. Clark[13] had his horse killed under him. At night we held our original line. Posted our sentinels some 50 yards in advance of the works. The boys must have felt ticklish standing in the weeds waist high listening to the plaintive cries of the wounded

Negroes calling to their comrades for help that never came. One poor fellow in particular made me feel sorry for him, as he called all night for Company H without receiving any assistance. I posted the picket one-half the night and Lt. A. W. Reese the other.

July 8, during the night the enemy brought up their artillery and placed it in position in front of the two rifle pieces of the Washington Artillery. Just after sunrise, they opened on our line and shelled us for about three hours, wounding several men and horses, our battery replying several times. Reinforced by 200 of the 4th Ga. Cavalry who took position on the extreme right of the line. The rest of the day passed off quietly. Guess Mr. Nig don't want to pay us a visit again, and we are still too weak to assume the offensive. After night we were reinforced by the 32nd and 47th Ga. regiments with Maj. Bonaud's 28th Ga. Battalion, all of the troops on the island numbering 1,500 men with Gen. Robertson in command.[14]

On the morning of the 9th, just as the first gray streaks of dawn showed themselves on the eastern sky, our forces were formed in line of battle with the Regulars and the 32nd Ga. Regiment on the right of the road with the 5th and 47th Ga. regiments with the 28th Battalion on the left. Our skirmish line was deployed in front of the works and the line of battle in the works. The skirmish line was ordered forward, advancing in the darkness. Could not see a man 20 feet away, but they were not long in attacking the enemy's works, which returned the fire. One of the first shots struck Pvt. Helms of Company M in the wind pipe and ranged down in his shoulder, causing his death some time later.[15] Gen. Robertson remarked, "A few shells will bring them out of that," then gave to his line of battle the command "Forward," and we advanced over the works and through the open field. Can't say how the rest felt, but can speak for myself. As we advanced through the field square down on the enemy's artillery, expecting every moment to see the flash of the enemy's artillery light up the heavens. The cold chills crept up my back and I felt decidedly shaky. When within 100 yards of the works, our line was halted, the 32nd Georgia firing several volleys before they could be stopped from firing. Maj. Wayne ordered his orderly to ride forward and ascertain where our skirmish line was. He dashed through our skirmish line, then jumped his horse through an embrasure in the enemy's works and returned telling Maj. Wayne there was not a d——d yankee over there. The line of battle then advanced on the works where our skirmish line was still firing away. When within

10 feet of the works, a large snake was discovered and the boys gave him the benefit of their bayonets. The enemy had removed their artillery back to their first line of works and could not use it when we charged the works because the infantry was in front of it. After we had captured the works and the enemy retired to the first line, the artillery opened shelling on us for some time.

On the left of the road, the troops had a pretty lively time capturing the works, losing about 100 men in killed and wounded. On the right there was several killed in the skirmish line who were shot by our own men, as they were shot in the back. The enemy's artillery had no effect on our line behind the enemy's works which were built for a fence around the field being at least six feet high, the enemy having to shave down a place to stand on to enable them to shoot over them. Our skirmish line followed them far enough to find out that the first line was too strong for our forces to attack. So we remained behind the works we had captured. After everything quieted down a lot of the boys went back into the field where our artillery had played havoc with them on the 7th, finding numbers of their dead, but nothing worth depriving them of. The Negroes found out that the troops in front of them were the ones they fought at Olustee, Fla., and did not carry in the fight as much as a pocket knife.[16] As they were pretty well shod, the boys decided to pull off their shoes and brought them back to the line, but they smelled so bad, could do nothing with them. Tried washing them in the branch, but the more they rubbed the worse they smelt and finally had to throw them away. You may know the boys wanted shoes pretty bad to take them off a dead Negro's feet.[17]

July 10, early this morning our scouts were thrown forward and discovered that the enemy had evacuated the island during last night, going on board of their transports and leaving in considerable disorder, burning a large amount of their commissary stores. July 11, marched out of the enemy's works before light and crossed the Stono River on the steamer *DeKalb* on to James Island.

JAMES ISLAND, SOUTH CAROLINA

After crossing the Stono River, the Regulars marched down to Battery Tatum where the right wing of the regiment remained, the left going to Battery Hascal. July 13, the right wing of the regiment from Battery Tatum joined the left at Battery Hascal and remained on duty all night. July 14, at light this morning marched to the 19th Georgia's old camps where we remained during the day and on picket at the batteries at night.

July 15, the Regulars taken up their quarters at Secessionville on James Island. This place is said to be where the first secession flag was raised, so we will take a view of our surroundings. In the first place, there is five or six houses all in a row along the edge of the marsh running north and south. In rear of the houses is a tubb [?] tower or lookout to watch the surrounding country in the day time. South of the houses we find Fort Lamar mounting several heavy guns. North of the houses is another battery of several guns. In the rear is a long bridge spanning a stream you can step over when the tide is in, but when the tide is out makes a broad expanse of water.[18] About halfway the houses and not far from them is a mound of earth known as a bomb proof which is made by digging a trench in the ground, say four feet deep by six in width. Timbers or posts are then arranged on the sides with cross timbers on the top. The sides are then planked up on the outside and over the top. It is then covered over in the shape of a mound some 10 or 12 feet deep in dirt and you have a place of refuge out of range of the shells. Lying due east is Morris Island, a long, bleak sand ridge almost destitute of vegetation.

On the north end of the island is three of the most noted batteries in the South, Wagner, Gregg, and the Middle Battery. Just north of them is grim old Fort Sumter, now in ruins on its entire sea front, with guns dismounted. West of Fort Sumter is Fort Johnson. East is Fort Moultrie on Sullivan's Island. A little southeast of Fort Lamar on Morris Island is Battery Joe, said to have a Negro gunner. And due east of Secessionville is the U.S. monitors and gunboats. So you see, while off duty in the day we can watch the yankee batteries on Morris Island as they bombard Fort Sumter. There is not over five minutes during the day or night that a shell is not fired at it. During the day you can see the puff of smoke as the cannon fires, then if you will look at the sea face of Fort Sumter you will see a cloud of dust and smoke as the shell strikes and explodes. At night if you feel inclined, you can see the shells from the mortars as they circle over by the fuse attached to them until they drop into the fort, when you will hear a terrific explosion. (This firing was kept up over two years and six months, day and night until the city was evacuated by the Confederates in 1865.)

We are having a hard time. During the night, everybody is on picket duty. During the day we remain at the houses. One day, Battery

Joe opened on the men in the lookout. You bet he scrambled down in a hurry, the shells seeming to drop with him, but he landed on terra firma all right. Fort Lamar then taken old Battery Joe to task, and such a shelling as they had of it. Lamar finally dismounted his guns which taken some two or three days to replace. While the two batteries were popping away, the Regulars were watching the fight from the breast-works in front of the houses. Some of the boys asked if we had not better get away from there. Someone said no, that Joe's guns could not bear on our position. Pretty soon, the gunboats opened on us. We would watch for the puff of smoke as the gun fired, then fall off the works until the shell exploded or passed over us. Then we would mount the works and watch for the next one.

Guess old Joe must have had his weather eye on us, for pretty soon, while we were sitting on top of the works, he put a shell right outside of the works. We tumbled off in a hurry. The next one entered the works a little farther on and the third one passed under one of the houses. His fifth one went through the roof knocking a lot of shingles off. Several of the boys were in the house cooking at the time and by the time the shingles had reached the ground, the boys were out after them to put them around the pots, as the wood we received on the island was green pine and almost impossible to burn it. About that time, I made for the bomb proof thinking Old Joe was getting most too familiar on so short an acquaintance. A bomb proof is not a pleasant place to stay in, as the air is close and stifling.

One morning while occupying my customary seat on the bomb proof, watching the yankee batteries firing on Fort Sumter, I saw a large frame building had been erected near the yankee batteries during the night. On inquiry I learned it was built to confine Confederate prisoners in to retaliate for the yankee prisoners placed in Fort Sumter by the Confederate Government to keep the batteries on Morris Island from firing on Fort Sumter. To say that I was shocked is but a feeble expression. The idea of placing helpless prisoners under the fire of their own guns is a disgrace to any nation who will dare to do it. Could not find out by whose authority they were placed there, but well knew it would have to be approved by the president and secretary of war before anyone else would dare to do such a thing. It certainly made me think little of the Confederacy to resort to such an underhanded trick. I could not blame the Federals for retaliating. (Have seen one officer since the war who was confined on Morris Island and that was Capt. John P. Allen of Dawson, Ga. He told me there was none of less rank than captain in the prison and from that up to generals.) It was, in my estimation, equal to raising the black flag and if anything, worse.[19]

Sometimes Forts Johnson and Moultrie turn loose on the yankee batteries and they have a warm time of it. The batteries on Morris Island are all the time pegging away at Fort Sumter. Can't see any use in it as the sea face of Sumter is in ruins. Nothing but a mass of brick and mortar. Poor old Sumter, how sad it makes me feel to watch the bombardment. Can't resent it or say enough, but has to stand and take it. How I would like to see gallant old Fort Sumter rise up in her might and hurl defiance at her enemies. The first shell of the war was burst at this gallant old fort.[20]

August 1 about dark, the Regulars marched to the nearest station to Charleston and boarded a train for Savannah, Ga. We leave the Palmetto State with no regrets, as we have had a pretty lively time of it, besides it is anything but pleasant on the islands. When the wind is blowing, you can't keep your eyes open without getting them full of sand and when it is not blowing, the flies will eat you up. Besides, coast duty is hard to keep up with as you are on duty all the time.

SAVANNAH, GEORGIA

The second day of August, 1864, the Regulars landed back in Savannah and went into camps near the park. Relieved the new issue [militia] guarding 600 yankee officers who were confined in the city hospital. We are again in possession of our tents and are enjoying ourselves in camps, our duty being light. Simply guarding prisoners, who on several occasions have come very near getting out by digging under the brick walls surrounding the hospital grounds. They will dig under the walls concealing the dirt in various ways. When near the surface, would stop so as to finish and make a break early in the night. On one occasion a cow caved in the hole they had dug, giving them away. They have to be watched very close to keep them from getting out. I don't blame them, would get out too if I was in the same condition and could get out. Some of them have been prisoners for a long time with no prospects of liberty before the war ends. The U.S. Government refuses to exchange prisoners of war, their commander-in-chief Gen. Grant claiming that it takes five yankee soldiers to capture or kill every Rebel soldier turned loose. So his idea is to hold them in prison while he has them, so the Confederates have no alternative but to hold to the yankees. Hope I may never be a prisoner of war.[21]

Our soldier boys are as full of mischief as a cat is of fleas. The other night after taps, Gus Clower, John Toddy,[22] Alvin Parr, and a host of others come round to my tent, pulled me out into the company parade ground, formed a circle around me by all hands round as they call it, and proceeded to sing, "Old Father Grimes, that good old man that wore the long tail blue all buttoned down" before marching around in a circle with myself in the middle feeling like a fool, whether I looked like one or not. No use to say anything, it only makes matters worse. After singing "Father Grimes," they sing their favorite revival tune, "Rye Straw," which has 99 verses in it and all just alike. When through singing would all shake hands with me as they marched round. They called that joining me in. They would then leave me to worry some other poor devil in the same way. While it annoys me, like to see them worry someone else.

The boys are going to have their fun, and the best you can do is to take it like a little man, because if you get mad and want to fight, you will certainly be accommodated. The boys mean no harm, and if it was not for the mischief carried on in camps, all would die of the blues. So here is hoping our mischievous boys may live long to enjoy the pranks they play on the rest of us. Alvin Parr, better known as Joe Dutton, and Gus Clower are two of the best soldiers in the regiment, and the most mischievous. They never get tired or in the blues. When the rest are completely tired out, they are ready for a frolic.

We are in camps opposite the city park which is a beautiful place, and on Sundays especially, patronized by the citizens. Quite a contrast between our ragged soldier boys and the well-dressed people promenading in the park. Everybody is represented, from the baby in its carriage to old age ready for the grave. So far as the soldier element is concerned, the officers predominate in their handsome uniforms. While we ought not to envy others, it does look hard that we have nothing in common with those well-dressed people who seem to be enjoying life to the fullest extent while we are dragging out a miserable existence, but such is war, and we can't all be well-dressed officers. Guess we will have to grin and endure it the best we can.

September 8, between 1,200 and 1,500 prisoners arrived from Andersonville, Ga., this morning and were confined in the new stockade in rear of the jail and built for their special accommodation. The stockade is built of plank set up and down and about 12 feet high with sentry boxes at proper intervals to overlook the prison. Some of the prisoners are fine-looking men, but others are sick, mostly with scurvy caused by lack of vegetables and other proper food and medicines which the Confederacy is unable to furnish on account of the blockade. Our own soldiers being destitute of nearly everything in the way of medicine.

The prisoners were sent here on account of Gen. Sherman having taken Atlanta on the 2nd instant.[23] The Regulars are guarding the stockade as well as the officers in the hospital grounds. There is six pieces of artillery bearing on the stockade. September 11, several thousand more prisoners have arrived within the last few days. The first Sunday after the prisoners arrived, the citizens of Savannah made quite a demonstration in behalf of the sick. There must have been between 500 and 1,000 women and children visited the stockade carrying baskets of provisions. They became so numerous, the guard could not keep them back. Maj. Wayne turned out the rest of the regiment and surrounded the whole crowd keeping them until sundown before letting them go. If the prisoners had made a break, would have had to of fired among the women and children or let the prisoners escape.

Sent off a carload [of prisoners] to Charleston, S.C., this morning, September 13. The yankee officers were sent by railroad to Charleston this morning. They went with a light heart, believing they were going to be exchanged. Some of them had a good clench of greenbacks, but it is against the law to pass them. But our boys found purchasers for them in the city, getting Confederate money in return which they could use in buying something to eat and other things they stand in need of. Some of them sold diamond rings and watches to get money. How cruel to keep men in prison when they could be paroled and allowed to return home until exchanged. But they have no one to blame but their own government, for the Confederacy would jump at the offer and be glad of the chance to get rid of them.

WHITMARSH ISLAND, GEORGIA

September 24, 1864. Regulars relieved from duty at Savannah and proceeded on the steamer *Ida* to Turner's Rock on Whitmarsh Island. Marched to Gibson's Point and pitched our tents. September 29, ladies of Savannah presented the Regulars with a new battle flag; our old one is getting the worse of wear. At the same time, we hate to give up our old flag on account of past associations, it having been thrown to the breeze on every field the Regulars have ever fought on.

Picket duty is very heavy, but the cool weather has sent the troublesome insects into winter quarters. November 7, the Regulars commenced building winter quarters at Gibson's Point, Turner's Rock, and Fleetwood, Col. Wayne's headquarters. Anyone visiting our camps would say the boys were hard up for something to eat, and they would not be far wrong. If they could see the boys catching rats and parching acorns. I have tried the acorns but am not quite hungry enough to go the rats. The wharf rats are very numerous about our quarters and make way with our rations unless put where they cannot get it. The boys first commenced killing in self-defense, but afterwards killed them to eat. You can hear the boys every morning yell, "Turn out your rat details," and at least 50 men will turn out with sticks and spades. The rats burrow under a row of cedars near the camps and the boys will dig them out and then let them run for their lives. They don't get far before they are knocked on the head. After the boys kill about 50, they turn too and dress them, each man cooking to suit his taste. Some fry, some stew, while others bake them, and the boys say they eat as well as a cat squirrel, but I am willing to take their words for it and let the rats alone. At the same time, eat my share of acorns parched. There has been a right smart sickness among the soldiers caused from so much exposure doing so much picket duty at night. The boys are having a good time gathering oysters and crabs. While I like the oysters very well, don't like the crabs. They are just about as much like meat as a maypop is like a vegetable.

The Regulars have had a good many conscripts sent to the companies. They are good, bad, and indifferent. Some of them make good soldiers, while others are incapable of performing military service. The government seems to have set a net and hold all they catch whether good or bad. Some have been sent to Company M on crutches and various other drawbacks in the way of making a good soldier. Guess the women will be called out next, as the boys down to 16 years and the men to 60 have been sent to the front. Well everything certainly looks squally, but we will hope for the best.

Some of our boys while out in a boat gathering oysters the other day, deserted and went to the enemy at Fort Pulaski. Well it will be a cold day in August when I go to the enemy. I would as soon go to the devil and be done with it, for I have about as much love for one as the other. That is saying a great deal, but there is no love between the two armies. You can hear the boys say, "Damn the yankees; if it was not for them I would be at home instead of being in the army suffering like I am." And no doubt the yankees feel the same way about us.

December 1, 1864, the yankee exchange fleet, after delivering 3,100 hundred [sic] sick and wounded Confederates, has returned north carrying 11,000 sick and wounded yankees.[24] Gen. W. T. Sherman of the Union Army cut loose from Atlanta, Georgia, on the 9th day of November, 1864, and is marching for Savannah, Georgia.[25]

SIEGE OF SAVANNAH, GEORGIA

December 9, Regulars evacuated Whitmarsh Island and marched to Savannah. December 10, marched out four and one-half miles from the city between the Central Railroad and the Little Ogeechee River where we were assigned to Gen. Lewis' Brigade of dismounted cavalry.[26] Heavy skirmishing along the line during the day. The Confederate lines extend from Fort McAllister[27] below the city to the Savannah River above, and must be several miles in length. Sherman's troops are fronting our entire line of works. Gen. William J. Hardee is in command of the Confederates.

December 11, considerable picket and artillery firing on the line in front of Lewis' Brigade. About the center of the Regulars position is a sand battery made of sacks of sand. In this battery is a 60-pound Seacoast Howitzer and just in front of us is a gum pond so thick you cannot see 20 yards in the swamp. About 150 yards in front of our regiment, the yankees have two six-pound rifle pieces and when they open on our battery, they certainly make the wool fly. Our 60-pound piece sends a shell through the gum swamp making noise enough to wake the dead. We can hear the yankees tell one another when they get to making too much noise, "Better keep quiet or the Rebs will turn that wash tub loose on you again." The yankees always have the last shot. If you were to shoot a month, it would be all the same.

On our right is a regiment of junior reserves, boys 'tween 16 and 18 years of age. Can't help feeling sorry for the boys, as the hardships of camp life is new to them and most of the time they are out of rations. If they draw three days' rations at one time, will sit down and eat it all up and then have to go hungry until they draw again. Have seen some of the Regulars sell them cornbread at one dollar a cake. I could not do that. If I have any to spare, will give it to them, but could not sell it to them. Poor boys, they have not found out how to make their scanty rations hold out. Home would be the proper place for them. At the same time, boys are hard fighters, don't seem to have any better sense than to go right into it. But it is hard, on account of their being so young. Numbers of them will contract diseases they will never get over if they are lucky enough to get out of the army alive.

One day [I] saw a soldier to the right of us trying to secure a piece of plank in front of the line. The yankees opened on him. He stopped and stood the plank up in front of him for protection. Two balls were put through the plank and the soldier too. A dear piece of plank to cost him his life.

While we were in the works an Englishman by the name of Loyd in Company M[28] came stalking into the trenches with a set of plough gear swung on his shoulders. On being asked what he was going to do with them, said he was going to sell them. What is it that fellow would not have stolen?

We are having some cold, wet weather. Nothing unusual on the lines outside of the picket and artillery firing. Some of our boys are shooting from positions up in trees. I prefer staying on the ground so if I get shot, won't have so far to fall.

Some 300 yards in our front is a long range battery of six guns that shoot over our lines in the direction of the city. The boys say they are hunting for our commissaries in the rear. And sure enough, they were.

Capt. Payne, our quartermaster, had a large sorrell horse he had rode through the war and had finally gone blind, but the captain thought so much of him, he still retained him in service. During one of the shellings, his horse broke loose from where he was hitched and stampeded the camps. Most of the men had dug holes in the ground to hide in during the shelling. The captain's horse fell in one of these holes where two doctors were in hiding, and killed one and badly injured the other. Blind horses are more dangerous than shells. At least I would take the shells in preference.

Tuesday night, December 20, 1864, the forces under Gen. Hardee evacuated the city of Savannah, Ga. The Regulars were withdrawn from the works about eleven o'clock, and I will never forget passing through the city which was sealed [?]. Doors were being knocked down, guns were firing in every direction, the bullets flying over and around us. Women and children screaming and rushing in every direction. All combined made it a night never to be forgotten by them who witnessed it. We finally reached the river where a string of rice barges strung end to end formed a bridge for us to cross on. The bridge was a poor makeshift, but the army succeeded in crossing it. While crossing the bridge, our way was lighted up by the burning of the Confederate gunboats and other vessels lying in the Savannah River. Sad to look at, but at the same time made a beautiful picture on the water. After the army had crossed, the barges were cut loose and destroyed. It was reported that several hundred of our men was left in the city. Most of them stayed on their own account, preferring being made prisoners to fighting any longer.

December 21, resumed the march up the Savannah River. During the morning there was a shower of rain, and the boys commenced firing off their guns on the line of march, which was ordered stopped by the officers. A lieutenant on Gen. Jackson's[29] staff ordered it stopped and jumped off his horse, jerked a rifle out of a soldier's hands, and shot one of the boys dead who had fired off his gun. I saw the dead soldier soon afterwards lying by the roadside where his grave was being dug. He belonged to the reserves. Had it been one of the Regulars he shot, he would have struck the ground nearly as soon as his victim did. It was simply an outrage, and he deserved death at the hands of the boy's comrades. The lieutenant was placed under arrest, and I suppose that was the last of it. Marched to Hardeeville on the Savannah and Charleston Railroad and went into bivouacs near the station.

December 23, the Regulars left Gen. Lewis' Brigade and marched five miles to Perrysburg on the Savannah River where we were put to guarding commissary stores. Perrysburg is where Gen. Francis Marion fought a battle during the Revolutionary War. One of his cannons is still lying where it was dismounted by the British, and in a graveyard close by sleep his departed heroes. Little did I dream when a boy reading the daring deeds of Marion and his men that I would tramp over the same ground as a soldier fighting the battles of his country. But truth is sometimes stranger than fiction.

December 24, the Regulars assigned to Col. Fiser's Brigade composed of the 5th and 6th regiments of Georgia Reserves and 27th Ga. Battalion, Gen. McLaws' Division.[30] Would like to know what has become of the troops we had stationed in Savannah. Seems as though Gen. Wheeler's Cavalry[31] was about all there was in the city, besides a few small regiments of reserves. The Regulars being the only old infantry I have yet heard tell of. Can't see why Gen. Sherman taken 12 days to capture the city when he could have walked over our line at any point.

December 24, McLaws' Division marched 18 miles to Grahamville, arriving late at night. Such a march as it was, through rain and mud. Expressed my feelings in no complimentary terms. I certainly felt like cursing somebody, and did not care who, for which Capt. DuBose reprimanded me for the want of patience. Sorry I have not the patience of my commanding officer, but he has help from on high to assist him along through this hungry and muddy world. If there is any Christians in the army, my captain is one of them. He never complains, suffer what he will, but is always that ever-ready brave and reliable soldier. While he makes no show of his religion or bravery either, he is as cool on the battlefield as he would be at home in his parlor. Makes me feel small to think I can't be like Capt. DuBose and do my duty like a man without complaining. But I am not Job, and if Job had to take my place on the march through mud and water without anything to eat, think he would have said something bad too. Another dreary Christmas day in the army, making four I have spent in the army. Hope I may never spend another one in the war, but from the looks of everything now, there is no prospects of the war coming to an end.

December 26, marched to the Coosawhatchie River where Gen. George P. Harrison's Brigade were holding the enemy in check, they having advanced to within one mile of the railroad and thrown up a battery of 16 heavy guns. December 27, marched three miles to Pocotaligo Station. December 28, bivouacked in the woods between Old Pocotaligo and the Coosawhatchie River, where we remained doing picket duty. Some nights when the Savannah and Charleston trains are passing, the fire of the yankee battery is something terrible. I used to think I would like to be an engineer, but not on that train. Think the engineer turns on all the steam and lets her go, [illegible]. Strange to say, he gets by without being killed or knocked off the track.

A Streak
of Misery

Battle of Pocotaligo, South Carolina

The year 1865 found the Regulars doing picket duty near Pocotaligo Station on the Savannah and Charleston Railroad, and on the north side of the Coosawhatchie River, Gen. Harrison's Brigade being on the south side. While on picket the other night, Pvt. Loyd of Company M deserted to the enemy, having to cross a wide marsh with Negro pickets on the other side. He was the fellow that stole the plough gear at Savannah, and while on the march to this place begged a lady for his dinner and then stole the knife and fork he ate it with. So the yankees had better look out or he will steal the sweetening out of their coffee. We are glad he is gone, but would have been better pleased if he had been killed by the Negroes when he went to them.

January 14, Gen. Sherman's 17th Army Corps landed at Port Royal from Savannah, and marched for Pocotaligo Station.[1] About one and a half miles east of the station is Old Pocotaligo, a few old houses being all there is of the place. Nearby, running east, is a creek with a public road running north and south and crossing the creek south of the houses. North of the houses, or nearly in front of them, is a line of works facing the east. On the evening of the 14th of January, our brigade, with a battery of artillery, taken position in the works. In our front is an open field extending to a piece of woods some three-fourths of a mile distant. We had not been in position long before we saw our cavalry enter the field deployed as skirmishers and gradually falling back. Pretty soon the enemy's skirmish line of infantry entered the field. Our forces were ordered to lie low to keep the enemy from seeing us. Our cavalry continued to fall back, and when about half way [across] the field fired the grass, but the enemy jumped over it and continued to drive our men back. When the yankee skirmish line had crossed over about halfway of the field, a line of battle emerged from the woods and advanced through the open field. Our cavalry rallied, formed company, and marched out when within 200 yards of our works. In our front was a marshy piece of ground, some distance in width that the enemy could not have crossed if they had succeeded in getting to it. But when they arrived within 200 yards of the works, our whole line of infantry and artillery belched forth one solid sheet of flame. The enemy was taken by surprise, and about one-half dropped to the ground while the other turned and fled in the wildest confusion. Those that dropped down that was not killed or wounded also made to the rear, having to retreat back to the woods under the combined fire of the infantry and artillery. Never knew what their loss[es] were, as night was approaching. After night, our brigade moved several hundred yards to our left where we remained until twelve o'clock at night, the enemy shelling the most of the time.

January 15 just before day, all the troops crossed the railroad bridge at Salkehatchie River and burned it, taking our position in the swamp above the bridge. Bearing on the bridge is a line of heavy batteries to hold the enemy in check. Since crossing, have some idea about our forces. We have Gen. Harrison's Georgia Brigade, Col. Fiser's Brigade of reserves and regulars, Col. Hardy's North Carolina Brigade,[2] and Gen. Conner's South Carolina Brigade,[3] in all, some 3,000 or 4,000 men.[4] As to the artillery and cavalry, don't know how many there is of them, but suppose Gen. Wheeler's command is somewhere in South Carolina. We are having some miserable weather. Don't do anything but rain, and the weather is cold with it. Guess we will go wild if we stay in this swamp long.

BATTLE OF THE SALKEHATCHIE

After crossing the bridge, our brigade went about one-half mile up the river swamp where we went into bivouacs. Some little time after sunrise, an old Negro with a wooden leg crossed the river and come to our regiment informing Capt. DuBose that on the other side of the river was a farm house that had been deserted by its occupants, leaving behind a fine lunch[?] of fattening hogs, turkeys, chickens, and ducks which our hungry boys could have by going after them, offering his services as a pilot to conduct them to the house. Capt. DuBose detailed eight men to accompany the old Negro, thinking that such a lunch was not struck up with every day. Besides, knowing that if we did not get them, the yankees would. So the boys and the old Negro struck out, managing in some way to cross the river. When on the other side, discovered a small trail leading out of the swamp. At one place discovered where a fire had been built in the path and had not gone out. That looked a little suspicious to the boys, and they decided to keep a sharp lookout. On getting through the swamp, they come to a field and found themselves not far from a home. They could hear hogs squealing and chickens squalling, and seemingly a general disturbance of everything. So the boys thought they smelled a rat and halted. After holding a council of war, they decided to send two of the boys forward to reconnoiter and see what was going on. By making a circle around the field they approached the house to find the yard full of yankees. The boys beat a hasty retreat back to their comrades and were just in time to keep from being cut off by a detachment of yankees who were slipping around to cut them off. It is needless to say the boys made quick-time in recrossing the river. The same old Negro succeeded afterwards in getting another crowd to undertake the same thing, with the same result. The old Negro ought to have been shot, as it was a trial of the yankees to capture some of our boys holding out the tempting allurements of something to eat.

One or two days afterwards, my messmates Sgt. Humphries, Cpl. Harris,[5] and Pvt. Frasier[6] succeeded in capturing four fine hens and a hog from an old darkie, besides taking his wash pot to cook them in. Stole his ax to make a fire with. As the 1st sergeant, I have no chance[?] to forage, but have to make it up in cooking. I certainly had a good rich pot one time; the hens were the fattest I ever cooked, besides a ham of the hog. What a time I had boiling that pot and how my mouth watered as the delightful odors filled the air. It certainly was rich, and smelt most appetizing. On top of the pot the grease was about one inch thick. After taking out the meat what a time we had eating cornbread and chicken gravy. We hung the chickens up in a bush to drip and a soldier came stumbling along and run over the bush, knocking our chickens down on the ground. Liked to have had a shooting scrape. My messmates were so mad, [they] wanted to shoot the poor devil for his carelessness. We got the dirt off as best we could. The only difference it made [was that] we had to chew that much easier to keep from finding the grit. We forgot to thank the old Negro or carry his pot and ax back. Very unthankful that, but soldiers don't stand much on politeness, and more especially so when something to eat is concerned. Have always heard it said, touch a man's pocket and you touch his soul. But if I wanted to find a soldier's soul, I would touch him on his stomach.

January 20, Col. Fiser with about 60 men (30 from the 27th Ga. Battalion, 30 from the Texas Rangers, Gen. McLaws' escort) went up the river on a scouting expedition. After going up the river road some distance, turned into the swamp and come down along the bank of the river. The swamp is almost impassable, with numbers of lagoons; besides the swamp is covered in a dense forest of trees. The undergrowth being so thick, you can scarcely see 20 feet in advance. While they were tramping down the river bank, the rain was falling in sheets. In making a turn in the bend of the river, Col. Fiser's men discovered the enemy on the same side. The enemy discovering [discovered] them at the same time, and pretty soon the merry crack of the rifles enlivened the swamp. Col. Fiser sent a courier round to camps with an order for Col. Hardy of the North Carolina Brigade to take the 1st Ga. Regulars of Col. Fiser's Brigade and charge them in the rear as he had the enemy cut off.

The Regulars, under command of our gallant Col. R. A. Wayne, were soon on the double-quick, splashing through the rain and mud. Sometimes waist deep in a lagoon and then again over head and ears in a brier patch. After going through the swamp for one or two miles, we arrived on the field of action. The regiment was halted and Capt. DuBose was ordered to deploy Company M as skirmishers and advance to the attack. When we arrived on the scene, everything was quiet, both sides resting on their arms waiting for the Regulars to arrive and scare them up. As it happened, we were deployed against Col. Fiser's Command instead of what he supposed to be the enemy. After the company was deployed, Capt. DuBose placed me in command of the right while he took command of the left. He then gave the command "Forward skirmishers" and we advanced. The swamp was a dense thicket, and we had not advanced many steps before we received the enemy's fire almost in our faces. They were not more than 15 feet in our front, concealed behind trees. Pvt. Cole[7] had his left arm shot off, or so badly mangled it had to be cut off. I ordered the boys on the right to fall back, which we did some 30 steps when we halted behind trees. Some of the firing was considerably to my right, showing that the enemy line overlapped ours. I then sent word down the line to Capt. DuBose that we were flanked on our right. He sent Sgt. Charley Bruce of Company I[8] to act as a scout on the right and ascertain the strength of the enemy.

When Bruce reached me I ordered my men to hold their positions and remain quiet until myself and Sgt. Bruce would reconnoiter the position of the enemy and locate their lines. To be old soldiers we acted very foolish. Instead of crawling through the underbrush where we would have been concealed, we made our way along a very dim old road running in the direction of the enemy lines. We had not made our way on our hands and knees many yards before about 20 caps, some of them not more than that many feet from us, were busted at us. Bruce and myself did not crawl in getting away from there, but we covered the ground between us and our men in a few bounds. I then sent word down the line for Capt. DuBose to come up to the right of the line.

I have always believed that a kind providence watches over we poor sinful mortals here on earth, and after Capt. DuBose succeeded in reaching the right believed it stronger than ever. The enemy were but a few yards distant, concealed behind trees. While the rain was pouring down so it was almost impossible to see anyone until you were right on them. Capt. DuBose in coming up the line made his way by jumping from tree to tree. When he reached the tree next to me he barely halted, and passed on. As he cleared the tree, a minié ball crashed through it and must have brushed his coat. The tree looked solid, but was nothing but a shell and if he had made a full stop, would have been a dead man. When he reached the right, Col. Hardy with the rest of the Regulars arrived on the scene. And about the same time, someone come from the left of the line and informed Capt. DuBose that we were fighting our own men and to call off the fight. But Col. Hardy paid no attention to it and ordered a charge with the skirmish line in front and the regiment in rear.

As we charged Sgt. Bruce and myself got within 20 yards of a man behind a tree. I called Bruce's attention to him telling him it was one of our men. Bruce said not. I then told Bruce to look at the light-colored overcoat he had on and the Confederate canteen hanging at his side. Still Bruce refused to be convinced. "Well Bruce," said I, "if nothing else will convince you, I will shoot him and prove it to you afterwards." So placing my rifle to my shoulder, I took deliberate aim and pressed the trigger. My gun being wet, failed to fire. Just at that time, the regiment that was charging in the rear of the skirmish line dashed up with Bruce and myself. The soldier with the light overcoat on blazed away at the regiment and beat a hasty retreat. As he left his tree, saw two others jump up from behind the same tree and run.

Company M continued the charge for a half mile or more. Saw some deer and wild hogs but no yankees. Col. Hardy told the regiment to bear to the right and give them the bayonet. No telling where Company M would have stopped at if we had not encountered a large ditch we could not jump over. After we stopped, Col. Hardy rode up and looked at us then turned and rode back. The regiment had stopped several hundred yards behind the skirmish line. Company M remained in that ditch all night and until ten o'clock the next morning without fire or anything to eat. And would probably have been there yet if Capt. DuBose had not made his way back to camps and let Col. Wayne know where his company was at. We were then ordered back to camps. It was a night never to be forgotten. Without anything to eat or fire to warm by. Without a dry thread of clothing on us. Had to dance all night to keep from freezing.

When we got back to camps, found out we were fighting Col. Fiser and his party of scouts who had attacked the pickets of the North Carolina Brigade. One man was killed and eight wounded. Somebody acted the fool and ought to have been punished for it. It was said that Col. Hardy was drunk and I don't doubt it. About twelve o'clock at night, the regiment was marched back to camps by Col. Wayne, and Col. Hardy made him march them back into the swamp and wait for his orders to move them out, when at the same time he was lying in his tent drunk. So the poor soldiers have to suffer for some drunken officer's wrongdoings.

Several days afterwards, two of my messmates, Sgt. Humphries and Cpl. Harris, were out foraging and killed a hog. While they were bringing the hog to camps, were arrested and carried to Gen. McLaws' headquarters where the hog was taken from them, their names and regiments taken, and then turned loose threatening to deal with them afterwards. The boys lost the hog and never heard anything more about it. Guess the fellows who took the hog knew what to do with it.

Sgt. William G. Humphries was a trump. He could not weigh more than 100 pounds and carried the largest knapsack of any man in the company. Could march farther and forage more than one of Gen. Wheeler's buttermilk cavalrymen. He was never absent at roll call or missed a fight his company was ever in. Had all of our soldiers been of the same stripe, the yankees would have had all of them to kill before they got rid of them.

The rains continued so long the swamps were overflowed and we had to take to the hills, having to march at least half a mile knee deep in water before we got out. January 30, Fiser's and Hardy's brigades left camps at 8:00 P.M. and marched up the Salkehatchie River towards Brocton's Bridge, leaving Gen. Conner's Brigade at the railroad bridge, Gen. Harrison's having preceded us a few days before. Marched 13 miles and stopped for the night. January 31, marched nine miles farther up the river and camped for the night.

Gen. Sherman's forces are burning the woods as they march up on the other side of the river, having seen one continuous line of smoke all the way. February 1, marched to Brocton's Bridge, which Gen. Harrison's Brigade had strongly fortified. February 2, Col. Fiser's Brigade relieved Gen. Harrison's at Brocton's Bridge. Gen. Harrison's going to River's Bridge five miles farther up the river. Sherman's forces arrived early in the morning and sharpshooting continued throughout the day. February 3, the enemy crossed the Salkehatchie River between Brocton's and River's bridges, scattering our forces and causing them to retreat in the direction of Branchville on the Augusta and Charleston Railroad. The Regulars were cut off from the rest of the command and marched all night by themselves.

During the night the boys got to stealing horses. Two of the boys secured an old horse just before day, sold him to a cavalryman who was conducting the regiment through the country. About one hour before day, we halted and dropped down by the roadside to rest and to sleep after our hard night's march. Just about light I roused up and could hear someone busily tramping about on the other side of the tree I was resting against. On looking around, discovered our guide busily fixing up his new charger he had just purchased from our boys. He had taken his bridle and saddle off his horse and turned him loose in the woods, and put his bridle and saddle on his new purchase. After getting the saddle all right, proceeded to trim his mane and then started to fix up his tail. Cavalry horses have their tails either tied in a knot or swabbed off short to keep the mud from clotting it up. About the time he started to fix the horse's tail, an old farmer hove in sight. He yelled out to our guide, "For God's sake Mister, don't swab his tail off, that's my old blind horse, have owned him for the last 21 years and he is everything me and the old woman has to make a crop with." The yell that went up from the boys was enough to make the poor fellow feel bad, and he certainly looked like he was badly sold. He never said a word, but slipped his saddle and bridle off and caught his own horse that was worth at least six of the one he had purchased. The old farmer seized his horse and returned home happy. Whenever the boys would get in sight of him during the day, would yell, "For God's sake Mister, don't swab his tail off," and he would ship out of sight.

February 4, 1865, marched 12 miles to Branchville, crossing the Edisto River. We saw several brigades of the Western Army.[9] Bivouacked in the streets all night. February 5, Regulars boarded a train for Georgia Station 15 miles towards Charleston, S.C. Marched from Georgia Station to Racer's [?] Bridge on the Edisto. The piney woods extends to the river bank, not a sign of swamp. We are merely guarding the bridge. I suppose in case the enemy comes we will set fire to it and skedaddle.

February 12, we evacuated our lines on the Edisto and marched 20 miles to Rosser's Station on the Augusta and Charleston Railroad. February 13, crossed the Four Hole Swamp and camped. February 15, marched three miles down the river to the railroad bridge. Relieved the 10th N.C. Regiment on picket duty. February 17, the Regulars rejoined the brigade three miles up the swamp. February 18, brigade marched 20 miles in the direction of the Santee river. February 19, marched 16 miles. The Confederate forces at Charleston evacuated the city yesterday, retreating on the Northeastern Railroad, the enemy entering the city at twelve midnight.

February 20, marched eight miles to St. Stephen's Station on the Northeastern Railroad and made a junction with Gen. Taliaferro's Division[10] from Charleston. Crossed the Santee River on cars, three miles of the swamp being covered in water. This is a great country for water. Sometimes we have to wade gum ponds from one-half to a mile in width and break the ice as we go. February 21, marched 19 miles to King's Tree, crossing the Black River. February 22 about dark, [the] brigade boarded the cars for Cheraw where we arrived on the 23rd. Passed through Florence. Cheraw is a beautiful little town on the banks of the Big Pee Dee River.

We went into camps until our artillery and transportation wagons could catch up. February 28, Col. Fiser's Brigade marched 12 miles to

Chesterfield, a little town on Clinch's Creek. Brigade halted at the Northeast Bridge about three quarters of a mile from the center of the little town. February 29, [the] Regulars marched through Chesterfield going to Craigg's Mill on Clinch's Creek. The creek makes an elbow and the little town is in the circle. Craigg's Mill is on the west side of town while the remainder of the brigade is on the north side. March 1, Regulars captured three prisoners belonging to the 17th Army Corps of Sherman's Army.

March 2. This morning Col. Wayne ordered his baggage wagon to rejoin the brigade at the Northeast Bridge, and to see that it passed through the town safe, he went with it. On entering the town Col. Wayne found it occupied by the yankees. An officer on horseback dashed up to the colonel and ordered him to surrender. He put the spurs to his horse and made his escape. From the bridge up town, the road is perfectly straight with considerable slope towards the creek. It certainly was worth a dollar of any man's money to have seen the race between Col. Wayne, his skillet wagon, and the yankee officer. It was nip and tuck. When the race commenced, Col. Wayne's skillet wagon was in the lead, the colonel next, and the yankee officer, on a white horse, brought up the rear. The colonel and his skillet wagon made good their escape by dashing back to the regiment. The colonel remarked on reaching his men, "You think a d——d yankee did not have the impudence to order me to surrender. I told him to go to h–ll, and made my escape." Several of the boys took a shot at the pursuing yankee without hitting him as he dashed back to town. Our gallant colonel had to take to his heels one time at least. I know it went hard with him, but it was either to run or be made prisoner.

The colonel is dead [?] game and has been with the regiment in every battle it was ever engaged in except Olustee, Florida, and he was then president of a court-martial in Tallahassee. The boys claim that the colonel cries sometimes because he missed that battle. He deserves spurs, and stars too, for he has rightly earned them.

At first the boys did not like Col. Wayne. He is naturally of a gruff disposition and speaks short and to the point. But since we have found him out, we love and admire him for that brave and fearless heart that beats in his bosom. The boys know the colonel can be depended on in any emergency. Besides, he has always been with the regiment and we can take from a brave man what we would not like in someone who had never done any fighting with us.

The Regulars rapidly retreated down Clinch's Creek to rejoin the brigade at the Northeast Bridge where we arrived after night, the brigade having had a brisk fight across the creek during the evening. Rations of rifle whiskey was issued to the boys, warranted to kill [at] 400 yards offhand. It certainly was a bad mixture and made the boys want to fight. About nine o'clock at night, retreated in the direction of Cheraw, and after going a few miles halted by the roadside until nearly day, when the retreat was continued.

About sunrise, we met a couple of women going in the direction of Chesterfield. One of them was carrying in her arms the remains of a small child, say three years old, that had died and she [was] walking and carrying the child back home to bury it. What a sad sight it was. No doubt [but] she had to bury it. How her heart must have bled as she performed the last sad rites. But such is war times.

About seven o'clock, halted and cooked breakfast some three miles from Cheraw, where we remained for several hours. When we moved forward again, it was at the double-quick, holding that gait until we reached the city. When the brigade was about halfway through the city, it was halted and the Regulars were ordered back to the edge of town to hold the enemy in check until Gen. Butler's Cavalry[11] from Chesterfield could enter the town.

BATTLE OF CHERAW, SOUTH CAROLINA

We formed line of battle with the left wing of the regiment, the right wing being in reserve. The enemy opened a brisk fire on us through an open field [?]. Capt. DuBose of Company M ordered Lt. F. B. Palmer to take three men and go to a piece of woods some 250 yards to our right to watch the movements of the enemy to keep them from flanking our position. I asked Capt. DuBose to let me go with the lieutenant, but he declined and Sgt. Watson of Company F and Cpl. Musgrove and Pvt. Overman[12] of Company M went with him. About the time the lieutenant arrived at his destination on our right, Gen. Butler's Cavalry dashed past at full speed entering the town and was soon out of sight. On looking to our left, discovered the yankees as thick as black birds flanking us. The order was given to retreat, and we had a running fight through the town. The screams of the women and children, the report of the rifles, and the familiar zip of the minié balls made it a scene not to be forgotten soon.

I was amused at our color bearer, Sgt. Bennett. The citizens were waving handkerchiefs, newspapers, or anything else that was white.

It seemed to enrage Bennett and he would yell, "You may wave your handkerchiefs and newspapers, but I will be d——d if this is not the battle flag," and he would wave it around his head nearly knocking my hat off. Company M being the sixth company, placed me beside the color bearer, a position I don't want because it is the most dangerous place in the line as everyone in front of the colors think it would be glory enough for one day to shoot the color bearer down and then I would have them to raise to the breeze.

When some distance in the town, the regiment formed and moved forward at a brisk rate. A little to our right and front, we could hear the rapid discharge of artillery. Someone remarked, "We are all right yet boys, as we have artillery on this side of the river." As we got opposite to and several blocks from the bridge, we filed left down a street. As we did so, a battery of the enemy's artillery up the street about 200 yards opened on us. My but it was terrible, as it taken the regiment lengthwise. We did not take time to see what was going on in our rear as the rapid fire of the artillery and the shells bursting in our midst made us have a hankering for the opposite bank of the river. It certainly looked like Gen. Hardee had made a sacrifice of the 1st Ga. Regulars as everybody else had long since crossed the river and were out of danger. The cavalry that we had held the enemy in check for dashed past us, as much as to say, "Take care of yourselves boys, if you can. We have pressing business on the other side of the river." As the regiment run down the street, we entered a bottom out of sight of the batteries except our colors, which the enemy was firing at. Capt. DuBose ordered Sgt. Bennett to lower his colors. Bennett swore he would die and then he would not trail his colors, but the captain got him to lower them. We then dashed out to our left in an alley and made around some building to the bridge.

On entering the bridge, found rosin piled all the way along on either side of the bridge ready to be fired as we crossed. Before we had got more than halfway [over] the bridge, the yankees entered behind us. We had a lively time as we fought through the bridge, some cavalrymen firing the rosin as we fought through. It was a terrible long bridge, or at least I thought so as it looked like we would never get out of it. We left the bridge on fire and full of yankees trying to put it out. The road makes a bend down the river and then turns to the left, the woods being at least one and a half miles distant.

When the regiment had made the bend in the road some 300 yards from the bridge, Gen. Butler dashed up and asked for the commanding officer, who was pointed out to him (Col. Wayne had rode on after we had crossed the bridge). Gen. Butler ordered him to face his regiment about charge and retake the bridge. The officer replied to him by saying his men were broke down and unable to charge. Gen. Butler told him he must retake the bridge as that was the only thing that would save our army. The regiment was halted and a line of battle formed facing the bridge. As we did so, a yankee battery on the bluff and below the bridge on the opposite side of the river numbering six pieces unlimbered, and before the command "Forward" was given to the Regulars, opened fire on us. The first shell passed to my right and took off one of the gallant Sgt. Bruce's legs. The order was then given to charge, and away we went charging in the face of those six pieces of artillery. Gen. Butler ordered the men to bear to the right and get the bridge between them and the battery, but most of them charged square down on the battery. Some six or eight of us bore up to the right so as to get the bridge between us and the enemy, Sgt. Alex Clemency of Company G being among the number.

As we were making for the bridge, Clemency was about 10 feet in front of me. A shell struck the ground and burst between us. As the shell exploded, Sgt. Clemency fell. I passed on by him remarking as I did so, "Alex old boy, you are done for, but you are a d——d sight better off than I am." I thought he was dead and envied his position. We were at that time desperate after running at least five miles. I would not have dodged a shell if I could have seen it coming at me. I still made for the bridge, but it seemed like I must have been jumping up and down in the same tracks, I got along so slow. I was one of the first men at the bridge and Sgt. Clemency was at my heels, having fell in a hole when I passed him instead of being killed.

We found just within the bridge a captain of the Marion or Washington Artillery from Charleston, S.C., defending the bridge all alone. His horse was lying in the bridge dead, and he was as deliberately firing away with his pistol as if he was being backed by 10,000 men. The farther end of the bridge was full of yankees who were trying to put the fire out. Some 20 of the Regulars got to the end of the bridge lying down and shooting over the abutment. We soon opened the bridge and the fire seemed to leap for joy as it spread from one end of the bridge to the other. The bridge was soon in a mass of flames. While we were at the end of the bridge, the artillery was directed on the end of the bridge, and you can safely bet, made the timber fly. But the Regulars went back to see that bridge burn and were not going to be disappointed, from the simple fact we knew if the bridge was not burned, Sherman's forces would take us in out of the wet. But by burning, it would give us several days the start of him as he would have to place his pontoons before he could cross the river.

Soon after the bridge fell in, the Regulars were ordered out, but getting out was another question, as most of the men was below the bridge and in full view of both the artillery and a double line of skirmishers on the opposite bank of the river. While I was at the bridge, saw Col. Wayne sitting on his horse in rear of a tree and the artillery firing at him. Sgt. Clemency, myself, and several others at the bridge crawled out a washout near the river bank and continued up the river until out of sight of the enemy, when we made for and gained the road. That was about 10:00 A.M., and the rest of the regiment had to remain until after dark before they could escape and rejoin the brigade some three miles from the bridge. Lt. Palmer with his detail was captured, besides a number of killed, wounded, and missing. Several of Company M was missing after the fight. We never knew what became of them.

The most of the men were below the bridge and when nearing the river bank, the enemy skirmish line opened on them. A sergeant of Company I was shot down some 20 steps from the river bank. Several men were ordered to bring him in and place him behind the trees for protection. When they reached him, had to put down their guns to carry him. Pvt. John Smith of Company M was sent after the guns. As he started to return with them, the yankees opened on him and he dropped down in a small sink in the ground, but not deep enough to hide him from the enemy, who continued to fire at him throughout the day without hitting him. The balls would strike the ground and glance over him. Capt. DuBose says he believes that Smith had his weight in lead shot at him.

Altogether, Cheraw was a mighty bad place, and one I don't wish to see again. At the same time, the 1st Regulars performed a gallant feat in charging and retaking the bridge.

At night, while in camps, we watched the angry flames as they devoured the best portion of Cheraw. Looked to be several blocks on fire at one time. Old Sherman's march has been illuminated by his fires on the way. First Atlanta, then Columbia, and now comes Cheraw.[13] Besides he burns the woods as he goes when dry enough.

March 4, our brigade received five days' rations of corn meal and nothing to cook it with. I cooked my bread last night on a piece of bark. The boys are hot and you can depend on it. Just about one-half mile back from us is a large barn filled with provisions: bacon, flour, crackers, meal, hens, sugar, and everything else kept in the commissary. That barn was fired to keep [it] from falling into the hands of the enemy. Why is it the rations could not have been issued to our half-famished troops instead of firing them? Don't all answer at once.

We marched off from camps, leaving our meal behind and with nothing to eat in our haversacks. Marched 20 miles to Rockingham, N.C. March 5, army under Gen. Hardee retreated towards Fayetteville, N.C., where we arrived on the 9th without being molested by the enemy. Ordered back several miles this side. During the night, Gen. Hampton's Cavalry[14] attacked Gen. Kilpatrick's, routing them. Gen. Kilpatrick made his escape in his night clothes on a bare-back mule.[15]

The next morning as we were marching out from camps, quite an amusing incident occurred. Each brigade has its place in the line of march. Our brigade had marched out ahead of time and halted by the roadside until some other brigades could pass us who belonged in front. As we were waiting, a soldier belonging to a North Carolina brigade passed some distance in rear of his command. He was an old straggler with his knapsack swung on his gun. He was singing a song about a little pig going a courting. He would sing a verse and then whistle the chorus. I don't think I ever heard so much laughing at any fool thing in my life. He tramped along the road as though perfectly oblivious of everything around him. Could account for his singing, but could not see how he could whistle in front of that roaring crowd of fun-loving soldiers.

We marched back to Fayetteville. I saw Gen. Wade Hampton. We crossed the Cape Fear River about ten o'clock at night, the cavalry crossing the next morning and burnt the bridge. March 12, the brigade marched to Smith's Ferry on the Cape Fear and went on picket. March 13, relieved from picket at Smith's Ferry and marched out two miles on the big road. March 14, regiment paid six months' wages at 18 dollars per month. I sent 50 dollars home, [with] which my mother purchased 50 pounds of lard. Pretty good money that. The only wonder is that it passed at all.

BATTLE OF AVERYSBORO, NORTH CAROLINA

One of Sherman's Army Corps having followed Gen. Hardee up the Cape Fear River, we formed what the boys call a streak of misery and offered them battle. Considerable skirmish and artillery firing during the evening. March 16, Gen. McLaws' Division formed on the left of Gen. Taliaferro's early in the morning. Threw up breastworks of logs and light wood knots, covering over with dirt. Using spades and bayonets to dig it up with. Soldiers are as careful to carry their spades along as they are to carry their guns.

Company M was ordered to the front. Advanced some 250 yards and deployed as skirmishers on the left of Gen. Harrison's Brigade. Captain gave me the following instruction which he had received when ordered out. "There is a [Confederate] line of battle in front. You are not to fire a gun under any circumstance until that line retreats and passes you. You will then fight for every inch of ground as you fall back and not to retire on the works unless the enemy go with you." "Alright captain, will try and obey orders." Capt. DuBose then left me in command of the right while he went to the left which was in a swamp covered with a dense undergrowth. Sometime afterwards, I saw a line of yankee cavalry about 100 strong charging square down on our position. When in 200 yards of us, I saw a line of infantry rise up and deliver a volley into their ranks. The cavalry without changing their gait obliqued to the right. At the same time, the infantry moved by the left flank still firing on them as they passed. After they had passed to the left of the infantry in our front, I ordered the right of Company M to fire on them, which was kept [up] until they disappeared behind the swamp to our left. I got in three shots as they went by. I saw numbers of horses with empty saddles, but still retaining their places in line. The firing on the right of the company soon brought Capt. DuBose up the line to see what the trouble was. He gave me Hail Columbia for disobeying orders. I told the captain I could not help it for the cavalry was too tempting a shot to let pass. The infantry in our front was the 32nd Georgia from Gen. Harrison's Brigade, who after firing on the cavalry, retreated back to the works.

Not long after the cavalry charge, the infantry in skirmish line attacked our right, which joined Harrison's left. Sharpshooting soon became pretty rapid. I saw an officer in command of Harrison's left that I pointed out to Capt. DuBose. He remained some 50 yards in rear of his line when everything was quiet, but when there was shooting on the line, he would get back at least 100 yards. When the shooting would cool down a little would advance again to retreat at the first fire. Capt. DuBose said he would prefer charges against him for cowardice.

Sometime in the afternoon, a line of battle, about one regiment of infantry, advanced opposite Company M's positions. As they hove in sight, we opened fire on them. Gen. Harrison's Brigade skirmishers retreated to their line of works. As the enemy still advanced, I ordered the right of Company M to fall back which brought Capt. DuBose again to the right, and when he saw the enemy advancing ordered the whole company to fall back. When we started to fall back, I thought we had to carry out orders and go in with the yankees, so I never paid any more attention to the men but fought my way back from tree to tree. When I arrived at the little branch in front of the works, the yankees were not 50 yards to my left and rear. I crossed the little stream and taken a position behind the root of a tree that had blown down. After firing several shots from that place, I thought it was about time the regiment was opening on the enemy's line. So I made for the works which were not more than 30 yards distant. When I jumped on top of the works, I was worse scared than I ever was in my life. I expected to find the Regulars where I left them, and therefore was in no hurry to get to the works, believing that our officers were then watching me. Would have preferred being shot in front of the works than to have rushed over them like I was scared. Instead of the Regulars in the works, I found it occupied by a line of boys who would have killed me before I could have entered the works if they had commenced firing before I entered the works. There was not a Regular in sight. So jumping over the works [I] took my stand in rear of them and opened fire on the yankee line not more than 40 yards distant from our works to the left of me.

The troops in front of the yankees brought them to a halt and finally forced them back. The boys where I jumped over wanted to know if the yankees were coming. I told them yes, and if they did not go to shooting like rip, the yankees would be over the works and kill the last one of them. I got them to shooting, but don't think one of them ever saw the yankees and they were not more than 40 yards away. They stuck down in the trenches and poked their guns over the works and fired. One officer lying stretched at full length tried to make me lie down. Said I would be killed if I did not. The enemy having accomplished his undertaking (feeling our lines), retreated back some 200 yards.

I saw a company on my right from Fort Gaines, Ga., under Capt. Cullens and Lt. Turnipseed. Among them were the McArthurs[16] and Andy Clemens[17] from near Cotton Hill [in Clay County, Ga.]. I was glad to see the boys. It was then getting dark and the troop in the works were ordered to throw out a picket line. I then saw the effects of regular discipline. There was a detail made from each company and nearly every one the 1st sergeant detailed had some excuse to make. Had either been on duty last or was sick and did not feel able to go. Finally some good soldier who had probably been on duty last would volunteer and go. Not so in the Regulars. Whenever the orderly sergeant details a man for duty, nothing short of the surgeon of the regiment can keep him from going. And he goes without grumbling about it either.

While watching the discipline among those troops, Capt. DuBose sent back after me. The company, on arriving at the works and not finding the Regulars, had formed and marched about one-half mile to our left, where our brigade was in position. By dark our entire line was confronted by the enemy some 200 yards in front, where they built fires and were busy cooking, perfectly indifferent to the proximity of our lines. About nine o'clock at night, our lines were withdrawn, marching in the direction of Black River with the rain coming down in sheets and the mud knee deep.

BATTLE OF BENTONVILLE, NORTH CAROLINA

March 17, continued the retreat towards Bentonville, marching 10 miles and crossing one prong of the Black Water River. While wading this stream Gen. Hardee and staff rode past us. He certainly looks dejected and care worn, his uniform being badly soiled and riding a poor rawboned horse. March 18, Hardee's troops marched five miles towards Bentonville. March 19, Gen. Hardee's troops crossed the Black Water River at Bentonville and formed a junction with Gen. J. E. Johnston's forces by way of Columbia, S.C., and Gen. Braxton Bragg's forces by way of Wilmington, N.C. Line of battle was formed across the Goldsboro Road on which Gen. Sherman's forces were marching. A general engagement ensued about 2:00 P.M. The Confederates, led by Gen. Hardee in person, captured two lines of the enemy's works and attacked the third line, but had to retire after several hours of hard fighting. Gen. Hardee led his old Western Corps, leaving Gen. Bragg in command of Hardee's Sea Coast Troops.[18] I saw Gen. Bragg for the first time on his horse sitting in rear of our brigade, which was held in reserve.

The rattle of musketry and the deadly roar of artillery told us there was some desperate fighting in our front. I saw the fewest men running out of battle I have ever seen while lying in the rear as reinforcements. While everyone knows that the Confederacy is on its last legs, still our boys fight as desperate as ever. It makes me feel sad to hear the old soldiers talk about the hopelessness of the cause [and] their hard and faithful service to the Confederacy. Now to have to give up everything and probably lose life itself in the windup makes it still harder to bear. While there was hope of our independence at some future day, life was held lightly in comparison to the cause we were fighting for. Now it seems like life is being thrown away as it will accomplish nothing.

March 20, heavy skirmishing throughout the day. Gen. Sherman trying to flank us on our left. McLaws' Division ordered from the right to the left of the line where we threw up heavy works out of logs and light wood knots, then covering over with dirt. We then placed on top of the works a line of head logs, believing that the pine timber was too heavy for the enemy to use artillery.[19]

March 21, heavy skirmishing in front of Gen. McLaws' Division. The enemy captured our rifle pits and drove our skirmishers in on the works. The yankee skirmishers charged up nearly to our breastworks. Some of the 5th Georgia boys jumped over our works and collared several of them and brought them into the works. On discovering our works, the Federals beat a hasty retreat. Our skirmish line was then ordered forward to retake our rifle pits. As the boys mounted our works and advanced, a private in Company C lagged behind his comrades and finally got behind a tree and stayed. Col. Wayne ordered the 1st sergeant of his company to shoot him, but he begged the colonel to excuse him. Col. Wayne told the sergeant to hand him his rifle, which he did. Col. Wayne placed the gun to his shoulder and called to the fellow behind the tree to advance, which he did in double-quick time. He knew it was death in the rear and he might stand some showing on the front.

The skirmishers recaptured their rifle pits and the very thing we thought impossible was what happened. The enemy turned their artillery on us, firing solid shot. The first one grazed one of our head logs. Almost in the twinkling of an eye every log was on the ground and the shelling was kept up for some time. On our extreme left the yankees tried to cut our forces off from the bridge across the Black Water, but were handsomely repulsed.

March 22, Gen. Johnston had withdrawn his army across the Black

Water River by sunrise, and marched 10 miles in the direction of Smithfield. Gen. Sherman continued his march unmolested to Goldsboro, N.C. March 23, crossed the north prong of the Black Water and went into bivouacs. March 24, the army crossed the Neuse River, passed through Smithfield and beyond the Raleigh and Goldsboro Railroad, going into camps two miles beyond.

Now That
Is All Over

ARMY REORGANIZED

Rations are getting extremely scarce. For instance, since being in this
camp I have paid one dollar per ear for corn to parch, and thought I
was extremely lucky to get it for that. At the same time, knew it had
been stolen from some poor old horse that needed it as bad as I did,
but hunger does not make a man feel very charitably inclined. April
3, Gen. Hardee's Corps, composed of McLaws', Hokes',[1] and
Taliaferro's divisions, was reviewed by Gens. Johnston and Hardee.
The generals and their staffs make a fine display in their new and
flashy uniforms, but the poor soldier boys in their rags don't cut much
of a shine. April 4, 1865, Gen. Johnston reviewed the Western Army,
composed of five divisions.

April 7, Gen. Johnston and Gov. [Zebulon B.] Vance of North
Carolina reviewed Gen. Hardee's Corps. Gen. Hardee is a very
conspicuous-looking officer mounted on a large, fine-looking dark
chestnut charger, and had the reputation of being the finest horseman
in the 4th U.S. Cavalry[2] before the war. Gen. Johnston is quite a
dashing-looking officer, and rides a small but well-groomed charger.
Gov. Vance is a brainy-looking man, and represents the Tar Heel
State.

April 9, Gen. Johnston's Army was reorganized and consolidated.

The 1st Ga. Regulars, 47th Regiment, and Bonaud's 28th Ga. Battalion was placed in one regiment. The 1st Regiment of Georgia Regulars formed five companies of the 1st, three of the 47th, and two of the 28th, with R. A. Wayne colonel, H. D. D. Twiggs lieutenant colonel, and the Maj. Hazzard[3] from the 47th Regiment placed in Gen. George P. Harrison's Brigade, Gen. Walthall's[4] Division, Stewart's[5] Corps. The 47th and 28th kicked like anything on being assigned to the Regulars, but it was of no use.[6]

April 10, [the] army left camps near Smithfield and marched 15 miles towards Raleigh. Considerable shelling in our rear said to be at the Neuse River (the last hostile gun I heard during the war). April 11, marched two miles beyond Raleigh. Officers rode along the line of march telling the men that Gen. Lee was holding his own along the banks of the Appomattox, after causing the enemy the loss of 30,000 men. "So cheer up boys, don't let your spirits go down, for there are many a girl that I know well, waiting for you in town." April 12, marched 16 miles towards Hillsborough. April 13, marched 16 miles, camped in two miles of Hillsborough. Sherman's Army said to be in hot pursuit. April 14, marched 18 miles in the direction of Greensboro. Rained all night.

While on the march, I saw quite a laughable incident occur. A division of cavalry was passing in the column of infantry on the march and on reaching a creek that we had to cross, the cavalry forded the stream and the infantry crossed on some rails just above the ford. The crossway being narrow, the column had to undouble, causing them to crowd up. Some of the cavalry asked the boys if they did not wish to ride over. At least a half dozen would make for the horsemen to ride. He would tell them to get on behind him. The cut in the road was about level with the horse's back, and by riding up close the foot soldier could get on. The cavalryman was very kind and seemed anxious to carry the poor fellow over the creek. But just as the soldier made a movement to put his foot over the horse's back to sit down on him, the horseman would stick spurs to his horse and jump from under him, leaving him sitting in the creek and the horseman dashing up the hill on the other side. The boys would have to lie down and roll over and yelled themselves hoarse. I saw while standing there at least three ducked in the same way.

April 15, marched 12 miles through rain and mud and camped for the night. We learned here for the first time that Gen. Lee's Army had surrendered to Gen. [Ulysses S.] Grant on the Appomattox the 9th day of April and were paroled on the field and allowed to return home. We found it out by seeing some of Gen. Lee's men on their way home. The announcement ruined the morale of Gen. Johnston's Army, as it was nothing more than a howling mob after that. April 16, marched within five miles of Greensboro where we went into camps. Here I obtained Gen. Lee's farewell address to his army which I will give you in full, as anything in connection with our most illustrious general will be of interest.

Headquarters, Army of Northern Virginia
April 10, 1865

General Order No. 9

After four years of arduous service marked by unsurpassed courage and fortitude, the Army of Northern Virginia has been compelled to yield to overwhelming numbers and resources. I need not tell the brave survivors of so many hard-fought battles who have remained steadfast to the last that I have consented to this result from no distrust to them, but feeling that valor and devotion could accomplish nothing that would compensate the loss that would have attended the continuance of the conflict I determined to avoid the useless sacrifice of those whose past services have endeared them to their countrymen. By the terms of agreement officers and men can return to their homes and remain until exchanged. You will take with you the satisfaction which proceeds from the consciousness of duty well performed and I earnestly pray that a merciful God will extend to you blessings and protection.

With an unceasing admiration of your constancy and devotion to your country, a grateful remembrance of your kind and generous consideration of myself. I bid you an affectionate farewell.

Signed R. E. Lee
General[7]

ARMISTICE AT GREENSBORO, NORTH CAROLINA

April 19, an armistice [is] agreed to between the two armies while negotiations are pending between the two governments. All order and discipline was lost in the army when an armistice was agreed to. The camps are nothing more than a mob. Nearly all of the ammunition was destroyed, the men tearing up the cartridges, putting the powder in sacks, and running the balls into bars of lead. The army supplies were carried five miles below our camps towards Raleigh. The soldiers confiscated everything they could get their hands on, consisting of bacon, crackers, chewing and smoking tobacco, leather, and various other things.

Gen. Harrison's Brigade was camped in a grove near the railroad, and the saplings were all weighted down with sides of bacon. What a crazy camp we had. One morning I paid five dollars for one pound of tobacco, and before I had made up one pipe full, Cpls. Smith[8] and Harris of my mess came into camps with as much as they could carry on an army blanket between them. Plug tobacco you can buy for five cents a plug in silver. Wild rumors of all kinds are flying through camps. Grapevine and haversack dispatches are in demand.

Every soldier in the army knows how the army is situated. Gen. Sherman is said to have 80,000 men on our trail. Gen. Grant has 130,000 men by way of Danville, Va., and Gen. Stoneman[9] has cut our line of communication between Greensboro and Charlotte with 20,000 cavalry. To contend against the Federal armies, Gen. Johnston has all told about 30,000 men. At one time rumor will have it that Gen. Johnston will make an attempt to cut his way through the enemy lines. Another will say Gen. Johnston is going to surrender his army and all will be sent to a Northern prison. And as the rumor spreads it gains influence, and by night the soldiers will begin to call at headquarters in howling mobs asking our generals to enlighten them. And all of them will respond when called upon, but the boys are not any wiser than they were before. All of the officers tell the men to stand to their colors as they have always done and meet their fate like men. I have heard Gen. George P. Harrison talk to our brigade and cry like a baby, begging his men to stand firm to the last.

At night I can hear the tramp of soldiers' feet on the railroad leaving the army to try and make their escape homewards, which is a desperate undertaking as Gen. Lee's Army has just passed through the country and cleaned up pretty much everything to eat, besides the risk of being captured by the enemy. Two companies of the Regulars went to Col. Wayne's headquarters to tell him goodbye, but he persuaded them not to go.

One morning the sergeant major called on me for a guard detail of one noncommissioned officer and three privates. I detailed the men and all of them refused to go on duty. I reported the matter to Capt. DuBose, who talked to them, but they still refused. And it was the same thing in every company in the regiment. I made sure Col. Wayne would have them all arrested, but he did not. He talked and reasoned with them, stating that the guard was not as a punishment but to keep order and cleanliness in the camps. But it was all no go, as the boys had decided they had done their last guard duty and stuck to it.

April 25, armistice between Gens. Johnston and Sherman ended at 11:00 A.M.[10] The Confederate forces were ordered into line and marched six miles beyond Greensboro where we went into camps. While on the march thousands of men left their guns by the roadside. Could have followed the line of march by the abandoned guns. The march was simply a rabble. No order, ranks scattered from one side of the road to the other. When we halted at night, the men were notified that all without guns would be arrested. That did not have any effect. Orders were then issued that all men without guns would not be allowed to draw rations. That order cooked their goose and you ought to have seen them making back for a gun.

GENERAL JOHNSTON'S SURRENDER

April 26, the Army of Tennessee under the command of Gen. Joseph E. Johnston, was surrendered to Gen. W. T. Sherman commanding the United States Army. Below is a copy of Gen. Sherman's order:

Headquarters, Military Division of the Mississippi
In the field near Greensboro, N.C., April 27, 1865

Special Field Order
No. 65

The general commanding announces a further suspension of hostilities and a final agreement with Gen. Johnston which terminates the war as to the armies under his command and the country east of the Chattahoochee. Copies of the terms of convention will be furnished Maj. Gens. Schofield,[11] Gillmore,[12] and Wilson, [13] who are specially charged with the execution of its details in the Department of North Carolina, Department of the South, and at Macon and Western Georgia. Capt. Jasper Myers, Ordnance Department U.S.A., is hereby designated to receive the arms &c. at Greensboro, and any commanding officer of a post may receive the arms of any detachment and see that they are properly stored and accounted for. Gen. Schofield will proceed [procure] at once the necessary blanks and supply the army commanders, that uniformity may prevail, and great care must be taken that the terms and stipulations on our part be fulfilled with the most sempulous [scrupulous] fidelity whilst those imposed on, our hitherto enemies, be received in a spirit becoming a brave and generous army. Army commanders may at once loan to the inhabitants such of the captured mules, horses, wagons, and vehicles as can be spared from immediate use, and the commanding generals of armies may issue provisions, animals, and any public supplies that can be spared to relieve present events and to encourage the inhabitants to renew their peaceful pursuits and to restore the relations of friendship among their fellow citizens and countrymen. Foraging will forthwith cease, and when necessity or long marches compel the taking of forage provisions or any kind of private property, compensation will be made on the spot, or when the disbursing officers are not provided with forms, vouchers will be given in proper form payable at the nearest military depot.

By Order of Maj. Gen. W. T. Sherman
D. M. Dayton
A. A. General

Headquarters, Army of Tennessee
Near Greensboro, N.C.
April 28, 1865

A true copy
Kinlock Falconer
A. A. General[14]

April 27, Gen. Johnston's Army was paid one dollar and 16 cents in silver and Gen. Johnston sent his chief of staff to Charlotte to

President Davis to get more money for his men, but failed to get any.[15] Frasier and Harris, two of my messmates, secured two old geese and I tried my hand at cooking them. The longer I boiled them, the tougher and blacker they got. Finally I had to give it up and eat them the best we could. My first and last geese.

April 28, the army turned over their guns to our ordnance officers, who turned them over to Gen. Sherman's ordnance officers. So we surrendered our guns without seeing a Federal soldier. Gen. Johnston was allowed to retain a fifth of his arms until each regiment marched to the capitol of its state so as to keep order while on the homeward march. Besides, the army was allowed sufficient transportation to carry them home. May 1, army paroled, and each regiment was ordered to march to the capitol of their respective states and there be disbanded. Below is a form of parole:

Greensboro, N.C.
May 1, 1865

In accordance with the terms of the military convention entered into on the twenty-sixth day of April, 1865, between Gen. Joseph E. Johnston commanding the Confederate Army and Maj. Gen. W. T. Sherman commanding the United States Army in North Carolina, 1st Sergeant W. H. Andrews, Company D, 1st Ga. Regulars, has given his solemn obligation not to take up arms against the government of the United States until properly released from this obligation, and is permitted to return home and not to be disturbed by the United States authorities so long as he observes this obligation and obey the laws in force where he may reside.

J. L. Dow   James R. DuBose
Capt. and Prov. Marshal U.S.A.   Captain, C.S.A.
Special Commissioner   Commanding

THE HOMEWARD MARCH

May 3, 1865. The Army of Tennessee started on its homeward march going 18 miles in the direction of Salisbury. At night the boys were pretty badly wasted, as scarcely a halt had been made to rest. Orders were issued that all soldiers not up when the roll was called at night would not receive any rations. We had rice bread and pickle pork which Gen. Sherman issued to our army to march home on. Rice bread does very well when warm, but when cold would do to make solid shot out of. But we ought not to grumble as it will preserve life until we get home. No one but a soldier can imagine how we felt starting home. I have been in the army since February, '61. Over four years hard service, never knowing what day would be my last. Now that is all over and we can look forward with the hopes of a brighter day coming, for we have seen nothing but dark ones during the war.

While it is a bitter pill to have to come back into the Union, don't think there is much regret for the loss of the Confederacy. The treatment the soldiers have received from the government in various ways put them against it. The army has been half clothed and half starved, besides they have received but little of the worthless money due them. Numbers of Confederate soldiers who went home to aid their starving families and were afterwards shot for desertion would most likely be with us today if the government had fulfilled its contract by paying them off so they could have sent the money home to their needy families.

On May 4 marched 23 miles to the Pee Dee River. Most of the men are straggling, not able to keep up. When leaving camps this morning, the officers at the head of the column put their horses in a brisk walk and kept it up, not halting to rest. Consequently they are scattered along the road for miles, and some of them will be late in the night getting up with the command if they get up at all.

May 5. This morning in company with Capt. James R. DuBose and J. D. Anthony, with 11 noncommissioned officers, left the Regulars and are marching as a special escort to Gen. Walthall. He has our baggage hauled for us, while we guard the wagon trains at night to keep our soldiers from stealing the stock. Every man is making for home, and the railroads being torn up, have to walk. So if he can press a horse or mule into service, he can ride. And the only way to keep the stock is to guard them with loaded guns during the night.

Marched to Concord Station, passing through Salisbury making 25 miles. May 6, continued the march by way of Charlotte, Yorkville, Unionville, Laurens, Cokesburg, Abbeville, and Washington, Ga., where we arrived on the 14th. May 15, left our guns where we camped. Thought if the yankees wanted them, they might go and get them.

Went to J. R. DuBose, Sr., where we bid farewell to Capt. James R. DuBose and Capt. J. D. Anthony. A sad farewell having served together since July, '61. Both were kind and gallant officers, and the boys honored and respected them for it. I certainly felt strongly attached to Capt. DuBose, having been in service so long and passed through so many dangers and hardships together. He was a brave man, a gallant soldier, and a Christian gentleman. What more could I say for him. He was the same at all times. Whether on the march, in bivouac, or on the battlefield, ever the brave, cool, and considerate officer. Always striving to relieve the hardships and wants of his men. While he made no outside show or pretention to religion, he was a devout Christian man and I believe left the army as pure and unsullied as when he entered it.

James Rembert DuBose was born the 7th day of January, 1837, near Washington, Wilkes County, Georgia, and was named after his father. His mother's maiden name was Martha Pope Hill. He was educated at Washington, Ga., and started to farming about 13 miles from Washington when 19 years of age. He married Miss E. Caroline Spann of Mississippi the first day of October, 1857.

In the winter of '60 and '61, he joined a volunteer company known as the Irwin Guard. In June, '61, his company was ordered out to Richmond, Va., where they were mustered into the Confederate States' service as a company [Company A] in the 9th Regiment Ga. Volunteers. In July, '61, he was commissioned by President Davis 2nd lieutenant and ordered to report to the 1st Regiment of Georgia Regulars for duty, which he did at Camp Walker near Bull Run, Va., and was assigned to Company M sometime in August. Afterwards promoted to 1st lieutenant, and in the winter of '64 was promoted to captain of Company M, Capt. Hill having been promoted to major, and Capt. Miller Grieve to lieutenant colonel. As a man and a gentleman, I am proud to have served under him. In all of our hardships and dangers we passed through, he was never heard to complain. (He is now an honored and useful citizen of Asheville, N.C. I receive letters of the kindest consideration from him which I more than appreciate, holding him in greater respect and admiration than any man I have ever seen. As you find a man in the army, you can take him that way all the time. I certainly wish Capt. DuBose a long and happy life, and when we pass over the river, hope to meet him on the other shore.)

After bidding them goodbye, we boarded the train for Camak where we saw the Federal Guard on their way back from Augusta, Ga., where they had been to carry President Davis who had been captured in the lower part of the state.[16] They told us they had the rope ready to hang him with. Would have let him off if he had given the Confederate soldiers the money he left Richmond with. We then boarded a freight train for Atlanta. It was packed as long as men could get on it. Mostly men going to the nearest military post to get paroled. Our boys said some of them had moss on their backs they had been hiding out in the swamps so long. Can't swear to that, but it might have been so.

May 16, sometime during the night, the train arrived in Atlanta. The sunrise gun at the yankee headquarters roused me up, and on looking out of the car the scene that met my eyes will never be forgotten. The cars had stopped in the street and just opposite the end of a triangular block. On the other side of the street south of where I was, there was a large building in which was the yankee headquarters. In front of the door was a small field piece, the firing of which had disturbed my slumbers. Near the cannon was a tall flagstaff with the Stars and Stripes floating to the breeze. Most of the buildings had been burned by Gen. Sherman and nothing but blackened walls remained standing. On the ground were a number of siege guns scattered about. Altogether it was a sad and gloomy scene to look upon, and one I hope to never see again. Boarded the train for Macon at 5:00 A.M. and arrived there at half past one. Macon is full to overflowing with Negro troops, and as impudent as the devil himself.

May 17, went on the cars from Macon to Cuthbert, Ga. Home, sweet home. How well I can appreciate it after four years and nearly three months' service. Four of the best years of my life thrown away, or at least nothing in return for it except a shattered constitution. At the same time *I have no regrets to offer. I believed I was right and acted accordingly.* I have tried to make a good soldier and perform all duties required of me, but since the war is ended will try and be as good a citizen for Uncle Sam as I was a soldier for the Confederacy.

W. H. Andrews, 1st Sergeant, Company M
1st Regiment, Georgia Regulars

Epilogue

We do not know a great deal about Andrews' postwar life. He apparently worked as a carpenter for a while. He is known to have lived in Dawson, about 40 miles northeast of Fort Gaines, where he married Amanda Avent. (We do not know if she was the little sweetheart mentioned in the memoir.)

Not long after his marriage, he and his wife moved to the Atlanta area. He lived in Fulton and then DeKalb County until 1896, when he moved to Sugar Valley in Gordon County. For a while he was a farmer. Meanwhile, his wife, Amanda, had died in or before 1888.

In 1900 when Andrews applied for a veteran's pension, he testified that he was then unable to work because of a "double Hernea" that had weakened his back. The certifying doctors called the condition a hernia "of the very worse form." Andrews stated that he, his son, and his two daughters had been supported by help from friends, neighbors, and his wife's mother. His friend and old wartime commander J. R. DuBose, writing in support of his application, praised Andrews as "a born soldier always." The pension was granted.

As late as 1909 Andrews listed his post office as Sugar Valley, but some time that year or the next he moved to the Atlanta area. Eventually he settled into a house on Grant Street, and there he died on November 14, 1920, after a long illness.

Andrews' return to Atlanta may have been prompted by a desire to be near his children. His son, J. W. Andrews, and one of his daughters, Mrs. R. S. Cox, both lived in Atlanta. The other daughter is not mentioned in Andrews' obituary and may have predeceased her father.

William Hill Andrews was buried in his daughter's family plot in Hollywood Cemetery. The graveyard is in northwest Atlanta, not far from the Chattahoochee River.

Appendix

Publications by William Hill Andrews

The following chronological list contains all known publications by William H. Andrews.

"1st Georgia Regulars Through the War Between the States." Atlanta: N.p., 1891. (A copy of this pamphlet is in the Huntington Library, San Marino, Calif.)

Articles from the Atlanta *Journal*

"The Fight at Garnett's Farm." February 23, 1901.

"'Tige' Anderson's Brigade on the Rappahannock." May 11, 1901.

"Gen. 'Tige' Anderson's Brigade at Thoroughfare Gap." May 25, 1901.

"Tige Anderson's Brigade at Second Manassas." June 8, 1901.

"Tige Anderson's Brigade at Ox Hill." June 22, 1901.

"Tige Anderson's Brigade at Crampton's Gap." July 27, 1901.

"Gen. 'Tige' Anderson's Brigade at Sharpsburg." August 24, 1901.

"An Incident at the Battle of Sharpsburg, Maryland." October 19, 1901.

"Tige Anderson's Brigade at Fredericksburg." November 16, 1901.

"First Georgia Regulars at Fort Pulaski, Ga." December 21, 1901.

"First Georgia Regulars at Lewisville, Va. Other Reminiscences of the Campaign." February 1, 1902.

"First Georgia Regulars at Siege of Yorktown, Va." March 1, 1902.

"First Georgia Regulars at the Nine Mile Road, Virginia." April 26, 1902.

"First Georgia Regulars from Nine Mile Road to Turkey Bend." May 24, 1902.

"First Georgia Regulars at the Battle of Olustee, Florida." June 21, 1902.

"First Georgia Regulars at the Battle of Waterloo, S.C." July 12, 1902.

"The First Georgia Regulars at the Siege of Savannah." August 16, 1902.

"The First Georgia Regulars in the Swamps of South Carolina." September 6, 1902.

"First Georgia Regulars at the Pee Dee Bridge." September 27, 1902.

"First Georgia Regulars at Averysboro and Bentonville." October 18, 1902.

"First Georgia Regulars at Johnston's Surrender." November 15, 1902.

ARTICLES FROM THE *CONFEDERATE VETERAN*

"Tige Anderson's Brigade at Sharpsburg." 16, no. 11 (November 1908), pp. 578-80.

"Hardships of Georgia Regulars." 17, no. 5 (May 1909), pp. 230-32.

"Honor Roll of the First Georgia Regulars." 17, no. 8 (August 1909), pp. 412-13.

(As noted in the section on the memoir, all of the articles in the *Journal* and the *Confederate Veteran* were taken from the corresponding chapter in the memoir.)

NOTES

INTRODUCTION

1. Four of the boys served in the Confederate army, and their fates are told in the memoir. James L. Andrews is known to have died as a child, and he may have predeceased his father. John Franklin Andrews was listed in the 1860 census as a twenty-year-old "watchman" for a house (perhaps a mercantile house or other business establishment). Why he did not serve in the Civil War is unknown. He could have been physically disqualified, or he might have died between the time of the census and the outbreak of the war.

2. Amanda Malvina Andrews (born c. 1845 or 1846), who is mentioned briefly in the memoir, and Sarah Jane Andrews (born c. 1846 or 1847).

3. Jane T. Andrews' fate is unknown, although the memoir indicates that she was alive during the war. On May 26, 1861, a "Mrs. Jane Andrews" married Charles N. Johnston. Cross-Index of Marriage Records, Clay County, 1840-92, copy in the Clay County Public Library, Fort Gaines. It is not certain that this Mrs. Andrews was the mother of the memoirist. Efforts to obtain information on Johnston have yielded nothing.

FEATHERBED SOLDIERS

1. Brig. Gen. (Bvt. Maj. Gen.) Edmund Pendleton Gaines (1777-1849) established the fort in 1816 as one of a series of military posts intended to protect whites in the lower Chattahoochee Valley against Indians who often raided the area from Spanish-held Florida. The records are not clear, but it seems that there may have been another military post on the site as early as 1814. The town was chartered in 1830; the county formed in 1854. See James W. Silver, *Edmund Pendleton Gaines: Frontier General* (Baton Rouge, 1949), pp. 54-88; P. C. King, Jr., *Fort Gaines and Environs* (Auburn, Ala., 1976), pp. 13-14, 16, 19, 23, 30-31; and Clay County Public Library (comp.), *The History of Clay County* (n.p., 1976), pp. 2-11.

2. The Southwestern Railroad ran southwest from Macon, through Fort Valley, to several termini, one of which was Fort Gaines, which the railroad reached in 1858.

3. Mount Gilead Baptist Church, seven miles northeast of Fort Gaines, was organized in 1822. The grave is unmarked.

4. Georgia seceded on January 19, 1861. By early February a total of seven Deep South states had withdrawn from the Union. The remaining four Confederate states (Virginia, North Carolina, Tennessee, and Arkansas) did not secede until after the war began in April.

5. Unidentified. No officer named Brown or Browne is listed in the service records of the 9th Georgia. This may be a reference to "Col." J. E. Brown who commanded the company in the 1830s when it was first organized. Andrews did not formally enlist in the Fort Gaines Guards or, if he did so, he left the unit before it formally went into service.

6. Richard A. Turnipseed became colonel of the 9th Georgia in April 1862. He resigned effective July 26, 1862, for medical reasons (measles and chronic diarrhea). Andrews met him again in the summer of 1863 in Tallahassee, Fla., and again in 1865 in the closing military operations of the war.

7. John G. Webb, who became lieutenant colonel of the 9th Georgia and lost an arm at Reams' Station, Va., August 25, 1864.

8. William A. Tennille was elected 1st lieutenant in the 9th Georgia June 11,

1861, and promoted to captain in 1863. He served on the staff of Brig. Gen. George T. Anderson and of Lt. Gen. James Longstreet until retired by a medical board in January 1865 for chronic diarrhea. (Orig. Tennell.)

9. Francis T. Cullens became captain of Co. K, 1st Ga. Regulars. He resigned for medical reasons (rheumatism) on January 11, 1862. Andrews was to meet him again in 1863 and 1865. Hereafter, unless otherwise specified, all men below general officer grade were members of the 1st Ga. Regulars, and only their company will be used in designating their unit.

10. Orrin W. Cone, later 1st sergeant of Co. K. On December 17, 1861, he was discharged because of rheumatism. The first name is Owen in some records. (Orig. O. H. Cone.)

11. Hiram A. Morgan became 1st sergeant of Co. K and served through the war, surrendering with the regiment at Greensboro, N.C., in April 1865.

12. Lewis B. Wheeler became a corporal in Co. B and surrendered with the regiment at Greensboro, N.C., in April 1865.

13. Boyle, a private in Co. M, was killed at Yorktown, Va., April 5, 1862.

14. L. B. Standifer (initials only in records), a private in Co. D, was transferred to the 1st Ga. Regular Art. (also called Read's or Maxwell's Battery) in August 1862. (Orig. Stendifer.)

15. Thomas C. Beall served as a corporal in Co. M. He was later quartermaster of the regiment. Elected 2d lieutenant April 30, 1862, he resigned because of disability two months later. Andrews wrote in 1909 that Beall was killed in the summer of 1862 when he fell (or jumped) from a train. (Orig. Bealle.)

16. Unidentified. As Andrews relates below, he was never officially in the regiment.

17. Washington L. Andrews, private in Co. M and brother of William H. Andrews. Washington's fate is detailed below in the account of the Seven Days' Battle.

18. Lavin, private, Co. M, was transferred to the 1st Ga. Regular Art. (also called Read's or Maxwell's Battery) in July 1862. He deserted that month.

19. Probably William G. Rowland, corporal, Co. K, who deserted from the regiment at Salkehatchie, S.C., February 4, 1865.

20. John Ash was detailed for duty at Oglethorpe Barracks. He was reduced to private on November 27, 1861, and transferred to Capt. Charles Daniell's Ga. Art. Battery in November 1863. He was reappointed a sergeant in 1864.

21. Unidentified. One F. E. Charlton, of Clarkesville, Ga., appears in Confederate service records (but not in those of the 1st Georgia) as a hospital steward, pharmacist, and assistant surgeon. It is possible that he was in state service in 1861 and was the doctor to whom Andrews refers.

22. William G. Gill is not in the regiment's records, but he was a former U.S. Army officer in Georgia service early in 1861 and was stationed in the area. He was later assigned as ordnance officer on the staff of Gen. P. G. T. Beauregard. He died in service at Columbus, Miss., on June 27, 1862, and seems never to have been on Bragg's staff.

23. Gen. Braxton Bragg commanded the Army of Tennessee in 1862 and 1863. In 1864 and 1865 he served as military adviser to President Jefferson Davis. At the end of the war he commanded troops in North Carolina where Andrews and the 1st Ga. Regulars served with him.

24. John L. Branch was appointed 1st lieutenant May 22, 1861. As Andrews indicates below, he transferred to the 8th Georgia and was killed in action at First Manassas on July 21, 1861.

25. George P. Harrison, appointed adjutant of the regiment April 8, 1861. In 1862

he became colonel of the 5th Ga. State Troops (a six-month regiment) and then colonel of the 32d Georgia. He reappears in the latter part of Andrews' narrative, commanding a brigade in the last year of the war.

26. Almost certainly Lt. Lawrence Cecil Berrien, who seems to have been briefly with the regiment in the spring of 1861 prior to joining, on May 21, the 9th Georgia. In March 1863 he was elected a 2d lieutenant in Co. E. He was a native of Savannah, and it would have been natural for him to have been with the regiment there in 1861.

27. Harrison was among a group of Rebel officers who may or may not have been generals. Several officers who acted in the capacity of general officers, were often called "general," and even signed themselves as such, never completed—and in some cases did not begin—the formal legal process that was necessary for becoming a Confederate general. That procedure required appointment by the president to general officer grade and confirmation of the appointment by the Confederate Senate. (A few officers were appointed under a May 21, 1861, law that did not require Senate approval of the appointment.) Some officers serving in the distant Trans-Mississippi Department were "promoted" to general by the commander of that department but never appointed by the president or approved by the Senate. Ezra J. Warner does not list Harrison as a Rebel general. For a discussion of the problem, see Warner's *Generals in Gray: Lives of the Confederate Commanders* (Baton Rouge, 1959), pp. xiv-xix; and for Harrison's case in particular, Mark Mayo Boatner III, *The Civil War Dictionary* (New York, 1959), pp. 378-79.

28. William Duncan Smith, Jr., who graduated from West Point in 1846 and served in the 2d U.S. Dragoons until he resigned to go with his native Georgia into the Confederacy. He served briefly with the 1st Ga. Regulars and then on the staff of Brig. Gen. A. R. Lawton at Savannah. He soon became colonel of the 20th Georgia and then brigadier general. He died of yellow fever at Charleston, S.C., in October 1862.

29. Unidentified. Four Cpl. Joneses are listed as having served in the regiment: James L. in Co. A; Robert H. in Co. H; Thomas in Co. F; and Willis R. in Co. A.

30. Maj. Gen. (Bvt. Lt. Gen.) Winfield Scott, commanding the U.S. Army and a very large man, well over six feet in height and, by 1861, weighing more than 300 pounds.

31. Alvin D. Parr (first name "Oliver" in some records) was a private in Cos. M and L who, as Andrews relates below, acquired the nickname "Joe Dutton." He was paroled at Augusta, Ga., May 23, 1865.

32. William W. Kirkland, a 1st lieutenant and adjutant of the 1st Regiment of the Georgia State Army from whence the 1st Ga. Regulars evolved. Kirkland was on duty at Oglethorpe Barracks early in 1861. Transferred to other duty, he became a brigadier general in 1863.

33. Edward Willis served briefly with the regiment at Savannah early in 1861. Later colonel of the 12th Georgia, he was mortally wounded May 31, 1864. He was never a general, as Andrews asserts below. See note 27 above.

34. John Milledge, Jr., 1st lieutenant, Co. C, resigned from the regiment May 21, 1862, to take command of a battery of Georgia light artillery of which he had been elected captain and which he commanded for the remainder of the war. He was state librarian at different times between April 6, 1888, and his death on November 6, 1897.

35. William R. Mansfield, Co. F, detailed to hospital duty March 20, 1861.

36. Pvt. William A. Clower, Co. G, enlisted at Athens February 23, 1861. He was promoted to corporal October 18, 1861. He was present for duty until the roll for May-June 1864 (last on file), which shows him under arrest.

37. Appointed colonel of the regiment March 15, 1861, Williams died February

6, 1862, while on sick furlough.

38. Probably Alexander McGhee Wallace, who became captain of Co. L, February 1, 1861. Later lieutenant colonel of the 36th Georgia, he was so badly wounded in November 1863 that he resigned for disability in April 1864.

39. Hamilton (initials only in records) was appointed captain February 1, 1861. On July 24, 1861, he transferred to Co. A. On July 14, 1862, he was elected major of Cabell's (Ga.) Art. Battalion. He was on medical leave from late 1864 to the end of the war.

40. Peyton L. Wise was appointed a 1st lieutenant in the company on March 21, 1861. He died of disease in Richmond, Va., on November 17, 1861. (Orig. Wade.)

41. J. F. Bass (initials only in records) was appointed a 2d lieutenant in the company on April 10, 1861. On October 3, 1861, he transferred to Co. F. He resigned in January 1861.

42. William Martin commanded Co. B. He was elected lieutenant colonel of the regiment in February 1862 and died while on sick leave in October 1864.

43. Paine (or Payne) was appointed a 1st lieutenant in Co. E on January 28, 1861. Elected captain January 24, 1863, he later served as assistant quartermaster of the regiment and was eventually detailed for ordnance duty at Savannah.

44. See note 28 above.

45. Fort Pulaski surrendered to Federal forces in April 1862 after a thirty-hour bombardment by Federal artillery on Tybee Island knocked great gaps in the masonry walls and threatened to detonate the magazine where most of the fort's ammunition was stored.

46. William J. Hardee had been a U.S. Army officer who had authored a widely used manual of infantry tactics. At the beginning of the Civil War he served briefly as colonel commanding the 1st Regiment of the Georgia Army from which the 1st Ga. Regulars evolved. Eventually he became a lieutenant general in the Confederate Army. In the winter of 1864-65 he commanded Rebel forces in the Savannah area and in the Carolinas. The 1st Ga. Regulars served under him then.

47. Brig. Gen. Alexander R. Lawton, then commanding Rebel forces at Savannah and later commander of a brigade that served with the Regulars in Virginia.

48. Unidentified. There are several single ladies named "Howard" listed in the 1860 census for Muscogee County (Columbus). The flag is now at the Fort Pulaski National Monument. (See frontispiece.)

49. Jacob J. Read commanded Co. D. The unit was left in Georgia and eventually was converted into the 1st Ga. Regular Art. (It was also called the Read-Maxwell Battery or Maxwell's Ga. Battery.) Read's name is spelled "Reed" and "Read" in the records. Fort Jackson was part of the river defenses below Savannah.

50. William Joseph Magill commanded Co. A. In February 1862 he became colonel of the regiment. In August 1864, wounds forced him to retire from the service.

51. John D. Walker commanded Co. C. Elected major in June 1861, he was mortally wounded August 30, 1862, at Second Manassas. He died October 3, 1862.

52. Richard A. Wayne commanded Co. E. He became successively major (October 3, 1862), lieutenant colonel (August 3, 1864), and colonel (September 3, 1864). He commanded the regiment in the closing months of the war.

53. John G. Patton commanded Co. F. He was killed August 30, 1862, at Second Manassas. (Orig. John M. Patton.)

54. Lewis H. Kenan commanded Co. I. He resigned July 18, 1864, after being wounded on Johns Island, S.C.

55. Cullens commanded Co. K. See note 9 above.

56. Miller Grieve, Jr., commanded Co. H. He was elected major of the regiment

(August 3, 1864) and lieutenant colonel (September 3, 1864). (Orig. Grieves.)

57. A. A. Franklin Hill served in the artillery until elected captain of Co. A of the regiment June 18, 1861. He served temporarily as captain of Cos. M and L in 1861. At the time covered here, he was with Co. L. In 1864 he was elected major.

Andrews omitted Capt. John S. Fain of Co. G, who later served with the 8th Ga. State Troops, Smith's Legion, and the 65th Georgia and Alexander McGhee Wallace of Co. L (see note 38). It is not certain, however, that Wallace was with the regiment in July 1861. Hill may then have been temporarily in command of Co. L.

58. On July 21, 1861, at Manassas (or Bull Run), Confederate forces under Gens. Joseph E. Johnston and P. G. T. Beauregard routed a Federal army commanded by Maj. Gen. Irvin McDowell. Scott was in Washington, D.C., and did not take part in the battle.

59. Patrick Brennan, Co. M, whose name last appears on the regiment's rolls for October 31, 1861. As Andrews notes below, he acquired the nickname "Mary Ann."

60. Davis often spoke briefly to units as they passed through Richmond on their way to the front. On July 23, however, he was away from the capital until late in the evening. He had been at Manassas and was greeted by wildly celebrating citizens on his return. He probably did not speak to the Regulars that day. Andrews probably confused this day's events with those of some other time or confused Davis with some other speaker.

61. Palmer's appointment as sergeant major was effective June 13, 1861. Prior to that date he had been 5th sergeant of Co. B. He was subsequently (July 18, 1864) elected a lieutenant in Co. M. He was captured at Cheraw, S.C., March 4, 1865, and held at Johnson's Island, Ohio, until released on June 17, 1865.

62. Lewis DeLaigle was a lieutenant when named quartermaster of the regiment effective May 1, 1861. He became a captain in 1864. The name is often spelled "De L'Aigle" or "Lewis D. Laigle." (Orig. DeLegle.)

63. Samuel McConnell was commissary of the regiment in 1861. He resigned in May 1863.

SOME PRETTY HARD CASES IN THE ARMY

1. Brig. Gen. William Henry Talbot Walker was assigned to Confederate forces at Pensacola, Fla., in the summer of 1861, but he spent some time in Virginia during those months. He became a major general and was killed July 22, 1864, in the Battle of Atlanta.

2. Toombs, a Georgia politician with virtually no military competence, served briefly as Confederate secretary of state before being appointed brigadier general July 19, 1861. He resigned from the army in the fall of 1862.

3. On July 18 Confederate and Federal forces clashed along Bull Run in a preliminary engagement that the Southerners called "Bull Run" to distinguish it from the larger Battle of Manassas fought three days later.

4. The Washington Artillery of New Orleans was one of the most famous Confederate artillery commands. Four of its companies fought in Virginia. The Second Company of the battalion was commanded by Capt. Thomas L. Rosser (probably a lieutenant when Andrews saw him). Later transferred to the cavalry, Rosser finished the war a major general.

5. Brig. Gen. Barnard E. Bee of South Carolina and Col. Francis S. Bartow (he was never a general but was often so called) of Georgia were both brigade commanders. The former was mortally wounded and the latter killed on July 21. For the monument see Robert E. L. Krick, "The Civil War's First Monument," *Blue & Gray* 8, no. 4 (April 1991): 32-34.

6. For an account of the family's ordeal see William C. Davis, *Battle at Bull Run: A History of the First Major Campaign of the Civil War* (Garden City, 1977), pp. 204-5.

7. At the Second Battle of Manassas in August 1862 the regiment was in the brigade commanded by Col. (later Brig. Gen.) George T. "Tige" Anderson.

8. Andrews, writing some three decades later, made at least one—and probably two—mistakes in this account. The 11th Alabama did not take part in the Battle of Manassas, and no Col. Williams was killed in that battle. He probably talked with troops from some other unit and simply did not recall either the regiment or the name of the officer.

9. James Ewell Brown ("Jeb") Stuart became a major general and commander of the cavalry of the Army of Northern Virginia. He was mortally wounded in May 1864. Andrews consistently misspelled the name as "Stewart."

10. Early in the war "Black Horse Cavalry" was a term often used for virtually any Confederate mounted unit serving in Virginia. More properly, it was applied to Co. H of the 4th Va. Cavalry.

11. Longstreet became a lieutenant general and commander of the I Corps, Army of Northern Virginia.

12. On May 24, 1861, soon after Federal troops occupied Alexandria, Va., Col. Elmer Ellsworth personally hauled down a Confederate flag flying above the Marshall House Tavern. On his way downstairs, Ellsworth was shot by James T. Jackson, proprietor of the tavern. Jackson, in turn, was promptly killed by one of Ellsworth's men. Ellsworth and Jackson both became martyrs for the cause for which they died.

13. Lewinsville was the scene of several minor affairs in late 1861. The only report of the engagement of September 25 is that of Federal Brig. Gen. William F. Smith printed in U.S. War Department (comp.), *War of the Rebellion: Official Records of the Union and Confederate Armies* (Washington, 1880-1920), ser. 1, 5:215-17. Hereafter this publication is cited as *OR*, with all references to volumes in series 1.

14. John Floyd King, 1st lieutenant, served with Cos. M, L, and A of the regiment before transferring to the 13th Va. Art. Battalion. A major at the end of the war, he served in the U.S. Congress in 1879-87.

15. Benjamin H. Hudson was elected a lieutenant in Co. M on September 2, 1861, and in Co. C on August 30, 1862. Last roll on file, for June 30, 1864, shows him present for duty.

16. Burns (or Berne) became 1st sergeant of Co. M in February 1861. He was later reduced to the ranks. His nickname was "Luney." (See chapter 3, note 16.)

17. Martin L. Brantley was 2d sergeant of Co. M. He later transferred to the 54th Georgia. Captured at Kennesaw Mountain in 1864, he was exchanged in March 1865.

18. See chapter 1, note 37. A Confederate colonel wore as the insignia of his grade three stars on his coat collar. All Confederate general officers wore three stars encircled by a wreath.

19. Technically the "Tigers" were the men of Maj. Chatham R. Wheat's 2d La. Battalion of Infantry. After Wheat was mortally wounded in June 1862, the battalion was broken up and the men reassigned. The name "Tiger" was adopted by the entire brigade (6th, 7th, 8th, and 9th La. regiments) to which Wheat's battalion had been assigned. "Tiger" was a term sometimes used to refer to any Louisiana troops serving in Virginia.

20. Maj. Gen. Gustavus W. Smith. After Beauregard was transferred in the winter of 1861-62, Smith was the second-ranking officer in the army. He was later assigned to the command of the Richmond area, and Andrews had an unfortunate encounter

with his provost guards early in 1863. Smith resigned from the army in February 1863 and spent the remainder of the war in Georgia. In 1864 and 1865 Smith commanded the Georgia Militia.

21. Eli M. Andrews, Co. D, 9th Georgia. As Andrews relates below, Eli died in Chimborazo Hospital in Richmond on April 12, 1862.

22. Joseph DeKalb Andrews, Co. D, 9th Georgia. Wounded and captured at Knoxville, Tenn., in late 1863, he was not exchanged until the war was almost over. He died January 14, 1915, in Montgomery, Ala.

23. DuBose served briefly in the 9th Georgia. He was then elected 1st lieutenant in Co. M of the regiment on July 25, 1861. Later he became captain of the company, and he figures prominently in Andrews' account of the last months of the war. After the war he and Andrews were close friends. Some biographical details on him are included near the end of Andrews' narrative. He died in 1906.

24. William Kearnes, a private, who last appears in extant records as of October 31, 1861. (Orig. Kearns.)

25. Andrew Sloven (also as Slaven), a private, who was wounded at Second Manassas, August 30, 1862. In May 1864 he transferred to the navy.

26. Either James or John Reilly, both privates, who last appear in extant records as of October 31, 1861.

27. Either James R. or John Smith, both privates, who last appear in extant records as of June 30, 1864. John, as Andrews relates below, was with the regiment in 1865.

28. Patrick McCann, a private, who transferred to the navy in May 1864.

29. W. L. Andrews' service record shows that he was detailed as a teamster for Toombs from March 5 to June 1, 1862.

30. Eli M. Andrews died of typhoid fever on April 12, 1862. He is buried in Oakwood Cemetery in Richmond (where many of the Chimborazo dead are buried) in section A, row H, grave 75.

SUCH IS LIFE AND SUCH IS WAR

1. Maj. Gen. John B. Magruder who in 1861 and the first half of 1862 commanded Confederate forces on the peninsula—the area between the James and York rivers east-southeast of Richmond.

2. Civil War artillery was often designated by the weight of the projectile. Hence the gun was a twelve-pounder, not a "12 pound" gun (it was more likely to be a 1,200-pound gun). Napoleon guns, named after the French emperor Louis Napoleon, were the workhorse artillery pieces of the war. Canister was a particularly nasty type of ammunition, designed for close-range use against formations of enemy troops. A gun firing canister spewed out hundreds of small pieces of iron or lead.

3. Copeland, the tallest member of the regiment, was appointed 2d sergeant of Co. F early in 1862 and 1st sergeant in 1864. He surrendered with the regiment on April 26, 1865.

4. Sgt. Thomas J. Lyon, Co. G, was wounded in 1862. He later served with the 37th Ga. Militia Regiment and surrendered at West Point, Ga., in April 1865. (Orig. Lyons.)

5. Andrews obviously meant twenty-four.

6. Thomas Carolen (or Carolan), who last appears in extant records as of October 31, 1861. (Orig. Carolin.)

7. William Garrett, Co. M, was wounded at Malvern Hill, July 1, 1862. In 1863 he was detailed as a hospital steward. The last extant roll on which he is reported, June 30, 1864, shows him present for duty. He figures at several points later on in Andrews' narrative.

8. William A. Bonds, Co. M, was killed near Yorktown on April 5, 1862. Andrews has confused the sequence of the events he describes.

9. James T. Armstrong, Co. I, was appointed 1st sergeant on August 20, 1861, and elected 2d lieutenant on February 6, 1862. He was killed near Yorktown on April 30, 1862.

10. On May 4-5, 1862, the Confederate rear guard under Longstreet fought pursuing Yankees at Williamsburg.

11. On May 7 Federal troops who had ascended the York River landed and clashed with Confederates in the Battle of Eltham's Landing (or Barhamsville, or West Point). After driving back the Yankees, the Rebels continued the retreat to Richmond.

12. E. D. Cherry (initials only in records) served as the regiment's surgeon throughout the war.

13. The Battle of Seven Pines (or Fair Oaks) was fought basically as Andrews describes it. Confused marching and bungled orders hampered Johnston's effort to strike part of McClellan's army while it was isolated by high water in the Chickahominy River. Casualties in the battle were 6,100 Confederates and 5,000 Federals. Gustavus W. Smith temporarily succeeded Johnston, but President Davis wisely decided upon Lee as the permanent replacement.

14. As part of the constant reorganization of the army the regiment was transferred to Andersons' Brigade to replace the 1st Ky. Infantry, which was mustered out of service at the expiration of its one-year enlistment. Anderson was a colonel at the time the transfer was made. He was not promoted to brigadier general until November 1, 1862. The brigade was in the division of Brig. Gen. David R. Jones, which was part of Magruder's command.

15. Toombs was a politician, not a general, and his unprofessional antics doubtless owed much to the fact that there were more voters among the enlisted men than among the officers. They may also have owed something to a reported fondness for alcohol.

16. It is not certain that this word is "break." If so Anderson probably meant that the company had stacked arms prior to being dismissed and Burns was suggesting that the men not unstack their weapons—break the stack (i.e. they would perform no more military duty)—until they were paid. Although Andrews does not so state, it may have been his role in this affair that led to Burns being reduced to private. See chapter 2, note 16.

17. James J. Craft, who last appears on extant rolls as of October 31, 1861.

18. Castle Thunder was a military prison (a converted tobacco warehouse) in Richmond.

19. Sgt. William Jasper won fame in a 1775 battle at Fort Moultrie, S.C., when he raced outside the fort under heavy enemy fire to retrieve a flag that had been shot away by the British. He was killed in November 1779 in a Franco-American assault on the British fortifications at Savannah.

20. Pay for soldiers in both armies—but more so for the Confederates—often lagged months, or even years, behind.

21. When the Confederate government enacted conscription early in 1862, it permitted men called for military service to hire a substitute from among those who had not been called. It also exempted one white man for every 20 slaves. The thinking was that the white man was necessary to supervise the labor of the slaves. Both provisions were longtime features of American military law. The 1863 U.S. draft legislation also permitted the hiring of substitutes and, as Andrews subsequently discovered, the payment of $300 in lieu of military service. This last practice was also a traditional feature of military law.

22. Originally a lieutenant in Co. D, Twiggs was elected captain of Co. G on February 6, 1862. He was probably the lieutenant colonel of the regiment at the end of the war—as Andrews records below—although there seems no extant official record of his promotion to that grade.

23. George W. Toole was paroled at Albany, Ga., May 22, 1865.

24. William Parish's records show he was last paid at Richmond on July 15, 1862. All extant records of his service are for 1861 and 1862. Andrews has again confused the chronology. (Orig. Parrish.)

25. The "Sherman Battery" was Battery E, 5th U.S. Artillery. The gun that became known to the Confederates as "Long Tom" was from Battery E, 2d U.S. Artillery. It was used at First Manassas near the position of the Sherman Battery, and hence the confusion. "Long Tom" was a 30-pounder Parrott gun and was abandoned by the Federals at Cub Run during their flight after the battle of July 21, 1861. The Confederates used it in the river defenses at Quantico, Va., before moving it to Richmond.

26. Both sides used observation balloons during the 1862 operations near Richmond. For a survey of their use, see Judith L. Anthis and Richard M. McMurry, "Rebels in the Sky: The Confederate Balloon Corps," *Blue & Gray* 8, no. 6 (August 1991): 20-24.

27. Maj. Gen. (later Lt. Gen.) Thomas J. "Stonewall" Jackson.

28. Maj. Gen. John Charles Frémont.

29. Brig. Gen. James Shields.

30. Maj. Gen. Nathaniel Prentiss Banks.

31. "Foot cavalry" was a term often applied to Jackson's hard-marching infantry. In the Shenandoah Valley in the spring of 1862 Jackson defeated Frémont, Shields, and Banks, whose combined forces outnumbered him about four to one. The foot cavalry's ability to make long marches was a major factor in Jackson's success.

32. As Andrews states, Lee's basic plan was to bring Jackson's 18,500-man force from the Shenandoah Valley and use it to strike the exposed right flank of McClellan's army on the north side of the Chickahominy River. Jackson's column would be joined by the 45,000 troops under Longstreet, Maj. Gen. Daniel Harvey Hill, and Maj. Gen. Ambrose Powell Hill. Meanwhile, Magruder and Maj. Gen. Benjamin Huger were to hold the rest of the Federal army in place by feints and demonstrations south of the river. Jackson was delayed, and the Battle of Mechanicsville was begun on June 26 by an impatient A. P. Hill. Jackson did not take part. The 1st Ga. Regulars were with Magruder south of the river.

33. First Cold (or Coal) Harbor, better known as the Battle of Gaines' Mill, was the key engagement of the campaign and one of the most important of the war. Jackson finally arrived, and the resulting Confederate victory led McClellan ("Little Mac") to decide to withdraw to the James River—a retreat (McClellan called it a "change of base") that took him across Magruder's front. Most of the subsequent battles of the Seven Days came as the Confederates lashed out to the east, trying to intercept McClellan's retreating army.

34. Lucius Mirabeau Lamar was wounded and captured at Savage Station on June 28, 1862. Once again, Andrews has confused the chronology.

35. Jones did not become a major general until the following November.

36. Again, the chronology is wrong. Gaines' Mill was fought on June 27.

37. Originally a sergeant in Co. B, Palmer was regimental sergeant major until elected 2d lieutenant of Co. M on February 5, 1862. He was wounded in September 1862, elected 1st lieutenant in 1864, and, as Andrews relates later, captured in South Carolina in 1865. He was held in the prisoner-of-war stockade at Johnson's Island, Ohio, until June 1865.

38. Andrews' service record shows that he was wounded June 29, 1862, in the battle he called the Peach Orchard. It is more often referred to as Savage (or Savage's) Station. Andrews treats the two as separate engagements. McClellan was moving roughly from northwest to southeast to reach his new base on the James River. Magruder was probing east in an effort to delay the Yankees' retreat.

39. Gann transferred to Co. L in 1863. He was later wounded and lost a leg.

40. Either John or Michael Kelly, both of whom last appear in extant records on the roll for October 31, 1861.

41. Confederate service records indicate that eight Drs. Mayo served in the Rebel army. Nothing was found to indicate which one was connected with the regiment.

42. Probably 2d Lt. James Rembert Anthony, who served in the 9th Georgia until elected a lieutenant in the Regulars on September 5, 1861. He served in Cos. L and M and then as captain of Co. C of the Regulars. He surrendered with the regiment at Greensboro, N.C., in April 1865.

43. Stephen Shields, who last appears in extant records on the roll for June 30, 1864.

44. See chapter 2, note 27.

45. Charles Watkins, who last appears in extant records on the roll for June 30, 1864.

46. William Mahan died June 29, 1862.

47. Alexander Clemency served in both Cos. G and E. He surrendered at Greensboro, N.C., in April 1865.

48. See chapter 2, note 19. William Walker was an American filibusterer who had been active in the 1850s in schemes to gain control of several Central American nations and annex them to the United States.

49. Fought June 30 and also known as White Oak Swamp, Glendale, Charles City Crossroads, New Market Crossroads, Nelson's Farm, and Turkey Bend. Once again, the Rebels were attempting to intercept McClellan's retreat to the James. The Federals held back their pursuers and then continued their withdrawal to Malvern Hill.

50. Although he had been a major general in the Pennsylvania state forces in 1861, George A. McCall was a brigadier general in the U.S. Army when he was captured at Frazier's Farm. He was soon exchanged. One of the oldest officers to serve in the war—he was born in 1802—he resigned from the army in 1863.

51. Jackson won praise for his conduct in several Mexican War battles, including the September 1847 engagement at Chapultepec, just outside Mexico City. The size of his feet was often the subject of observers' comments.

52. Lewis B. Wheeler made it through the war and surrendered with the regiment at Greensboro, N.C., in April 1865.

53. The Malvern House, an ancient red brick structure, was a mile or so behind the Federal line. See the location on the map in Clifford P. Dowdey, *The Seven Days: The Emergence of Lee* (Boston, 1964), p. 324. It was used as a hospital in 1862.

54. It is not certain that Andrews wrote "jump." If he did, he seems to have meant what we would call "the jumping-off place" or from the start of the attack.

55. Thomas Beverly Baldwin of Co. M presents a mystery. In 1862 he enlisted as a private in Co. G, Cobb's Legion. On July 15, 1862, he was discharged, probably because of being under age. Records of the 1st Ga. Regulars show that he enlisted on January 3 (or 8), 1864, and became a corporal. Why he would be carrying the Regulars' colors at Malvern Hill is a mystery. Perhaps he did not, and Andrews confused him with someone else. The mystery gets more complicated. See chapter 4, note 19.

56. Confederate forces, attacking across an open area against a naturally strong

position, lost about 5,500 men. Union losses were about 3,200. After the battle McClellan withdrew to his new base at Harrison's Landing on the James.

57. In the entire Seven Days Battle the Confederates lost about 20,000 men; the Federals about 16,000.

58. Abraham Lincoln arrived at Harrison's Landing on July 8 and spent a few days visiting the troops and discussing the military situation with McClellan.

59. George Wythe Randolph, secretary of war March 22, 1862-November 15, 1863.

60. It is not certain that this word is "bower." If so, Andrews probably meant it in the sense of a sheltering limb. Lee once called Jackson his right arm. He referred to Longstreet as his old warhorse.

THE DANGER AND MISERY SURROUNDING ME

1. Lee had sent part of his army under Jackson to meet the threat posed by Pope's newly organized army in northern Virginia. On August 9 Jackson fought Pope's advance units at Cedar Mountain. Once convinced that McClellan's army—still on the James below Richmond—posed no threat to the Rebel capital, Lee hastened to join Jackson with most of the remainder of his force. By now Lee's army was informally divided into wings (often called corps). Longstreet commanded one; Jackson the other. Jones' Division was one of five in Longstreet's wing. Anderson's Brigade was one of three in Jones' Division.

2. Little Sorrel (stuffed) is now in the museum of the Virginia Military Institute in Lexington.

3. Brig. Gen. Nathan G. ("Shanks") Evans commanded an independent brigade that often operated with Longstreet's wing of the army.

4. Holcomb's Legion was a South Carolina unit assigned to Evans' Brigade. Legions were small, mixed (infantry, artillery, cavalry) commands. Such tiny armies were found impractical, and the artillery and cavalry parts were detached for service in those branches. The infantry part then functioned as a regiment.

5. This unit has not been identified. The term may be a reference to a time early in the war when the Confederates assigned horses to batteries by the animals' color. The hope was that such a practice would make identification of the unit at a distance possible.

6. Originally a 2d lieutenant in Co. G, Robert Hall Atkinson had been appointed adjutant of the regiment in 1861. In February 1864 he became captain of Co. C. He surrendered at Greensboro, N.C., in April 1865.

7. Evans' brief account of the affair of August 23 is in OR, 12, pt. 2, p. 628; that of Anderson in ibid., pp. 593-94.

8. Lee was moving his army around the right (west) of Pope's line to reach the Federal supply base at Manassas Junction. Jackson's wing had marched August 25-26 to Manassas. Longstreet, after demonstrating along the Rappahannock on the 25th, followed the next day. Thoroughfare Gap in Bull Run Mountain was the place at which Pope could have blocked Longstreet's march and kept the two wings of Lee's army apart while he dealt with each of them separately. Pope, however, was thoroughly confused. As a result, the Yankees made only slight resistance to Longstreet at the gap.

9. Andrews' appointment as 1st sergeant was made in June 1862.

10. Benjamin H. Hudson was originally a private in the 2d Georgia. He was elected a 2d lieutenant in Co. M of the Regulars September 2, 1861. He was promoted to 1st lieutenant on August 30, 1862. The roll for June 30, 1864 (the last extant record for him) shows him present for duty. (Orig. Hutson.)

11. It is not certain to which units Andrews referred. Federal forces in the campaign included the 10th Pa. Reserves, 11th Pa. Reserves, 11th Pennsylvania, 110th Pennsylvania, and 111th Pennsylvania. Andrews was probably referring to the 11th Pennsylvania. See note 13 below.

12. Lt. Seaborn J. Benning, elected 2d lieutenant, Co. C, September 18, 1861. In 1863 he was promoted to captain and assistant adjutant general on the staff of his father who was then a colonel commanding Toombs' Brigade of Jones' Division.

13. The Federal officer may have been Capt. William Shanks of the 11th Pennsylvania who was killed on August 28. Anderson reported that Patton shot five Unionists with his pistol, killing three of them. OR, 12, pt. 2, p. 594.

14. After winning several impressive victories in the West, Pope assumed command in northern Virginia. He issued a series of bombastic orders and dispatches dated "headquarters in the Saddle" and announcing that he was accustomed to seeing the backs of his enemies. The Confederates often joked that Pope had his headquarters where his hindquarters ought to be and that he would be frightened if he ever saw the backs of Confederate soldiers in Virginia because so many of their pants were worn out in the seat.

15. In July 1862 Pope had issued a series of orders directing his army to live off of the country, to use forced civilian labor to repair damage done to Federal property by Confederate guerrillas, and to arrest and punish civilians in areas where attacks were made on Union soldiers. See OR, 12, pt. 2, pp. 50-52. Most Confederates were angered by the policy that these orders represented.

16. Brig. Gen. (Later Gen.) John Bell Hood commanded a small division in Longstreet's wing. One of his brigades was the Texas Brigade (1st, 4th, and 5th Texas, 18th Georgia, and Hampton's South Carolina Legion). Hood's men were involved in the battle at Second Manassas, but he reported no such maneuver as that described here.

17. Almost certainly this officer was Lt. C. C. Hardwick, acting assistant adjutant general on Anderson's staff.

18. A 2d lieutenant as of February 1, 1862, G. B. Lamar, Jr. (initials only in records), became a 1st lieutenant and a member of the staff of Maj. Gen. Lafayette McLaws in 1863. Andrews later gives the name as "Gasaway B." The man was probably the son of Confederate banker and businessman Gazaway Bugg Lamar.

19. See chapter 3, note 55. The Baldwin mystery deepens, for T. B. Baldwin's service record indicates that he was present for duty in the early summer of 1864 and that he was admitted to a hospital in Charlotte, N.C., in February 1865.

20. The fact that he was wounded at Second Manassas is the last item in Cpl. Jonathan P. Herndon's extant records.

21. Probably Augustus H. Rutherford of Co. L, who became a 2d lieutenant on February 6, 1862, and a 1st lieutenant on August 3, 1864. He surrendered with the regiment at Greensboro, N.C., on April 26, 1865.

22. Nancy Hanks was a famous racehorse.

23. Henry J. Porter had first been a member of the 10th Georgia and joined the 1st Regulars just a few days before his death. He apparently was never assigned to a company in the regiment.

24. Originally 2d sergeant of Co. A, Crawford Tucker was transferred to Co. F in 1861. He became 1st sergeant in 1862 and on August 3, 1862, was elected a 2d lieutenant.

25. John Robertson. (Orig. Robinson.)

26. Soon after Second Manassas a rumor ran through the army that Lee had been wounded. This report may have stemmed from the injuries that he suffered on August 31 when his horse shied away while Lee held the reins. When he fell, Lee broke a bone

in one hand and sprained the other. See Douglas Southall Freeman, *R. E. Lee* (New York, 1934-35), 2:340; and John Hennessy, "'Near Killing Me,'" *Civil War* 9, no. 4 (July-August 1991): 40-42.

27. This was the same Alexander R. Lawton with whom the Regulars had served at Savannah at the beginning of the war.

28. Brig. Gen. Thomas Fenwick Drayton commanded a Georgia-South Carolina brigade in Jones' Division.

29. Maj. Gen. Philip Kearny was killed at Ox Hill. (Orig. Kearney.)

MOVED FORWARD INTO THE FIGHT

1. Probably because many men removed their clothes and held them aloft while wading across the river.

2. Although some of Jackson's troops camped near the bridge, they did not destroy it.

3. Under Federal draft laws, which like their Confederate counterparts reflected ancient military practices, a man called for military service could pay $300 and be excused from that draft call. He was liable for later calls. See chapter 3, note 21.

4. One of the long-lasting postwar myths with which Southerners consoled themselves was that their men—unlike the Yankees—did not rob civilians. In fact, Confederate soldiers did steal from citizens despite army orders forbidding their doing so. Andrews himself describes several instances of theft by Rebels—including one a few paragraphs below.

5. On September 10, near Boonsboro, Md., Jackson did have a close call when he was chased by Federal cavalry.

6. When Lee marched into Maryland, the Federals left their garrison at Harpers Ferry, Va., which was southwest of the area Lee's army occupied and so located that the Yankees stationed there were in position to threaten the Rebels' communication with Virginia. To neutralize the threat, Lee sent Jackson with a large part of the army to capture the town. Meanwhile, Longstreet moved his wing west of the Blue Ridge. Unfortunately for the Confederates, a copy of Lee's order directing these movements fell into McClellan's hands, and the Union commander realized how widely Lee had separated the parts of his army. McClellan pushed west to try to take advantage of his good fortune. As a result he clashed with the Confederates at several points along the mountains. Lee had to send Longstreet's men rushing to help the rear guard hold the mountain passes and thereby keep McClellan from getting between the halves of the Southern army. After the fighting at the mountain passes, Lee pulled back to the little town of Sharpsburg on Antietam Creek, where he was able to reunite his army and where the bloody Battle of Antietam (Sharpsburg) took place on September 17.

7. Francis Minus Myers was then a 1st lieutenant in Co. E. In July 1864 he was elected captain of Co. I. He surrendered at Greensboro, N.C., in April 1865.

8. Brig. Gen. William Nelson Pendleton.

9. It is not certain to which medical officer Andrews refers. Of the several who served with the regiment, William R. Bickers, appointed assistant surgeon August 22, 1862, and still with the regiment in October 1862, seems the most likely. See the comments below, p. 88.

10. Straggling did hurt the Confederates in the Maryland campaign. Many men were exhausted. Many others wore out their shoes on the hard Maryland roads. By some estimates as many as 13,000 of the 53,000 men with whom Lee had entered the state had dropped by the roadside by the time of the battle.

11. Jackson's troops were put into line on the left of the Confederate position; Longstreet's men held the right. The desperate fighting, however, forced Lee to shift

troops from place to place to bolster threatened portions of the line.

12. See note 4 above.

13. Brig. (later Maj.) Gen. Joseph B. Kershaw.

14. The weapon was a single-shot, muzzle-loader. The soldier poured powder down the barrel, put a bullet in the muzzle, and then pushed it all the way to the back of the barrel with his ramrod. He then placed a small cap filled with fulminate of mercury over a small hole above the trigger. When he pulled the trigger, the hammer struck the cap, detonating the fulminate of mercury, which in turn detonated the powder, sending the bullet (a minié ball) on its way. When the gun misfired, it had to be cleaned out and the whole process repeated.

15. First a lieutenant in Co. B, James G. Montgomery was elected captain of Co. K on January 15, 1862. The wound permanently disabled him, and he was retired from the army on August 25, 1864.

16. Benjamin B. Smith survived the war and surrendered at Greensboro, N.C., in April 1865.

17. The Yankee was Samuel Bloomer. He survived but lost his leg. For his account of this incident see his letter printed in W. H. Andrews, "An Incident at the Battle of Sharpsburg, Maryland," Atlanta *Journal*, October 19, 1901, p. 3; and "A Wounded Federal Color Bearer," *Confederate Veteran* 17, no. 4 (April 1909): 169.

18. Many Federal soldiers, especially among those from the Midwest, did not like blacks and were adamant that they were fighting to save the Union, not to free slaves.

19. Zachariah Ables transferred to the navy in May 1864. No further record found.

20. William G. Humphries became a sergeant. The roll for June 30, 1864 (the last on file), shows him present for duty. (Orig. Humphreys.)

21. Jordan J. McMullen was killed at Olustee (Ocean Pond), Fla., on February 20, 1864.

22. Losses at Antietam totaled about 10,700 Confederates and 12,500 Federals.

23. It is difficult to trace Lee's movements during the battle. It is known that once or twice that day he lost his temper with stragglers. See Freeman, *Lee*, 2:387-404; and Clifford Dowdey, *Lee* (Boston, 1965), pp. 311-12.

24. William M. Crawford became a corporal and in May 1864 transferred to the navy. He served on CSS *Palmetto State* in 1864-65 and was captured at Richmond, Va., April 3, 1865. He was released at Newport News, Va., June 26, 1865.

25. Pursuing Federals were driven back over the river on September 20. The Federals were commanded by Gens. Charles Griffin and George Sykes. The only Gen. Featherston was the Rebel Winfield Scott Featherston.

26. See note 9 above.

27. Soldiers tended to look down upon militia officers as less worthy to command.

28. Probably John H. Totty, sergeant in Co. E. The last extant record with a reference to him shows him on 60-day furlough as of August 31, 1864.

29. The 15th Georgia was assigned to what had been Toombs' Brigade and was then commanded by Brig. Gen. Henry L. Benning. The brigade was assigned to the same division as the Regulars.

30. Robert John Magill, 1st lieutenant, Co. E. He transferred to Co. B for a few weeks in 1864 but surrendered at Greensboro, N.C., April 26, 1865, as a member of Co. E.

31. Samuel P. Childers was a private when he surrendered at Greensboro, N.C., on April 26, 1865.

32. See chapter 2, note 27.

33. In the weeks after the Battle of Sharpsburg, Lee reorganized his army. Jones, who was suffering from heart trouble, had left the army. He died in Richmond on

January 15, 1863. Anderson's and Toombs' brigades (the latter now commanded by Henry L. Benning) were placed in Hood's Division. The division was one of five in Longstreet's Corps.

THE FATTEST TIME I HAD DURING THE WAR

1. Maj. Gen. Ambrose E. Burnside.
2. It is not certain that this word is "made." If so, Andrews probably intended it to mean that the fence ran down to the river.
3. Hamilton's Crossing is about four miles south-southeast of Fredericksburg on the railroad, north of the Massaponax River.
4. On December 13 Burnside launched his army in a series of futile assaults on Lee's strong position on the hills west of Fredericksburg. The Federals lost about 12,000 men; the Confederates some 5,500.
5. It is not certain that this word is "depot."
6. One of the favorite postwar Southern beliefs was the conviction that the Rebels had been overwhelmed by vast hordes of immigrant soldiers brought to the United States in the war years. In truth, both sides had units made up mostly of immigrants. Overall perhaps 20 to 25 percent of the Federal army was of foreign birth. Some 15 to 20 percent of the Confederates first saw the light of day in another country. Like the Federals, the Southerners gave bounty money to men who joined the army.
7. Choang T. Boggs was 2d sergeant of Co. H in December 1862. He became sergeant major of the regiment in 1864. He was hospitalized in Lake City, Fla., on March 1, 1864, and then sent on a furlough that was extended to June 30, 1864. No further record found.
8. Camp Lee was a "camp of instruction," or basic-training site, in Richmond.
9. The gentleman was obviously not the great chief justice of the U.S. Supreme Court, who died in 1834. Efforts to determine his identity have been futile. The best guess seems to be that he was some relative of Justice Marshall, or perhaps an unrelated man of the same name. So far as can be determined, no John Marshall lived in Richmond in 1860.
10. The ironclad Confederate warship *Virginia*, which was built using what remained of USS *Merrimack* after the Federals burned it in 1861, had been destroyed in the spring of 1862 to prevent its capture. Later the Rebels built a ship they named *Virginia II* (sometimes called *Merrimack II*). This, or some other ironclad, was obviously the ship that Andrews saw.
11. Smith, formerly with the army as Andrews relates above, was then commanding the defenses of Richmond, with his headquarters in the city.
12. George W. Posey, originally in Co. K, transferred in June 1861. He last appears in extant records as present for duty on June 30, 1864.
13. The decision to return the regiment to Georgia and to station it in the lower Chattahoochee Valley as well as its route home and the three-day sojourn at Danville may all have been the results of factors of which Andrews knew nothing. In late 1862 there had been a great deal of popular unrest in southwestern Georgia as citizens there took alarm at several threatening aspects. Many seem to have feared that a Federal force would establish itself on the Gulf Coast and strike into Georgia. See Richard M. McMurry, "Rebels, Extortioners and Counterfeiters: A Note on Confederate Judaeophobia," *Atlanta Historical Journal* 22 (1978): 45-52.

The men could have made the entire journey to Georgia by rail, changing trains because of different track gauges, had they gone via Wilmington, Charleston, and Savannah—the route by which they had come to Virginia in 1861. In such a case they would have been spared the overland march from Danville to Greensboro. (The

Danville-Greensboro gap was not closed until later in the war.)

On December 19, however, Lee had written to Adjutant and Inspector General Samuel Cooper that he would send the regiment to Danville, adding, "As far as I know the character of that part of the country, I am in no apprehension of a rising of the negroes" (OR 33:1068). It may have been that the regiment paused at Danville to allay white fears or to intimidate blacks who were rumored to be plotting a slave uprising.

PINE WOODS, WIRE GRASS, AND SAW PALMETTO

1. Brig. Gen. John Hunt Morgan was a "dashing" Rebel cavalry commander who, in the summer of 1863, foolishly took his command north of the Ohio River where he and most of his men were captured. Morgan escaped in November, returned to the Confederacy, and was killed at Greeneville, Tenn., on September 4, 1864.

2. Brig. Gen. Joseph Finegan, commanding the Department of Middle and Eastern Florida.

3. Andrews gives a description of and background on the arsenal on pp. 112, 114.

4. Maj. Gen. Howell Cobb, who commanded in Middle Florida from late 1862 until the fall of 1863. He was then assigned to command the reserve forces in Georgia, but he returned to Florida briefly in early 1864 to exercise overall command during the Federal invasion of the state.

5. Jacksonville changed hands several times during the war. As Andrews notes below, it was the Federal occupation of the town in February 1864 that led to the Battle of Olustee.

6. Eubanks was originally a private in Co. I. He was later transferred to Co. E and surrendered with the regiment at Greensboro, N.C., on April 26, 1865. He spent most of the war on detached duty as a wagonmaster.

7. George W. Wilf was wounded at Second Manassas but returned to the regiment and surrendered at Greensboro, N.C., on April 26, 1865.

8. Either Nathan Harris or Thomas A. Harris, both of whom are last accounted for in extant records as present for duty on June 30, 1864.

9. For details on the ship and the explosion see Maxine Turner, Navy Gray: A Story of the Confederate Navy on the Chattahoochee and Apalachicola Rivers (Tuscaloosa, 1988), pp. 99-107.

10. Unidentified. This may be Henry Eyels (Eylers in some records), who served as quartermaster sergeant of the regiment. The extant records of his service cover only 1861 and 1862. The only "Wylley" in the regiment was an officer in Co. G. See chapter 8, note 10.

11. Originally a 1st lieutenant in Co. H, Tomlinson Fort was elected captain of Co. L on April 24, 1862. On June 23, 1864, he was sent to the hospital in Savannah. No further record found.

12. See p. 109.

13. Entries in the "Record of Events" section of extant company documents indicate that the health of the command greatly improved in the early months of 1863.

14. Inflation was a major problem for the Confederacy. Andrews may have intended for some decimal points to appear in these figures.

15. Maj. A. Bonaud (initial only in the records) commanded the 28th Ga. Art. Battalion. The unit later served as infantry. (Orig. Bonneau.)

16. George W. and N. B. Norman, both privates in Co. E. George transferred to the navy in May 1864; N. B. last appears in extant records as present for duty on June 30, 1864.

17. A. Clayton Sorrel served as 2d lieutenant in Co. I. He was never a general. Andrews may have confused him with Brig. Gen. G. Moxley Sorrel. (Orig. Sorrell.)

18. John A. Lane, 2d lieutenant in Cos. L and A. He was elected captain of Co. C, 11th Battalion of Georgia Field Artillery, in late 1861. He became a major in 1863 and a lieutenant colonel on February 18, 1865.

19. Doubtless Capt. John C. Rutherford, formerly of Maj. Gen. Howell Cobb's staff but in early 1864 on the staff of Brig. Gen. William Montgomery Gardner, commanding the District of Middle Florida.

20. Henry A. B. Weldon was originally a private in Co. G. He surrendered at Greensboro, N.C., on April 26, 1865.

21. Hiram A. Morgan surrendered at Greensboro, N.C., on April 26, 1865.

22. The only Camp in the regiment was H. W. Camp, The last extant record regarding him (December 1863) shows him as a private in Co. L. He could have been promoted later.

23. Hungry Civil War soldiers often reported being attacked by such dangerous but edible beasts as chickens, cows, and hogs. Once the soldier had killed the animal in self-defense, it would be a waste not to cook and eat the carcass.

24. Three Walkers served in the regiment. Alfred was in Co. H; David J. and Elisha Covington Walker were in Co. G. Both Co. G men joined on January 3, 1864, and one of them would seem to be the man to whom Andrews refers.

25. Originally an enlisted man in the 9th Georgia, Fort was elected 2d lieutenant in Co. K in March 1863. Two years later he was promoted to 1st lieutenant.

26. Daniel A. McDuffie enlisted in Co. L in 1861. In late 1863 he transferred to Co. K and, in May 1864, to the navy. He served with the Savannah River Squadron in 1864 and seems to have been with the James River Squadron in 1865. He was captured at Jetersville, Va., on April 6, 1865, and held in the prison at Point Lookout, Md., until June 29, 1865. (Orig. McDuffey.)

27. The Chatham Artillery was an old Savannah artillery company named for the county in which that Georgia city is located. Most Confederate batteries were designated by the commanding officer's name—hence Andrews' confusion.

28. Brig. Gen. Alfred H. Colquitt commanded a brigade then serving on the south Atlantic Coast. He and his men had been rushed to Florida as part of the force that the Confederates were assembling to meet the Federal expedition advancing west from Jacksonville.

29. Beauregard was organizing and directing the Olustee concentration. The arrangement with the Regulars was probably made some time before the Union threat materialized, not—as Andrews implies—on the eve of battle.

30. Federal troops overran the camp of the Milton Light Artillery on the night of February 8-9. The Rebels lost four guns.

31. Henry A. Cannon was originally a lieutenant in Co. C. He was elected captain on June 19, 1861. In 1864 he was temporarily assigned to command Co. G. At Olustee he was killed in action while commanding the regiment.

32. As mentioned in chapter 1, note 27, Harrison was probably never a Rebel general. He certainly was not one at Olustee.

33. Brig. Gen. Truman Seymour.

34. Lt. Robert Francis Dancy of Co. B, who was acting as Harrison's ordnance officer (not adjutant) and who was killed by an artillery shell just as the Federals were beginning to give way. (Orig. Dancey.)

35. Most probably John H. Bennett, 2d sergeant, Co. C, who surrendered at Greensboro, N.C., on April 26, 1865. Extant service records do not mention the wound.

36. Samuel M. Hunter was captured and paroled at Athens, Ga., May 8, 1865.

37. The right of Finegan's line rested on a swamp and was not as exposed as Andrews thought. Union casualties were about 1,900; Confederate losses about 950. Each side had about 5,000 men in the battle.

38. His name is not on the roll of the Milton Light Artillery published in *Soldiers of Florida in the Seminole Indian-Civil-Spanish-American Wars* (reprint, Macclenny, Fla., 1983), pp. 304-6. The name Joel R. Andrews does appear on that roster, however.

39. During the winter of 1863-64 soldiers in the main armies in Georgia and Virginia often staged great snowball battles, complete with flags, mounted officers giving commands, strategy, and maneuvers. The fight that Andrews describes was a Deep South version of the battles that men in more northern climes fought with snow.

40. Capt. Robert H. Gamble's Company of Florida Light Artillery, also known as the Leon Light Artillery. (Orig. Gambol.)

41. In the Civil War the term "torpedo" was used to designate what is now called a naval mine—a submerged explosive device detonated either by contact or by electrical connection with a post on the river bank.

42. *Maple Leaf* was wrecked at McIntosh's Point on the St. Johns. The Confederate haste in leaving the area probably owed much to the fact that Grieve had been specifically cautioned against being cut off. OR, 25, pt. 2, p. 397.

43. The winter of 1863-64 was a time of great religious revivals throughout the Confederate armies. It was a common practice for men going into battle to throw away dice, playing cards, and other gambling paraphernalia so that if they were killed they would not die with those instruments of sin on their bodies. If a man survived the battle, however, one of the first orders of business was to retrieve the discarded equipment.

44. George W. Posey, who transferred from Co. K in 1861, is last on extant records as present for duty on June 30, 1864.

45. In early 1864 a shortage of sailors led to the transfer of many men from the army to the navy. As shown in several of these notes, a number of men transferred from the Regulars to the navy.

NO REST FOR THE WEARY

1. Often there was confusion in the designation of Rebel units. Three infantry regiments bore some version of the designation "1st Georgia." The 1st Ga. (Ramsey's) Volunteer Regiment served only during the first year of the war and was then disbanded. The 1st (Mercer's-Olmstead's) Ga. Volunteer Infantry was the unit relieved by the 1st Ga. Regulars. It was then sent to join the Confederate army defending north Georgia. Still other 1st Georgia units were found in various militia and reserve forces.

2. The extant service records on Garrett are from early in the war and show nothing concerning his desertion.

3. The Stono Scouts (also known as the South Carolina Independent Riflemen) operated as an independent company of infantry.

4. Originally serving in Co. D, Cheshire was transferred to Co. K in 1861. He was made acting sergeant major May 23, 1864. He later deserted and in March 1865 was sent to New York.

5. There was no such unit as the "26th N.Y. Colored Troops." The 26th U.S. Colored Troops, however, did participate in operations against Battery Pringle on James Island and on Johns Island in July 1864. Reports of the action are in OR, 25, pt. 1, pp. 16, 84-85, 263-64. Dye was probably Maj. Edwin P. Dye of the 26th USCT.

6. Anderson W. Reese first enlisted in the Troup (Ga.) Light Artillery. He was elected a lieutenant in Co. M in July 1863. He surrendered with the regiment at Greensboro, N.C., in April 1865.

7. There were several Confederate artillery units named after George Washington. This one was a South Carolina outfit, not the Washington Artillery that Andrews had seen in Virginia in 1861.

8. On July 6 Col. W. W. H. Davis of the 10th Pennsylvania, commanding Federal troops in the area, was wounded. He could have been the officer under the tree. His report is in OR, 25, pt. 1, pp. 104-6.

9. See note 5 above.

10. Charles Spalding Wylly was then a 1st lieutenant in Co. G. He was promoted to captain on August 25, 1864. He was wounded in action in South Carolina on February 7, 1865, and hospitalized, first in Augusta, Ga., and then in Florida where he was when the war ended. (Orig. Wiley.)

11. First a private in Co. M, Cpl. Thomas J. Musgrove was captured at Cheraw, S.C., on March 4, 1865. He was held in the prison at Point Lookout, Md., until released on May 14, 1865.

12. Hannibal D. Watson (H. B. Watson in some records) was captured at Cheraw, S.C., on March 1, 1865. He was released from Point Lookout, Md., on June 22, 1865.

13. Horace P. Clark (Clarke in some records) had served as a corporal in the 1st (Ramsey's) Georgia until elected 2d lieutenant of the 1st Regulars on October 15, 1861. He was promoted to 1st lieutenant on July 4, 1863, and to captain in August 1864. At this time he may well have been acting as adjutant. He was captured at Macon, Ga., on April 21, 1865.

14. Brig. Gen. Beverly H. Robertson.

15. Benjamin M. Helms' service record shows that he was mortally wounded in action on Johns Island on July 9, 1864.

16. Accusations were made that Confederate soldiers murdered wounded and captured black troops after the Battle of Olustee. See William H. Nulty, *Confederate Florida: The Road to Olustee* (Tuscaloosa, Ala., 1990), pp. 210-13.

17. Reports of the action of July 9 are in OR, 25, pt. 1, pp. 14-15, 84-86, 142-43, and esp. 254-56.

18. Andrews seems to have confused the ebb and flow of the tide.

19. In the summer of 1864 Confederate authorities placed Federal prisoners in Charleston where they would come under fire from Union guns outside the city. The Yankees retaliated by putting 600 Confederates (the "600 Immortals" in Southern lore) under the fire of Rebel guns. See note 21 below. John P. Allen of the 55th Georgia was one of these unfortunates. He was captured at Cumberland Gap, Tenn., on September 19, 1863.

20. The Confederate bombardment of the fort on April 12-13, 1861, touched off the war. The Federals outside Charleston bombarded the fort for most of the last two years of the war.

21. In the early part of the war the usual practice was for the two governments to parole captured enemy troops (to let them go on their promise not to fight again until they had been exchanged) and then to exchange them. This policy broke down in 1863 over Confederate refusal to accord captured black troops the status of soldier. In 1864 Federal authorities realized that many captured Yankees were men whose three-year term of service had expired, and exchanging them for Confederates who would immediately be sent back into the Rebel army was not in the interest of the Union cause.

22. See chapter 5, note 28.

23. A Federal army commanded by Maj. Gen. William T. Sherman had captured

Atlanta and was marching across Georgia to Savannah. The march threatened the great prisoner-of-war camp at Andersonville in southwest Georgia and prompted Confederate authorities to move the prisoners.

24. The exchange of prisoners was renewed in late 1864 when the Confederate government agreed to include blacks as prisoners.

25. Sherman was marching to Savannah both to slice across the Confederacy and also to open communication with the Federal navy off the coast.

26. Brig. Gen. John H. Lewis, whose Kentucky brigade (the "Orphan Brigade") had been converted into mounted troops.

27. Fort McAllister at the mouth of the Ogeechee River on the coast below Savannah.

28. John B. Loyd, who, as Andrews relates below, deserted at Pocotaligo, S.C., January 12, 1865. (Orig. Lloyd.)

29. Brig. Gen. John K. Jackson.

30. John C. Fiser was, on December 24, assigned to command a brigade composed of the 1st Ga. Regulars, William R. Symons's (1st) Regiment of Georgia Reserves, the 27th Ga. Battalion, and the Cobb Guards. The 5th Ga. Reserves was assigned to the brigade commanded by Col. John B. Cumming. The 6th Ga. Reserves is not listed with the brigade on returns for December 1864. It is included on the return for January 31, 1865. By that time the 5th Reserves had been transferred to another brigade. OR, 44:985, 999; 47, pt. 2, pp. 1069-70. Maj. Gen. Lafayette McLaws had previously commanded a division in the Army of Northern Virginia and had been more recently in charge of some of the Savannah defenses. He now commanded one of the two divisions made up of troops from the Savannah defenses. All of the Confederate forces were under Hardee. Other Rebel units joined as Hardee's command moved northward to unite with whatever reinforcements might be sent from other areas.

31. Maj. Gen. Joseph Wheeler's cavalry had been detached from the Confederate army in north Georgia and used to oppose the Federal march across the state to Savannah. Most of his men were then in the Augusta area.

A STREAK OF MISERY

1. While most of Sherman's force entered South Carolina by crossing the Savannah River, the XVII Corps and part of the XV Corps went by water to Port Royal, on the coast about halfway between Savannah and Charleston. They landed and moved inland to link up with the troops moving overland. Bad weather slowed the Yankee advance, and it was February 7 before the Federals reached the Charleston-Augusta railroad.

2. Col. Washington M. Hardy commanded a small infantry brigade consisting of the 50th N.C. and the 10th N.C. Battalion. (Orig. Hardee.)

3. A brigade of South Carolina reserve militia was part of McLaws' Confederate force "between Grahamville and the Combahee River" in late December. The name of its commander is not in the OR. Meanwhile, the governor of South Carolina had requested that the brigade of Brig. Gen. James Conner be returned to its native state from the Army of Northern Virginia. The brigade joined McLaws' command in mid-January, but Conner himself, who was recuperating from the October 1864 amputation of a leg, seems not to have been with it. Andrews may have referred to either of the two South Carolina brigades, but the latter seems more probable.

4. On January 31, 1865, McLaws' command (five infantry brigades and six batteries of artillery) reported 362 officers and 5,663 enlisted men present for duty. Wheeler's cavalry on that day numbered 678 officers and 7,079 enlisted men. Total

Confederate strength in the Department of South Carolina, Georgia, and Florida (Hardee's command) was 1,772 officers and 23,179 enlisted men. OR, 47, pt. 2, pp. 1069-70.

5. C. H. Harris (initials only in the records).

6. J. H. Frasier (initials only in the records) surrendered with the regiment at Greensboro, N.C., April 26, 1865.

7. The service record of George Cole of Co. M shows that he was wounded at Salkehatchie River, S.C., on February 6, 1865. Andrews dates the wounding January 20. His chronology is confused.

8. The last extant record on Sgt. Charles E. Bruce is from the summer of 1864.

9. Among the Rebel forces concentrating in the Carolinas for a last-ditch effort were some of the troops of the Army of Tennessee (the "Western army"). That army had been used to defend the area between the Appalachian Mountains and the Mississippi River. In Tennessee in December 1864 it had been all but destroyed in the Battle of Nashville. Some of its remnants were then sent to the Carolinas.

10. Maj. Gen. William B. Taliaferro. (Orig. Talifero.)

11. Maj. Gen. Matthew C. Butler.

12. Richard S. Overman transferred from Co. H to Co. M in 1861. He was captured at Cheraw, S.C., on March 4, 1865, and held at Point Lookout, Md., until released June 29, 1865.

13. Sherman burned much of Atlanta when he left that city in mid-November. He occupied Columbia in mid-February, and soon afterward vast portions of the South Carolina capital were aflame. A long dispute has raged over whether the fire was deliberately set by the Yankees or whether it spread from cotton bales ignited in the city's streets by retreating Confederates. After the Federals occupied Cheraw in early March, much of the city was destroyed. Some of the damage was deliberate, but some was the result of a Yankee getting careless with a match when he was too close to a large cache of ammunition.

14. Lt. Gen. Wade Hampton, who was now commanding Rebel cavalry in the area and trying to cover the retreat of the army.

15. Brig. Gen. (later Maj. Gen.) Hugh Judson Kilpatrick, commanding Sherman's cavalry. Hampton surprised the Yankees early on March 9 and sent Kilpatrick fleeing in his nightclothes.

16. Sgt. Littleton B. McArthur and Pvt. Newton J. McArthur were both in Co. A of Cobb's Guards.

17. Clemens does not appear in extant records of Cobb's Guards.

18. From early 1862 until September 1864 Hardee had commanded a corps in the Army of Tennessee (except for a brief period in late 1863). He had then been sent to command troops on the South Atlantic Coast. Bragg had been in command at Wilmington, N.C.

19. Troops in the trenches could fire through the narrow opening between the top of the earthworks and the bottom of the head log. Artillery could knock the head log onto the troops in the trench.

NOW THAT IS ALL OVER

1. Maj. Gen. Robert F. Hoke.

2. Hardee was never in the 4th U.S. Cavalry. He did serve with the 2d U.S. Cavalry in the antebellum army.

3. Probably Elliott H. or W. Hazzard, who last appears in extant records for June 11, 1863, as the captain of Co. H, 47th Georgia.

4. Maj. Gen. Edward C. Walthall.

5. Lt. Gen. Alexander P. Stewart.

6. Johnston's April 1865 reorganization of the forces under his command was characterized by the wholesale consolidation of units—a step made necessary by the reduced strength of the veteran regiments. Despite the obvious necessity for the consolidation, many veterans were demoralized when their units lost their identity.

7. Andrews' version of Lee's Farewell Order to the Army of Northern Virginia is not quite accurate. See the real thing in Clifford Dowdey and Louis H. Manarin (eds.), *The Wartime Papers of R. E. Lee* (New York, 1961), pp. 934-35.

8. See chapter 2, note 27.

9. Maj. Gen. George Stoneman, then leading a Union cavalry force into North Carolina from Tennessee.

10. Johnston and Sherman first negotiated what amounted to a general peace agreement between the two sections. The Federal government very properly overruled Sherman for trespassing beyond the military sphere and directed him to make an agreement that would be limited to the military forces commanded by Johnston.

11. John M. Schofield. (Orig. Scofield.)

12. Quincy A. Gillmore. (Orig. Gilmer.)

13. James H. Wilson.

14. As was the case with Lee's Farewell Order, Andrews did not get Sherman's order quite accurately. The order is in *OR*, 47, pt. 3, p. 322.

15. The Confederate government, fleeing south from Richmond, which had been evacuated on April 2, was then in Charlotte, N.C.

16. Following his capture near Irwinville, Ga., on May 10, Davis was taken through Augusta on his way to imprisonment.

INDEX

Ables, Zachariah, 82, 83, 84, 85, 204n.19
Allen, John P., 147
Anderson, George T. "Tige," 16, 37, 38, 42, 44, 48–49, 57, 61, 64, 69, 75, 78, 79, 83, 89, 99–100, 101, 192n.8, 198n.14, 202n.13; feelings of men for, 102
Anderson's Brigade, 16, 53, 56–57, 73, 88, 90, 94, 198n.14, 201n.1, 205n.33; First Georgia Regulars transferred to, 37–38; at Second Manassas, 62–68; at Sharpsburg, 74, 75, 77, 78
Andersonville, Ga., 149–50
Andrews, Amanda Avent (wife), 187
Andrews, Amanda Malvina (sister), 110, 191n.2
Andrews, Eli M., 25, 197n.21; death of, 28, 197n.30
Andrews, Ivey, 129
Andrews, J. W., 187
Andrews, James Highsmith, xi–xii
Andrews, James L., 191n.1
Andrews, Jane Tucker, xii, 191n.3
Andrews, Joel R., 208n.38
Andrews, John Franklin, 191n.1
Andrews, Joseph DeKalb, 25, 28, 93, 197n.22
Andrews, Sarah Jane, 191n.2
Andrews, Washington L., 2, 6, 25, 26–27, 41, 45, 192n.17, 197n.29; death of, 46
Andrews, William Hill: brothers of, 25; Civil War memoir of, xiv–xv; commended for bravery, 108; family background of, xi–xii, 191nn.1, 2, 3; homeward march of, 183–86; postwar life of, 187–88; religious beliefs of, 111; returns home, 108–10; sweetheart of, 108–9, 117
Anthony, James Rembert (J. D.), 46, 184, 200n.42
Antietam, Battle of. See Sharpsburg, Battle of
Appomattox: surrender at, 178–79
Armstrong, James, 35, 198n.9
Artillery, Civil War, 197n.2

Ash, John, 2, 8, 192n.20
Atkinson, Robert Hall, 58, 65–66, 90, 201n.6
Atlanta, Ga.: Andrews' return to, 186
Augusta, Ga., 106
Avent, Amanda, 187
Averysboro, N.C.: Battle of, 170–73

Baldwin, Thomas Beverly, 52, 65, 68, 200n.55, 202n.19
Balloons, observation, 40, 199n.26
Banks, Nathaniel Prentiss, 41, 199n.31
Bartow, Francis S., 16, 195n.5
Bass, J. F., 8, 13, 194n.41
Battery Hascal, 145
Battery Joe, 146–47
Battery Tatum, 145
Beall, Thomas C., 2, 192n.15
Beauregard, P. G. T., 13, 25, 102, 126, 195n.58, 207n.29
Bee, Barnard E., 16, 195n.5
Bennett, John H., 128, 166–67, 207n.35
Benning, Henry L., 61, 204n.29, 205n.33
Benning, Seaborn J., 61, 202n.12
Bentonville, N.C.: Battle of, 173–75
Berne, John. See Burns, John
Berryon (Berrien), Lawrence Cecil, 4, 193n.26
Bickers, William R., 88, 203n.9
Black Horse Cavalry, 17, 18, 196n.10
Bloomer, Samuel, 204n.17
Blue Ridge Mountains, 72–73; crossing of, 90–94
Boggs, Choang T., 101, 121, 205n.7
Bonaud, A., 118–19, 123, 206n.15
Bonds, William A., 34–35, 198n.8
Boyle, John, 2, 34, 192n.13
Bragg, Braxton, 4, 173, 192n.23, 211n.18
Branch, John L., 4, 5, 6, 192n.24
Brantley, Martin L., 21, 196n.17
Brennan, Patrick, 13, 26, 195n.59
Brown, J. E., 2, 191n.5
Brown, Joseph E., 6
Bruce, Charles E., 161–62, 168,

Sergeant [illegible] ...

... known on [illegible] it given me the greatest ...
you a letter expressing my entire satisfaction ...
conduct during the whole war. As a [illegible] ever ready ...
[illegible] soldier of our country any commander ...
he seems to have been ... call him 5 again th ...
Gallant brother Washington I [illegible] the [illegible] ...
[illegible] but he was at his post & like someone [illegible] ...
was [illegible] his duty. Wishes you a pleasant [illegible] ...
your [illegible] and [illegible]

I am with great Respect.

Your Obedient Servant

R. A. Franklin Hill. Capt.

Comm...